California's Desert Parks

A DAY HIKER'S GUIDE

John McKinney

WILDERNESS PRESS · BERKELEY, CA

California's Desert Parks: A Day Hiker's Guide

1st EDITION March 2006

Copyright © 2006 by The Trailmaster, Inc.

Front cover photos copyright © 2006 by Ed Cooper
Maps designed by: Hélène Webb
Cover design: Larry B. Van Dyke
Book design: Emily Douglas
Book production: Lisa Pletka
Book editors: Cheri Rae, Eva Dienel, and Jessica Benner

ISBN-13: 978-0-89997-389-0
ISBN-10: 0-89997-389-2
UPC 7-19609-97389-8

Manufactured in the United States of America

Published by: **Wilderness Press**
           1200 5th Street
           Berkeley, CA 94710
           (800) 443-7227; FAX (510) 558-1696
           info@wildernesspress.com
           www.wildernesspress.com

Visit our website for a complete listing of our books and for ordering information.

Cover photos: *(clockwise from top left)* Harmony Borax Works, Death Valley National Park; Mojave yucca and San Jacinto Peak, in Mt. San Jacinto State Park; Sunrise at Fonts Point, Anza-Borrego Desert State Park; Joshua Tree, Joshua Tree National Park

SAFETY NOTICE: Although Wilderness Press and the author have made every attempt to ensure that the information in this book is accurate at press time, they are not responsible for any loss, damage, injury, or inconvenience that may occur to anyone while using this book. You are responsible for your own safety and health. The fact that a trail is described in this book does not mean that it will be safe for you. Be aware that trail conditions can change from day to day. Always check local conditions and know your own limitations.

ACKNOWLEDGMENTS

For their cooperation, field- and fact-checking and for generously sharing maps and interpretive information relating to California's desert parklands, the author wishes to thank the rangers and administrators of the State of California Department of Parks and Recreation, the National Park Service, the U.S. Bureau of Land Management and the U.S. Forest Service. A special tip of the hiker's cap goes to some particularly dedicated individuals, wise in the ways of the desert, who have helped me repeatedly over the years to accurately portray our public lands and tell their special stories, including Jim Foote of the U.S. Bureau of Land Management, James Woolsey of Mojave National Preserve, Charlie Callahan of Death Valley National Park, Superintendent Joe Zarki of Joshua Tree National Park and author Diana Lindsay, who so cherishes Anza-Borrego Desert State Park.

PHOTO CREDITS

Roslyn Bullas, 6, 20, 151, 152, 213, 254 (bottom), 255, 256; Bob Howells, 148; Michael McKay, 150; National Park Service, 2, 18, 24, 27, 37, 53, 55, 63; State of California Department of Parks and Recreation, vi, 214; Cheri Rae, 73, 218, 244; U.S. Bureau of Land Management, 64, 192; all other photos by author.

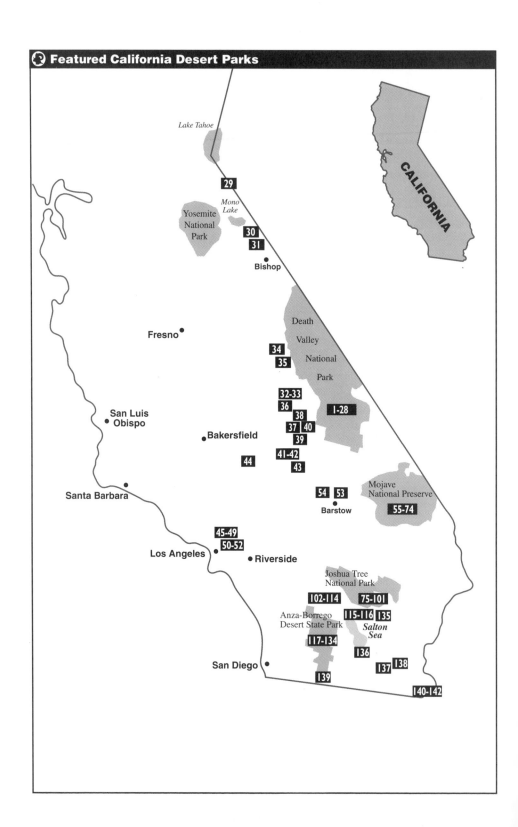

◯ Key to Locator Map

DEATH VALLEY NATIONAL PARK
1 Eureka Dunes
2 Scotty's Castle
3 Ubehebe Crater
4 Ubehebe Peak
5 Racetrack Valley
6 Titus Canyon
7 Fall Canyon
8 Death Valley Buttes
9 Keane Wonder Mine
10 Keane Wonder Springs
11 Death Valley Sand Dunes
12 Burned Wagons Point
13 Grotto Canyon
14 Mosaic Canyon
15 Salt Creek
16 Harmony Borax Works
17 Golden Canyon
18 Zabriskie Point and Gower Gulch
19 Desolation Canyon
20 Natural Bridge
21 Coffin Peak
22 Dante's View
23 Badwater
24 Panamint Dunes
25 Panamint City
26 Darwin Falls
27 Wildrose Peak
28 Telescope Peak

WEST MOJAVE AND THE GREAT BASIN
29 Bodie State Historic Park
30 Mono Lake Tufa State Reserve
31 Hot Creek Geological Site
32 Ancient Bristlecone Pine Forest / Methuselah Trail
33 Ancient Bristlecone Pine Forest/ Discovery Trail
34 Inyo Mountains Wilderness
35 Manzanar National Historic Site
36 Fossil Falls
37 Walker Pass
38 Little Petroglyph Canyon
39 Ridgecrest's Rademacher Hills
40 Trona Pinnacles
41 Red Rock Canyon
42 Red Cliffs Natural Preserve
43 Desert Tortoise Natural Area
44 Tomo-Kahni
45 California Poppy Reserve
46 Arthur Ripley Desert Woodland State Park
47 Saddleback Butte
48 Antelope Valley Indian Museum
49 Vasquez Rocks
50 Devil's Punchbowl Natural Area County Park
51 Devil's Chair
52 Big Rock Canyon

MOJAVE NATIONAL PRESERVE AND EAST MOJAVE
53 Calico Early Man Site
54 Rainbow Basin
55 Afton Canyon
56 Pyramid Canyon
57 Clark Mountain
58 Nipton
59 Kelbaker Hills
60 Lava Beds
61 Cima Dome
62 Keystone Canyon and New York Peak
63 Caruthers Canyon
64 Piute Canyon
65 Table Mountain
66 Mid Hills and Hole-in-the-Wall
67 Hole-in-the-Wall
68 Kelso Dunes
69 Granite Mountains
70 Mitchell Caverns Natural Preserve
71 Providence Mountains State Recreation Area
72 Crystal Spring Canyon
73 Camel Humps
74 Amboy Crater

JOSHUA TREE NATIONAL PARK
75 High View
76 Black Rock Canyon
77 Eureka Peak
78 Wonderland and Willow Hole
79 Indian Cove
80 Rattlesnake Canyon
81 Fortynine Palms
82 Contact Mine
83 Hidden Valley
84 Wonderland of Rocks
85 Desert Queen Mine
86 Pine City
87 Lucky Boy Vista
88 Ryan Mountain
89 Lost Horse Mine
90 Cap Rock
91 Keys View
92 Skull Rock
93 Live Oak and Ivanpah Tanks
94 Pinyon Well and Pushawalla Plateau
95 Arch Rock
96 Cholla Cactus Garden
97 Pinto Basin Dunes
98 Cottonwood Spring Oasis
99 Moorten's Mill
100 Mastodon Peak
101 Lost Palms Oasis

PALM SPRINGS AND THE COACHELLA VALLEY
102 Big Morongo Canyon
103 Coachella Valley Preserve
104 Palm Springs Desert Museum
105 Tahquitz Canyon
106 Murray and Andreas Canyons
107 Palm Canyon
108 Santa Rosa and San Jacinto Mountains National Monument
109 The Living Desert
110 Desert View
111 Mount San Jacinto State Park
112 Santa Rosa Wilderness
113 Toro Peak
114 Desert Divide
115 Painted Canyon
116 Sheep Hole Palms Oasis

ANZA-BORREGO DESERT STATE PARK
117 Borrego Palm Canyon
118 San Ysidro Mountain
119 Hellhole Canyon
120 Calcite Canyon
121 Yaqui Pass
122 Cactus Loop
123 Yaqui Well
124 The Narrows, San Felipe Wash
125 Pinyon Ridge
126 Harper Canyon
127 Pictographs
128 The Morteros
129 Ghost Mountain
130 Elephant Trees
131 Agua Caliente Springs
132 Mountain Palm Springs
133 Bow Willow Canyon
134 Carrizo Badlands

IMPERIAL VALLEY AND THE COLORADO RIVER
135 Salton Sea State Recreation Area
136 Salton Sea National Wildlife Refuge
137 Algodones Dunes
138 Mesquite Mine
139 Valley of the Moon
140 Picacho State Recreation Area
141 Ice Cream Canyon
142 Stewart Lake

The attractions of the California deserts have long drawn admirers.

CONTENTS

1 DEATH VALLEY NATIONAL PARK   19

2 WEST MOJAVE AND THE GREAT BASIN   65

4 JOSHUA TREE NATIONAL PARK 149

5 PALM SPRINGS AND THE COACHELLA VALLEY 189

6 ANZA-BORREGO DESERT STATE PARK   215

IMPERIAL VALLEY AND THE COLORADO RIVER   241

Stone-carved messages offer insights to long-ago cultures.

INTRODUCTION

Many travelers drive along California's coast or through the state's forests and feel inspired by the scenery. A drive through the desert, however, rarely provides similar inspiration. Many motorists consider the desert too flat, too barren, and too unaccommodating to inspire.

The desert demands a closer look. To fully appreciate the desert's beauty requires the visitor to slow down and take a walk: along a nature trail looping around a park campground, down a rocky canyon to a palm oasis, up a rugged mountain to a craggy peak. Without a doubt, the desert is most seductive—and challenging—when approached on foot.

But the desert, first in the hearts of the many who love it, was the last of the state's regions to be preserved. Early conservationists worked to preserve California's glorious mountains and forests first; next came the seashores and coastal ranges. And, finally, came the desert.

The desert's recreation potential followed a similar pattern. First Californians took to the mountains, then to the coast, lastly to the desert. At the beginning of the twentieth century, resorts were built and recreation of all sorts took place in the state's alpine and coastal regions, but only a few hardy prospectors roamed the desert.

It wasn't until the 1920s and the development of (somewhat) dependable autos that Americans began discovering the desert. During that decade, there was a worldwide fascination with the desert, prompted in part by exploration of the ancient Egyptian pyramids and a fascination with Egyptology. Many Southern Californians wanted a bit of desert for their very own and backyard cactus gardens became very much in vogue. Entrepreneurs hauled truckloads of desert plants into Los Angeles for quick sale or export. The Mojave was being picked clean of its cacti, yucca, and ocotillo. A wealthy Pasadena socialite, Minerva Hoyt, organized the International Desert Conservation League to halt this destructive practice. Through her lobbying efforts and crusade in Washington, D.C., Joshua Tree National Monument was established in 1936.

Horace Albright, a founding father of the National Park Service, was instrumental in the creation of Death Valley National Monument. In 1913, Albright interrupted his study of mining law at the University of California to take a job in Washington as confidential clerk to the secretary of the interior. He soon teamed with wealthy borax industry executive Stephen Mather to establish the National Park Service, serving as superintendent of Yellowstone National Park and as Mather's field representative. For two decades, Albright explored and evaluated dozens of potential parks and historical sites.

"Death Valley National Park was in many ways a tough sell," Horace Albright told me in a 1976 interview. After all, he explained, in the early 1930s, the general public—and most members of Congress—regarded the desert in general, and Death Valley in particular, as a trackless wasteland. And then President Herbert Hoover came from a mining background, and often tilted more toward industry than scenery.

Albright, who became National Park Service director in 1930, helped convince Hoover to sign an executive order to withdraw two million acres of the Death Valley region for inclusion in a national park or monument. Although Albright pushed for park status, Congress approved the designation of Death Valley National Monument in 1933. Not only did this legislation protect a vast and wondrous land, it helped to transform one of the earth's least hospitable spots into a popular tourist destination

Like a proud father with many children, Albright declined to name a favorite park, but he confessed that Death Valley had always occupied a special place in his heart. His upbringing in the nearby town of Bishop, his interest in mining, and his major role in the park's creation all contributed to his love of the valley. When I asked him what was it about Death Valley that attracted him, he adjusted his hat, pulled on his string tie, and said suddenly: "The rocks. You can see almost the whole history of the earth in those rocks."

Horace Albright, early National Park Service director, celebrates Death Valley's 50th anniversary.

By the 1930s, Southland roads carried more cars than any place in America except New York City. The Depression, although it brought much hardship, did not end the weekend drive, already a beloved habit of Southern Californians. Families managed to squeeze a little gas money out of tight budgets and hit the road. And the roads were getting better in the 1930s. Thousands of miles of dirt roads received a coating of asphalt and the Auto Club, under the leadership of Doug "Dusty" Rhodes put up hundreds of thousands of road signs.

In winter, Southlanders invariably headed for the desert. Travelers visited places we now know well—Indio and Palm Springs—and places we know less well—Nipton and Borrego Springs. These early desert travelers also journeyed to desert places that can't be found on a modern map. Whither Garnet, Vincent, Cinco?

During the 1940s and 1950s, the military became a major presence in the California desert. What the military viewed as worthless terrain was used for desert warfare training exercises, bombing and gunnery practice, and weapons testing. These military maneuvers and activities continue in designated areas today.

Public perception of the desert completely changed over the years. Land that had previously been considered hideously devoid of life was now celebrated for its spare beauty; places that once had been feared for their harshness were now admired for their uniqueness.

Congressional approval of the Federal Land Policy Management Act of 1976 required the Bureau of Land Management, the California desert's major land steward, to (1) emphasize outdoor recreation as a principal or major use of public lands; (2) evaluate desert lands for their wilderness values and make recommendations to Congress of Wilderness Area designation; and (3) begin a program of law enforcement and a ranger force to patrol its most environmentally sensitive properties. (BLM's first rangers were assigned to the California desert.)

The bureau began a four-year study that resulted in the California Desert Conservation Area Plan. The BLM gathered an astonishing 40,000 public responses from citizens offering their opinions about desert. This study is believed to have been the largest regional planning effort ever attempted in America.

While the plan called for increased protection for desert lands, most conservationists believed that the BLM emphasized commodity production and utilitarian use of the desert at the expense of wilderness preservation and wildlife management.

In 1987, California Senator Alan Cranston introduced his California Desert Protection Act to Congress. The bill called for national park status for Death Valley, Joshua Tree, and the eastern Mojave, along with wilderness designation for millions of acres of desert. This bill, which faced fierce opposition from mining and off-road vehicle interests, was modified and reintroduced again and again over the years.

In October of 1994, Congress finally passed the Senator Dianne Feinstein-sponsored California Desert Protection Act, which created the 1.6-million acre Mojave National Preserve. It also expanded Joshua Tree National Monument and Death Valley National Monument and "upgraded" them to national parks. Further, the desert bill designated another 3.5 million acres of land in sixty-nine different areas as wilderness to be managed by the BLM.

In signing the act, President Bill Clinton proclaimed: "The broad vistas, the rugged mountain ranges, and the evidence of the human past are treasures that merit protection on behalf of the American people."

Not everyone considers desert parklands treasures that need protection. A few years after passage of the California Desert Protection Act, one California congressman tried to strip Mojave National Preserve from the National Park Service and actually succeeded in convincing his colleagues to temporarily defund the preserve.

Today many threats are massed at the boundaries of California's desert parks. Joshua Tree National Park is under siege by a mammoth landfill operation on its eastern boundary, by sprawling cities on its northern boundary, by a proposed city of 10,000 people and ten golf courses at its southern boundary, and by military flights that constantly crisscross its skies. Nevada developers want to build a new Las Vegas airport on the outskirts of Mojave National Preserve, a huge facility that would altogether shatter the tranquility of this parkland.

Admirers of the California desert have contributed not only to the local ecology, but to the local economy as well. In recent years, Death Valley National Park, Joshua Tree National Park, and Mojave National Preserve have become part of a "Three Desert Park Tour" that attracts visitors from across the nation and around the world. Millions of tourist dollars are spent in and around gateway towns located at desert park borders. No wonder area business owners and local politicians have begun to see that it's in their enlightened self-interest to preserve the beauty and tranquility of these parks.

Even if certain Congress members and chamber of commerce members still cannot hear the silent symphony of the desert or appreciate the beauty of its composition, perhaps they will at least listen when money talks and cash registers ring. Our desert parks must be staunchly defended and legally protected so that those politicos and developers who are deaf to the desert's music and blind to its beauty keep their hands off our public lands.

CALIFORNIA'S DESERT PARKS

California visitors are fortunate to have not one, but two vast deserts to explore: the Mojave and the Colorado. The Mojave is referred to as a high desert, for reasons of latitude and altitude. There is (relatively) more rainfall in this region, and the hot season is neither as hot nor as severe as it is in the lower desert.

The West Mojave is that part of the desert bounded on the east by the Mojave River. It sweeps north and west from Barstow toward Death Valley and the southern Sierra Nevada.

The West Mojave takes in the burgeoning Antelope Valley, including Lancaster and Victorville. The East is the larger part of the Mojave and extends east to the Nevada border and to the Colorado River.

Topographically, the East and West Mojave are quite different. The West presents great sandscapes, with many flat areas and some isolated ridges and buttes. The East Mojave, too, has its flatlands—primarily in the form of big basins and wide valleys between mountain ranges—but it is the mountain ranges themselves that differentiate the East Mojave from other desert lands.

Along with the Colorado and Mojave deserts, California's other great dry land is the wild western fringe of the Great Basin. This forbidding land, located east of the Sierra Nevada and north of Mojave Desert proper, is a stark collection of mountain ranges and sandy-floored basins.

Death Valley, the largest national park outside Alaska, preserves more than 3.3 million acres of this Great Basin desert. One place to take in the enormity of the park is from the crest of the Black Mountains at Dante's View or Coffin Peak. A never-to-be-forgotten panorama unfolds. A vertical mile down lies Badwater, the lowest spot on the continent. Across the valley rises Telescope Peak and the snow-clad summits of the Panamints. Farther still, on the western horizon, loom the granite ramparts of the Sierra Nevada. North and south of Dante's View rise the Funeral Mountains. The names on the land are fittingly eerie for this otherworldly place.

Many of Death Valley's topographical features are associated with hellish images—Funeral Mountains, Furnace Creek, Dante's View, Coffin Peak, and Devil's Golf Course.

This is a place where mountains stand naked and unadorned; the bitter waters of saline lakes evaporate into bizarre, razor-sharp crystal formations; jagged canyons jab deep into the earth. Ovenlike heat, frigid cold, and the driest air imaginable combine to make this one of the most forbidding spots in the world.

Badwater, the lowest point in the Western Hemisphere, at 282 feet below sea level, is also one of the hottest places in the world, with regularly recorded summer temperatures of 120°F.

Southwest of Death Valley National Park is a region known loosely as the West Mojave. The West presents great sandscapes, with many flat areas and some isolated ridges and buttes. Some of the strange geology includes the oddly up-thrust Trona Pinnacles, so alien it actually was a location for one of the Star Trek movies, and the Devil's Punchbowl, a bizarre earthquake-fractured basin.

Situated south of the Tehachapi Mountains and northwest of the San Gabriel Mountains, the Antelope Valley makes up the western frontier of the Mojave Desert and hosts much of its human population. Natural attractions include a reserve for the state's official flower, the California poppy, and another reserve for the endangered desert tortoise, the state's official reptile.

Just a few hours' drive from Los Angeles is a virtually undiscovered gem of the desert, sometimes referred to as the East Mojave Desert or as "The Lonesome Triangle." Within the triangle—bounded by Interstate 15 on the north, Interstate 40 to the south, Barstow on the west, and Needles on the east—is Mojave National Preserve. It is a land of great diversity—of grand mesas and a dozen mountain ranges, sand dunes, and extinct volcanoes.

The view from the busy highway on the way to Las Vegas offers little hint of the unique desert environment beyond: cinder cones, dry lake beds, tabletop mesas. Beckoning the hiker are the magnificent 700-foot Kelso Dunes, along with with the world's largest Joshua tree forest.

The Colorado Desert, located in the extreme southeastern portion of California, is only a small part of the larger Sonoran Desert, which covers 120,000 square miles of the American Southwest. Lower in elevation than the Mojave Desert, it is therefore hotter and drier.

In places, the Colorado Desert appears too civilized. Extensive irrigation for agriculture and a host of water-reclamation projects create an unnatural green. In Palm Springs, imported water, land speculators, and eager developers have created a renowned resort area in what was once considered the middle of nowhere.

Prior to the 1930s, Palm Springs had successively been the domain of Cahuilla Indians, a stagecoach stop, and a healing place for those convalescing from illness, especially tuberculosis. When a paved road linked Palm Springs to Los Angeles, film actors and directors began wintering in the desert. Seventy years of growth have brought enormous changes to the resort, but it remains the most popular and widely known desert recreation center in the world. A 1930s description of Palm Springs by a *Los Angeles Times* travel writer still rings (at least partially) true: "Here one may laze away in the violet rays of the constant sun, swim in glorious pools, play golf, tennis, hike amid ever-changing scenery, motor, explore canyons on horseback, or do any of the hundred and one things that drive dull care away and renew the healthy corpuscles that make life worth living."

The hills and canyons bordering Palm Springs have the greatest concentration of palm trees in North America, and Palm Canyon just south of the city in the Agua Caliente Indian Reservation, has more trees than any other desert oasis. A meandering stream and lush undergrowth complement more than 3,000 palms, creating a jungle-like atmosphere in some places. Tree-lovers enjoy the California fan palms, some of which are estimated to be 2,000 years old.

Located just east of Palm Springs is Joshua Tree National Park. The park area is sometimes known as the "connecting" desert because of it location between the Mojave and the Colorado deserts, and because it shares characteristics of each.

Well known for its incredible granite boulders that attract rock climbers and for its forest of Joshua trees, the park lures visitors as a year-round destination for many outdoor activities, particularly hiking and camping.

One of the many fascinations of the national park is the Wonderland of Rocks, 12 square miles of massive jumbled granite. This curious maze of stone hides groves of Joshua trees, trackless washes, and several small pools of water.

California's largest state park, with 763 square miles of Colorado Desert, Anza-Borrego Desert State Park, is named for the Mexican explorer Juan Bautista de Anza and a bighorn sheep. De Anza traveled through the region in 1774, and the sheep still roam some parts of the park. This diverse desert park boasts more than 20 palm groves and year-round creeks, great stands of cholla and elephant trees, slot canyons, and badland formations. Numerous trails explore the park.

The California desert includes not only the three huge parks under National Park Service stewardship and mega-Anza-Borrego under State Parks administration, but millions of acres in the care of the U.S. Bureau of Land Management. Dozens of BLM locales are now managed as wilderness areas and offer breathtaking adventure far off the tourist track.

DESERT TRAVEL

Many notable travelers have journeyed through the hot, white heart of the Mojave since Father Francisco Garcés first passed this way in 1776. Other early desert explorers include Jedediah Smith, Kit Carson, and John C. Frémont. They had little idea of what to expect during their desert crossing. Traveling without detailed maps, high-tech equipment, or freeze-dried foods, they still managed to make the overland trek toward the coast.

Today, we enjoy the benefit of all sorts of undreamed-of modern accoutrements, making desert journeys more comfortable than they were in days past. But the most important aids to desert travel remain as simple as they were 200 years ago—common sense, advance planning, and packing the right supplies.

Planning Ahead

Individuals accustomed to spending their days in air-conditioned comfort are in for a surprise when they venture into the desert. It's a harsh environment that demands adaptation by inhabitants and visitors alike. Daily extremes of hot and cold are the norm; a 100°F day can become a 50°F night. It's important to be prepared—not simply for comfort, but for survival.

The unforgiving desert does not allow visitors to make many mistakes. Those ill-prepared may be unable to deal with threatening situations. Desert dangers are real, and using common sense is essential.

Planning ahead is the first rule of desert travel. Study maps and know where you're going. Become informed about weather patterns, and know what temperatures and climatic conditions to expect. Use this information to plan your trip.

As you study your maps, determine where to obtain services—food, water, gas, ice, etc. Anticipate when you'll need to replenish fuel and supplies, and purchase them whenever you have the chance, since gas stations and stores are few in the vicinity of most desert parks.

Before you depart on a desert journey, leave a detailed itinerary with a friend or family member. Be sure to indicate when you expect to return; call later if your plans change.

Water

Water is the essential life-sustaining substance in the desert. It's in short supply in this arid environment, and most natural water sources are probably unsafe to drink. Therefore, it's imperative that desert travelers be prepared at all times with sufficient quantities of water. At an absolute minimum, carry 1 gallon per person per day. Remember that a gallon of water weighs about 8 pounds.

Anytime you venture out into the desert on foot, for even a short period, bring a bottle of water. Plastic bottles sold in backpacking and outdoors shops are convenient and easy to carry. It's far better to carry water and not need it, than to be stuck in an isolated area without a drop to drink. Bring enough water for each member in your party.

The key to staying properly hydrated outdoors is to drink before you become thirsty; take a few sips every 10 to 15 minutes or so. Don't ration your water, and don't waste it. Fill up when you have the opportunity (at campgrounds and at roadside rest stops; purchase water at stores when you can); it's a good idea to have more than you think you'll need.

Food

When packing food for desert travel, consider the dry climate, heat, and cold you'll encounter. Additionally, consider nutritional requirements, tastes, and appetite. Leave the junk, the sugary "treats," and empty calories at home. Better yet, leave them in the store, and choose instead healthy, high-quality fuel foods that are simple to pack and transport and easy to prepare.

You needn't go the dehydrated food route unless you're planning a back-packing trip where weight is a major concern.

Always pack and carry some food with you when you venture out into the desert. Pack plenty of trail mix, dried and fresh fruit, cut vegetables, whole-grain crackers, and low-sugar cookies for trail snacks and light lunches. Cereal straight from the box, peanut-butter sandwiches, and other simple foods are camp staples. Boxes of juice pack and travel well. Remember that foods—especially bread, bagels, and rolls—dry out quickly in the arid desert environment; always wrap foods well before storing them.

Clothing

Heat, cold, wind, rain, cactus, and rugged terrain characteristic of the desert combine to make proper dressing essential for protection and comfort.

Pack simple, sturdy clothing that doesn't show the dirt. Natural fabrics, especially cotton and wool, are favorite choices because of their breathability and durability.

The simplest approach to desert dressing is to layer your clothing, adding to or subtracting from the layers as the temperature and wind allow. Make sure you choose roomy, comfortable clothing that doesn't bind anywhere. Classic long-sleeved, button-front shirts and sweaters, as well as T-shirts and tank tops, are all smart choices, as are jeans and khakis. In general, long pants are preferred in the desert for the protection they offer from cactus and the sun, but long socks and hiking shorts may be more comfortable. Sweats are comfortable and warm in the early morning and evening hours.

What you wear on your extremities is also important. In warm weather, head protection is a must. Popular choices include baseball caps and broad-brimmed canvas or straw hats. In cold weather, however, a knitted watch cap is best for keeping in your body heat; mittens or gloves make winter desert trekking more pleasant.

Selecting the proper footwear is always a question for outdoor adventurers. Desert hiking requires more substantial footwear than a pair of lightweight running shoes. The terrain is rough, and the temperature of the sand can really heat up during the day, making even short hikes literally a blistering experience. Sturdy hiking boots or the hiking shoes manufactured by running-shoe companies are good choices. Since waterproof materials are rarely required for desert hiking, the fabric-and-leather construction of these running shoe/hiking boot hybrids is ideal. These lightweight boots breathe and can be much more comfortable than heavy-duty waffle stompers. Look for long-wearing soles and stiff shanks for comfort and support.

Pack running shoes or other comfortable footwear to wear around camp.

Above all, when selecting footwear, get a proper fit. Improperly fitting boots or shoes will never be comfortable. Period.

Outerwear is largely a matter of personal choice. Synthetics have been fashioned into jackets, pullovers, and pants. They offer maximum protection from the elements, with minimal weight or bulk. Down jackets and vests are also popular and comfortable for cool weather or nighttime desert wear. Windbreakers offer inexpensive protection from the almost ever-present winds in the Mojave Desert; they are easily stuffed into a day pack or fanny pack.

Many desert rats swear that their most valuable piece of clothing is a bandanna. These brightly colored squares of cloth can serve as a handkerchief, neckerchief, towel, washcloth, headband, loincloth, bikini top, sweatband, head scarf, tablecloth, napkin—well, the list is limited only by your imagination. . . .

Gear
- **Flashlight** Bring extra batteries and a bulb.
- **Compass** This is an indispensable tool for geographical orientation. If you know how to use it, bring a compass. If you don't know how to use one, learn how; outdoors shops and many organizations frequently offer map and compass classes. Increasingly, outdoors adventurers are taking along various Global Positioning System (GPS) devices to help them stay oriented.
- **Cell phone** Phone coverage is expanding rapidly, but don't count on reaching out from every remote desert locale. For example, your basic cell phone could call out from less than one half of Mojave National Preserve at last estimate. Remember, Mojave is a desert of mountains, so don't expect miraculous coverage.
- **Sunglasses** They protect from the intense light, glare, and wind that are characteristic of Mojave. Polarized lenses and UV ratings between 50 and 80 ensure real protection, not just stylish looks. Attach a leash to your glasses for convenience.
- **Pocketknife** What comes in handy more frequently than a trusty Swiss Army knife? Enough said.
- **Emergency supplies** You may wish to keep extra food and water in your vehicle all the time. Waterproof matches, fire-starting tablets, a well-stocked first-aid kit, and a couple of blankets are also essential. Replenish as needed. One of the best ways to be prepared in a medical emergency is to have taken a Red Cross CPR class.
- **Toilet paper** and tissues.
- **Sunscreen** Get the SPF rating that's right for you, and use it. Reapply frequently.
- **Lip balm** To protect from chapped lips, look for one containing a sunscreen.
- **Skin lotion** Use this to counteract the drying effects of the desert.
- **Camera** Always bring more film than you think you'll need, along with an extra battery.
- **Insect repellant** Keeps the critters off you.
- **Sewing kit** Buttons pop off when you least expect it.

- **Notebook or journal and pen** You may want to scribble your thoughts and take notes about your desert observations.
- **Daypack or fanny pack** These are easy to carry on a day hike; keep an extra water bottle in each for convenience.
- **Binoculars** Great for bird-watching.
- **Telescope** Nice for for sky-watching.
- **Any prescribed medications.**
- **A good book** As you read through this guide, you'll notice quotes from some favorite desert classics.

Desert Driving

Because few amenities are available in and around California's desert parks, you must not only bring your own supplies, but consider your automobile a self-contained "survival module." Be certain that your vehicle is road-worthy and capable of withstanding harsh desert conditions. In case of emergency, your life could literally depend on it.

The image of bouncing across the desert in a dilapidated jalopy may have some romantic appeal; it symbolizes the highly cherished notion of the freedom of the open road. In reality, however, driving a well-maintained, comfortable, and reliable vehicle provides a sense of confidence and security—and a real measure of safety as well.

Naturalist Joseph Wood Krutch described venturing into the desert as "rewarding travel in an unfrequented land." Travel in the desert is rewarding for a number of reasons, not the least of which is the fact that it truly is an

Desert driving—long a popular pastime, but to really know desert lands, get out of the car and take a hike.

"unfrequented land." The wide-open spaces and lonely desert roads are particularly appealing to those seeking the solitude and quiet the desert offers.

But in an unexpected situation, such as a vehicle breakdown, that feeling of peaceful solitude can quickly become a fearful experience in a hostile environment. Therefore, driving a road-worthy vehicle is of utmost importance in the desert.

The perils of desert driving include extreme heat and glare (especially when driving east in the morning or west in the afternoon), winter cold, ice, and snow. The long, straight roads can become monotonous and sleep-inducing day or night. Dirt roads require special driving skills, and the unfamiliar territory demands navigational expertise. Weather conditions, including dust, wind, and thunderstorms, which can cause flash floods, are other difficulties faced by desert drivers.

Maps

An early twentieth century U.S. Geological Survey report noted: "With some persons, the faculty of getting lost amounts to genius. They are able to accomplish it wherever they are. The only suitable advice for them is to keep out of the desert. There are safer places in which to exercise their talent." If those words strike home, remember that map reading is a skill. And like any other skill, performance improves with practice.

Certainly there is nothing more nerve-wracking or upsetting than the experience of a frustrated driver demanding directions from an unsure navigator. Not only is it frustrating, it is potentially hazardous, especially when intensified by traffic, hot weather, fatigue, or confusing territory.

To avoid such disorienting and upsetting scenarios, spend time before departure planning and mapping out excursions. Write down directions, road names, and pertinent landmarks to prevent on-the-road confusion. While most of the main access roads in desert parks are well-marked, many lesser roads are not signed at all. Therefore, pay close attention to mileage on the odometer when following directions to locations throughout the desert.

Good desert maps are indispensable. I have a dozen favorites. Eight maps are issued by the Automobile Club of Southern California: Los Angeles County & Vicinity, San Bernardino County, Riverside County, San Diego County, Imperial County, Palm Springs, Colorado River, and Eastern Sierra. Along with these excellent maps, I like to use more detailed maps of the larger parks, including Tom Harrison's recreation maps of Mojave National Preserve, Death Valley National Park and Joshua Tree National Park, plus the Anza-Borrego Desert Region Recreation map that goes with the guidebook *The Anza-Borrego Desert Region*, written by Lowell and Diana Lindsay and published by Wilderness Press.

Desert Survival Safety Rules

- When planning a trip into the desert, always inform someone as to where you are going, your route, and when you expect to return. Stick to your plan.

- Carry at least one gallon of water per person per day of your trip. (Plastic gallon jugs are handy and portable.)
- Be sure your vehicle is in good condition with a sound battery, good hoses, spare tire, spare fan belt, radiator water, necessary tools, and reserve gasoline and oil.
- Keep an eye on the sky. Flash floods may occur in a wash anytime thunderheads are in sight, even though it may not rain a drop where you're standing.
- If caught in a dust storm while driving, get off the road. Turn off driving lights, turn on emergency flashers, and back into wind to reduce windshield pitting by sand particles.
- Before driving through washes and sandy areas, test the footing. One minute on foot may save hours of hard work or prevent a punctured oil pan.
- If your vehicle breaks down, stay near it. Your emergency supplies are here. Your car has many other items useful in an emergency. Raise the hood and trunk lid to indicate to other drivers that you need help. A vehicle can be seen for miles, but a person on foot is very difficult to find.
- When not moving, use available shade or make your own with tarps, blankets, seat covers—anything available to reduce the rays of the sun.
- Do not sit or lie directly on the ground. It may be 30°F or more hotter than the air.
- Leave a disabled vehicle only if you are positive of the route to help. Leave a note for rescuers that lists the time you left and the direction you are taking.
- If your must walk, rest for at least 10 minutes out of each hour. If you are not normally physically active, rest up to 30 minutes out of each hour. Find shade, sit down, and prop up feet. Adjust shoes and socks. Do not remove shoes; you may not be able to get them back on swollen feet.
- If you have water, drink it. Do not ration it. And don't waste it by pouring it over our head.
- If water is limited, keep your mouth shut. Do not talk, do not eat, do not smoke, do not drink alcohol, do not take salt.
- Keep clothing on; it helps keep the body temperature down and reduces the dehydration rate. Cover your head. If you don't have a hat, improvise a head covering.
- If stalled or lost, set signal fires. Set smoky fires in the daytime, bright ones at night. Three fires in a triangle denote "help needed."
- A roadway is a sign of civilization. If you find a road, stay on it.
- If hiking in the desert, equip each person, especially children with a police-type whistle. It makes a distinctive noise with little effort. Three blasts denote "help needed."
- To avoid poisonous creatures, put your hands or feet only where you can see them.

From the manual, *Desert Survival: Information for Anyone Traveling in the Desert Southwest*, Maricopa County Department of Civil Defense and Emergency Services:

Emergency Equipment
First-aid kit
Fire extinguisher
Blanket
Shovel
Knife
Flashlight
Signal mirror
Road flares
Matches

Repair Items
Jack and lug wrench
Tire pump
Tow chain
Tow rope
Electrical tape
Duct tape
Baling wire
Tool kit

Commodities
Water (absolute minimum, one gallon per person per day)
Extra oil and gas
Toilet tissue
Weatherproof matches
Concentrated food

Personal Items
Compass
Map of area
Protective clothing
Sunglasses
Hat
Sunscreen

Desert Hiking

The very notion of hiking the desert in general, and at a place like Death Valley in particular, is a surprising one to some people—even to some avid hikers. The desert that seems so huge when viewed from a car can seem even more intimidating on foot.

Apparently not that intimidating though; reader response to my *Los Angeles Times* hiking columns about the desert proved to be enthusiastic to say the least! More walks "way out there," readers demanded.

With such a desert, the visitor really needs two views: the broad view offered by an auto tour and the intimate view offered by a sojourn afoot. Some of the walks detailed in this guide are leg-stretchers, informal wanderings, part of the grand tour. Heed some of these suggestions, get out of car, and walk as much as possible.

Other selected hikes require a few hours or a half day to complete, while a few distant destination may take most of a day to visit and return. Many of these hikes are suitable for the whole family, and most can be enjoyed by the average hiker. A few treks are for experienced hikers only in good condition.

Compared to forest or mountain parks, desert parks (even the larger national parks) have a limited number of signed footpaths; nevertheless, hiking opportunities abound because roads (closed to vehicles), washes, and narrow canyons serve as excellent footpath substitutes. For the average day hiker, there's a week or two's worth of wonderful walking in each of the major parks (such as Joshua Tree National Park) and geographical areas (Palm Springs, for example).

Although it's quite tempting, don't over-schedule. California's deserts are vast, with an enormous number of sights to see and hikes to take. Planning a weekend whirlwind trip is likely to leave you feeling frustated and exhausted. Pick one or two areas to explore during each trip, and plan to return again.

For the very experienced desert hiker, there are many excellent Class 2 and Class 3 climbs and cross-country outings in the California desert. For example, Providence and New York peaks in the Mojave Preserve are two fine climbs; these peak-bagging expeditions are for experienced hikers in top form with route-finding abilities. By all means, if you are one of these experienced hikers, call a park or BLM office for access information, get yourself some topo maps and an ample water supply, and go for it!

The California desert has a way of making every trip an adventure. If you like the idea of hiking to places where it seems there's no one else for miles around, or where you could swear no one has ever been before, the California desert may be just the place for you.

Warm Weather Hiking Tips

Hot and bothered after a midday desert walk? Well, it's no wonder. Recent studies have shown that optimum temperatures for long-distance walks or hikes are in the 50°F to 55°F range. Above this, a hiker's performance degrades as much as 2 percent for every 5°F increase in temperature. Air quality, wind (or lack of same) and the amount and kind of reflective heat are also environmental factors that affect a walker's performance.

Pay attention to your physical responses in the desert. Temperature extremes and dryness make it a stressful environment. If you're overweight or out of shape, take it easy, and don't push yourself to keep up with your fitter friends.

As temperatures rise, hikers must adjust their routine. Here are five tips to beat the heat:

- Time your hike for the cool of the day—early morning is best, late evening second best. Avoid midday, when the sun's rays are directly overhead, and late afternoon, when the earth has absorbed the sun's rays but the heat hasn't dissipated at all.

- Wear a hat. A baseball cap will do, but only if you wear it with the bill in the front (hopelessly unhip, but effective). A better bet is an expedition-type hat that has protective flaps to cover the neck. Another style is the wide-brimmed hat made by Tilley Endurables. This classic lasts and lasts; Tilley offers a free replacement if it ever wears out.

• Apply sunblock (minimum SPF 15) on all exposed skin. Read the product directions: some varieties of sunblock need to be put on some time before exposure in order to be effective.

• Wear loose-fitting, light-colored, lightweight clothing.

• Carry—and drink—lots of water. You need to consume 16 ounces for every 20 minutes of exercise on a hot day.

With the right preparations and smart decisions on the trail, hikers can enjoy their adventures in California's desert parks.

Using This Guide

California's desert parks and preserves are grouped by geography into chapters, then further organized in rough north-to-south order. Most of the hiking locales clearly belong in their respective categories, but a couple of parks straddle geographical areas, and I've made a judgment call as to which chapter to place these parks. For example: Agua Caliente County Park is an island of San Diego County Parks Department land in the midst of vast Anza-Borrego Desert State Park, so I included this hot springs and hike in the Anza-Borrego Desert State Park chapter. Well, you get the idea.

Distance, expressed in round-trip mileage figures, follows each destination. The hikes in this guide range from 0.5 mile to 15 miles, with the majority averaging less than 5 miles. Gain or loss in elevation follows the mileage.

In matching a walk to your ability, you'll want to consider both mileage and elevation, as well as the condition of the trail, terrain, and season. Take a more conservative approach to walking in the desert than you might with more forgiving terrain. Hot sands, exposed chaparral, or miles of boulder hopping can make a short walk seem long.

Hikers vary a great deal in relative physical condition, but you may want to consider the following: an easy walk suitable for beginners and children would be less than 5 miles with an elevation gain of less than 700 to 800 feet. A moderate walk is considered a walk in the 5- to 10-mile range, with less than 2,000 feet of elevation gain. You should be reasonably fit for these. Preteens sometimes find the going difficult. Hikes of more than 10 miles and those with more than a 2,000-foot gain are for experienced hikers in top form.

Season is the next item to consider. Most of the hikes in this book are best done in autumn, winter, or spring. With the exception of a couple high mountain regions—Telescope Peak above Death Valley, the White Mountains, Mt. San Jacinto—summer hiking in the desert is far too uncomfortable and dangerous to consider.

For more hiking hints, visit the author's website at www.thetrailmaster.com and read *The Joy of Hiking: Hiking the Trailmaster Way* (Wilderness Press).

While the desert receives very little rain, when it does fall, dangerous flood conditions often result. A few trails in this guide may be impassable in winter and spring due to high water. Relevant flood information has been noted in the text.

An introduction to each hike describes what you'll see in a particular park, preserve, or forest area, and what you'll observe along the trail: plants, animals, panoramic views. You'll also learn about the geologic and human history of the region.

DIRECTIONS TO TRAILHEAD take you from the nearest major highway to trailhead parking. For trails having two desirable trailheads, directions to each are given. A few trails can be walked one way, with the possibility of a car shuttle. Suggested car shuttle points are noted.

After the directions to the trailhead, you'll read a description of **THE HIKE**. Important junctions and major sights are pointed out, but I've left you to discover the multitude of little things that make a hike an adventure.

About the Maps

The maps in this book support the author's mission, which is to provide an introduction for the day hiker to the state's best state, national, coastal and desert parklands.

Many of the Golden State's parklands are regarded by rangers, administrators—and most importantly by hikers—as true "hiker's parks." These footpath-friendly parks offer miles and miles of maintained trails, with plenty of options for great day hikes. For these adventures, in contrast with, say, easy "walks in the park," route descriptions are described in more detail and accompanying maps highlight more trails and park features.

It's a delight for me to share some of my favorite, often carefully selected, shorter California trails, too. Among these short but scenic paths are nature trails and history interpretation trails, as well as beach trails and informal footpaths along a river. These short hikes have correspondingly short route descriptions, and the accompanying maps chart a minimal number of features. A handful of the selected hikes are so short, and the on-the-ground orientation for the hiker so obvious, that mapping them would not add anything to the visitor's experience and, in a few instances, would be downright silly.

Fellow hikers, do give us a heads-up about any trail changes you notice or any discrepancies you observe between the map and territory.

For reasons I can't explain, during more than 20 years that I've been chronicling hiking trails, you hikers have been lots more vigilant about pouncing on errant or out-of-date prose and telling me about it than you have been about pointing out the need for any trail map updates. (Jeez, I can't even misidentify a rare plant or obscure bird without hearing about it from so many of you...) Anyway, your cartographic input is always welcome.

The magnificent panorama of Death Valley's diverse topography.

CHAPTER 1

DEATH VALLEY NATIONAL PARK

Entering Death Valley National Park at Towne Pass, State Highway crests the rolling Panamint Range and descends into Emigrant Wash. Along the road I spot the sign: Welcome to Death Valley National Park.

Park? Other four-letter words are more often associated with Death Valley: gold, mine, heat, lost, dead—and the four-letter words shouted by teamsters who drove the 20-mule-team borax wagons need not be repeated.

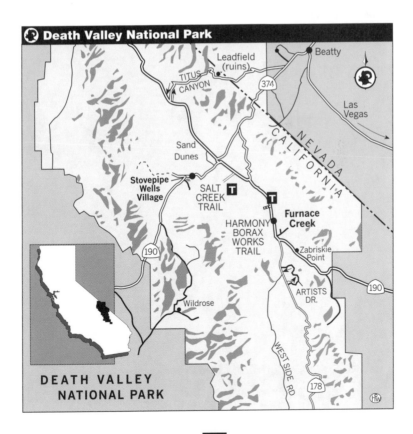

There is something about the desert, and especially this desert, that at first glance seems the antithesis of all that park-goers find desirable. To the needs of most park visitors—shade, water, and easy-to-follow, self-guided nature trails—Death Valley answers with a resounding "no."

And the word "park" suggests a landscape under human control. In this great land of extremes, nothing could be further from the truth. A bighorn sheep standing watch atop painted cliffs, sunlight and shadow playing atop the salt-and-soda floor, a blue-gray cascade of gravel pouring down a gorge to a land below the level of the sea—this territory is as ungovernable as are its flaming sunsets.

In Death Valley, the forces of the earth are exposed to view with dramatic clarity: a sudden fault and a sink became a lake. The water evaporated, leaving behind borax and, above all, fantastic scenery. Although Death Valley is called a valley, in actuality it is not. Valleys are carved by rivers. Death Valley is what geologists call a *graben*. Here, a block of the earth's crust has dropped down along fault lines in relation to its mountain walls.

At Racetrack Playa, a dry lake bed, visitors puzzle over rocks that weigh as much as 500 pounds and move mysteriously across the mud floor, leaving trails as a record of their movement. Research suggests that a combination of powerful winds and rain may skid the rocks over slick clay.

Open spaces and lonely places abound in Death Valley.

Looking west from Badwater, the lowest point in the Western Hemisphere at 282 feet below sea level, the eye is drawn to what appears to be a shallow stream of water flowing across the floor of the valley. But this flow is a *trompe l'oeil*, a mirage caused by the strange terrain and deceptive colorings. Light plays upon the valley floor and the mind spins as though caught in a color wheel, from the gray and gold of sunrise to the lavender and purple of sunset to the star-flecked ebony of night.

The park's steep-walled canyons beckon hikers.

Americans looking for gold in California's mountains in 1849 decided to cross the burning sands to avoid severe snowstorms in the nearby Sierra Nevada. Some perished along the way, and the land became known as Death Valley.

A multitude of living things miraculously have adapted to living in this land of little water, extreme heat, and high winds. Two dozen Death Valley plant species grow nowhere else on earth, including Death Valley sandpaper plant, Panamint locoweed, and napkin-ring buckwheat.

In spring, even this most forbidding of deserts breaks into bloom. The deep blue pea-shaped flowers of the indigo bush brighten Daylight Pass. Lupine, paintbrush, and Panamint daisies grow on the lower slopes of the Panamint Mountains, while Mojave wildrose and mariposa lily dot the higher slopes.

Two hundred species of birds are found in Death Valley. The brown whip-like stems of the creosote bush help shelter the movements of the kangaroo rat, desert tortoise, and antelope ground squirrel. Night covers the movements of the bobcat, fox, and coyote. Small bands of bighorn sheep roam remote slopes and peaks. Three species of desert pupfish, survivors from the Ice Age, are found in the valley's saline creeks and pools.

Death Valley celebrates life. Despite the outward harshness of this land, when you get to know the valley, you see it in a different light. As naturalist Joseph Wood Krutch put it: "Hardship looks attractive, scarcity becomes desirable, starkness takes on an unexpected beauty."

■ EUREKA DUNES
Eureka Dunes Trail
1 to 5 miles round trip

B etween the Owens Valley and Death Valley, isolated and often overlooked Eureka Valley holds many surprises, chief among them the Eureka Dunes. The dunes, formerly known as the Eureka Dunes National Natural Landmark and administered by the BLM, were added to the expanded Death Valley National Park in 1994.

The dunes occupy the site of an ancient lake bed, whose shoreline can be identified to the northeast of the dunes. The once-flat lake bed northwest of the dunes sometimes captures a little surface water; this happenstance delights photographers who focus their cameras on the water and capture the reflection of the Inyo Mountains.

The neighboring Last Chance Mountains get a fair share of the meager rains that fall in these parts—meaning the dunes are (relatively) well watered. Rain percolates downward, the water later nurturing some 50 different dune plants even in the driest of years. Three species of flora occur nowhere else: Eureka Dunes milkvetch, Eureka Dunes grass, and the showy, large white flowers of the Eureka Dunes evening primrose.

Like their cousins, the Kelso Dunes in Mojave National Preserve, the Eureka Dunes "boom." Low vibrational sounds are created when the wind-polished, well-rounded grains of sand slip-slide underfoot. The booming, which has been compared to the low-altitude airplane and a Tibetan gong, is louder in the Kelso Dunes.

However, it's not the noise of Eureka Dunes, but the silence that impresses the hiker. The massive dunes (3.5 miles long and 0.5 mile wide) are California's highest at nearly 700 feet high.

DIRECTIONS TO TRAILHEAD From the entrance station (fee) opposite Grapevine Campground, continue north on North Highway a short distance to a fork. The right fork leads to Scotty's Castle, but you continue toward Ubehebe Crater, 2.8 miles, then turn right onto dirt Death Valley Road. Drive some 21 miles northwest to Crankshaft Junction. Bear left, continuing on Death Valley Road, which heads southwest up and over the Last Chance Range. (A few miles of the road through Hanging Rock Canyon are paved; the rest are dirt.) After 12.3 miles, turn left (south) onto South Eureka Road and travel 10.7 miles to the north end of the dunes and a road fork.

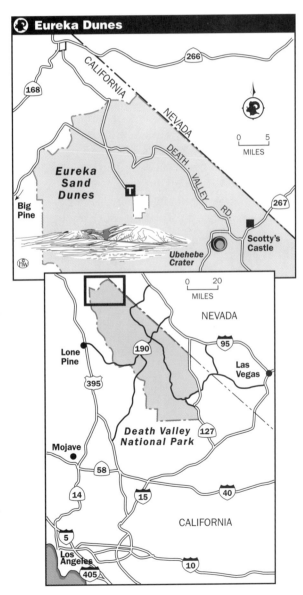

An ungraded road goes east to the north side (near interpretive signs) and primitive campsites.

THE HIKE The trail-less walking is strictly free-form up and across the dunes. If you get to the top of the island of sand, you'll get a unique vista of Eureka Valley and the many mountains that surround it: the Last Chance

Range to the northeast, the Saline Range to the west, and the Inyo Mountains to the southwest.

■ SCOTTY'S CASTLE
Windy Point Trail
From Castle to Scotty's grave is 0.75 mile round trip

Scotty's Castle, the Mediterranean-to-the-max, mega-hacienda in the northern part of the park, is unabashedly Death Valley's premiere tourist attraction. Visitors are wowed by the elaborate Spanish tiles, well-crafted furnishings, and innovative construction that included solar water heating. Even more compelling is the colorful history of this villa in remote Grapevine Canyon.

Construction of the "castle"—more officially Death Valley Ranch—began in 1924. It was to be a winter retreat for eccentric Chicago millionaire Albert Johnson. The insurance tycoon's unlikely friendship with prospector-cowboy-spinner-of-tall tales Walter Scott put the 2.3-million-dollar structure on the map and captured the public's imagination. Scotty greeted visitors and told them fanciful stories from the early hard-rock mining days of Death Valley.

The one-hour walking tour (fee) of Scotty's Castle is excellent, both for its inside look at the mansion and for what it reveals about the eccentricities of Johnson and Scotty. To learn more about the castle grounds, pick up the pam-

The opulent furnishings and grand architecture of Scotty's Castle—an unexpected desert pleasure.

phlet, "A Walking Tour of Scotty's Castle," which leads you on an exploration from stable to swimming pool, bunkhouse to powerhouse.

Another walk is the short hike through Tie Canyon Wash, which supplied tons and tons of sand and gravel for the castle's construction. Mixed with cement, these raw materials went into the castle walls and into the unique concrete fence posts, each bearing letters J and S—for Albert Johnson and Death Valley Scotty. Winters were cold in the canyon and much wood was needed for the castle's many fireplaces. Johnson bought 70 miles worth of railroad ties from the abandoned Bullfrog-Goldfield Railroad. The ties, thousands of which are still stacked in Tie Canyon, cost him about a penny apiece.

Windy Point Trail, which leads to a cross marking Death Valley Scotty's grave, is a self-guiding path keyed to an interpretive pamphlet that gives and overview of the desert flora.

DIRECTIONS TO TRAILHEAD Scotty's Castle is located some 53 miles north of the visitor center.

THE HIKE The path skirts the cookhouse, alas destroyed by fire in 1991 when a computer short-circuited. You'll see an intriguing solar water heater—very high-tech for its time and a useful conservation lesson for today.

Windy Point is, indeed, often windy, but it was actually named for Death Valley Scotty's dog, who lies buried next to his master.

■ UBEHEBE CRATER
Little Hebe Crater Trail
From Ubehebe Crater to Little Hebe Crater is 1 mile round trip with 200-foot elevation gain

Add volcanism to the list of cataclysms such as earthquakes and flash floods that caused high-speed changes to the Death Valley landscape.

Little Hebe and Ubehebe are sometimes called explosion craters. One look and you know why. After hot magma rose from the depths of the earth to meet the ground water, the resultant steam blasting out a crater and scattering cinders.

To the native Shoshone of Death Valley, the crater was known as *Temppin-tta Wo' sah*, "Basket in the Rock"—an apt description indeed. A half mile in diameter, Ubehebe is not the only "basket" around; to the south is Little Hebe Crater, and a cluster of smaller craters.

When measured by geological time, the craters are quite young—a few thousand years old. Most of the cinders covering the 6-mile area are from Ubehebe.

Although many visitors are drawn to the rim of the Ubehebe, few descend to the bottom of the crater. If you do, watch your footing; the crater wall is a loose mixture of gravel and cinders. The mud flat at the bottom of the crater is the site of many short-lived lakes.

The more interesting walk is along the half-mile rim-to-rim route from Ube-hebe to Little Hebe Crater.

DIRECTIONS TO TRAILHEAD From the Grapevine Ranger Station at the north end of the park, continue north (don't take the right fork to Scotty's Castle) 2.8 miles to the signed turnoff for Ubehebe Crater and continue another 2.5 miles to the crater parking area.

THE HIKE From the edge of 500-foot-deep Ubehebe Crater, join the south-trending path over loose cinders. The trail tops a couple of rises, then splits. You can either go down to Little Hebe or head farther south along the ridge.

Walk the perimeter of Little Hebe Crater and enjoy the views of the valley and of the Last Chance Range to the west.

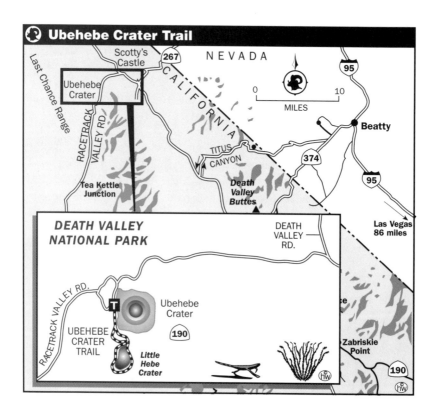

Ever-windy, ever-wondrous Ubehebe Crater—a must-see attraction of Death Valley.

■ UBEHEBE PEAK
Ubehebe Peak Trail
From Racetrack parking area to summit is 5 miles round trip
with 2,000-foot elevation gain

Marvelous vistas are the hiker's reward for climbing the steep trail to Ubehebe Peak, a remote summit in the equally remote Last Chance Range. The White Mountains, Saline Valley, and the High Sierra are among the sights visible from the peak.

Ubehebe means "big basket" in the Shoshone language; such a name seems more appropriate to Ubehebe Crater some 24 miles northeast of the rocky peak.

For most travelers, the attraction in this part of the park is not rarely visited Ubehebe Peak but a 3-mile-long mud flat known as the Racetrack. High winds push rocks along the sometimes muddy surface, leaving long, faint tracks. Most of the tracks you're likely to see on the playa are made by smaller rocks, but throughout the years there have been reports of rocks weighing several hundred pounds skidding for a quarter mile.

The Grandstand, a rock outcropping located at the northern end of the Racetrack, is an easy half-mile walk from the pullout off Racetrack Valley Road. This pullout is also the trailhead for the hike to Ubehebe Peak.

The old miners' trail that leads to the crest is in fairly good condition. To reach the very top of Ubehebe Peak requires some rock scrambling (Class 2-3); however, traveling only as far as the crest delivers equally good views.

DIRECTIONS TO TRAILHEAD From the Grapevine Ranger Station at the north end of the park, continue north (don't take the right fork to Scotty's Castle) 2.8 miles to the signed turnoff for Ubehebe Crater and continue another 2.5 miles. The paved road ends with a left turn into the Ubehebe Crater parking lot, but you continue south some 20 miles on the washboard-surfaced, occasionally rough Racetrack Valley Road to Tea Kettle Junction, colorfully decorated with tea kettles. Bear right, traveling another 5.7 miles to a turnout on the right (west) side of the road opposite the Grandstand and the Racetrack.

THE HIKE The path begins a moderate ascent through a creosote-dotted alluvial fan, then soon steepens as it begins climbing higher over the desert-varnished shoulder of the peak. Many switchbacks bring you to the crest of the range, 1.5 miles from the trailhead.

From the 5,000-foot crest, savor the panorama: the Inyo Mountains, the Racetrack, the Cottonwood Mountains, and the snow-capped peaks of the High Sierra.

If you want to bag the peak, follow the trail as it climbs steeply along the crest, switchbacks some more, and reaches a rocky shoulder, whereupon the trail fades away. You continue along the crest, dipping briefly, and then rock-scrambling up to the small summit area atop Ubehebe Peak.

■ RACETRACK VALLEY
Sliding Rocks Trail
2 to 3 miles round trip

Death Valley, the largest national park outside of Alaska, has more than its share of unusual features. Badwater, the lowest spot in the Western Hemisphere, and the desert pupfish, thriving against all odds in Salt Creek, are but two of the park's weird sights.

The amazing sliding rocks scooting across Racetrack Valley may just be the park's weirdest phenomena of all. While scientists have measured Badwater with great certainty and figured out how the pupfish endures in the middle of the desert, geologists have been unable to determine exactly how rocks migrate around the Racetrack.

An ancient lake bed, the Racetrack is a 2.5-mile-long, oval-shaped dry mud flat. A rock outcropping at the north end of the Racetrack is known as the Grandstand.

Rocks of various sizes (baseball to basketball) slide across the old lake bed leaving tracks in their wake. These tracks (about 6 inches wide or so, depending on the size of the rock) are straight, curved, and even looped, and extend as much as 600 feet.

Prospectors noticed the sliding rocks more than a century ago, earth scientists have studied them since the 1950s, and countless visitors have observed

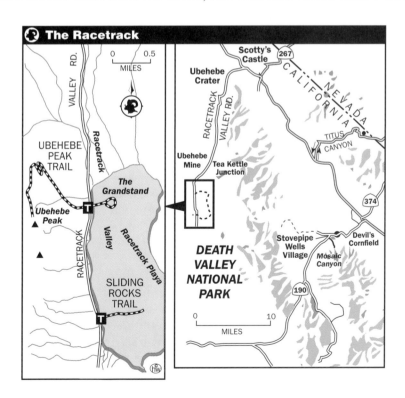

them. Sure, scientists have measured the rocks' changes of location, but no one, trained park naturalist or curious hiker, has ever seen the rocks actually move.

Scientists theorize that the rocks slide after rain moistens the top couple centimeters of the lake bed and a high wind (perhaps 70 miles per hour or more) arises to push them around the track. Do not hike on the Racetrack after a rainstorm.

Wind-pushed rocks across a rain-slicked mud flat sounds like a plausible enough explanation for such movement, but it does not explain why the rocks move in such peculiar patterns. Some rocks have made sudden right-angle turns; others have made complete loops and ended up almost exactly where they began.

The sliding rocks are not one of Death Valley's roadside attractions, so you'll have to take a short hike to visit them. Even if you're not fortunate enough to be the first human to observe the rocks move, you'll have a great time tracing the rock tracks and playing on the playa.

Two other hikes complement your day at the Racetrack. Don't just drive by Ubehebe Crater. Stop and walk a mile along the cinder-covered rim of this volcanic crater.

For grand views of the Racetrack, ascend the trail to Ubehebe Peak. This strenuous path begins at the turnout to the Grandstand, 2 miles north of the Racetrack trailhead. The hike to the 5,678-foot summit (5 miles round trip with 2,000 feet in elevation gain) is for experienced hikers and requires some rock scrambling. However, a more modest 1.5-mile hike up the trail to the ridge crest delivers great Racetrack vistas.

DIRECTIONS TO TRAILHEAD From the Furnace Creek Visitor Center in the heart of the park, drive 17 miles north on Highway 190, then bear right on the road to Scotty's Castle and proceed 32 more miles to the Grapevine Ranger Station and entry kiosk. Head north toward Ubehebe Crater (don't take the road to Scotty's Castle) for 5 miles.

The paved road ends with a left turn into the Ubehebe Crater parking lot, but you continue south 20 miles on the washboard-surfaced, occasionally rough dirt Racetrack Valley Road (not suitable for low-clearance passenger cars) to Tea Kettle Junction, colorfully decorated with teakettles. Bear right, and travel another 6 miles to the Grandstand, on the left side of the road, and 2 more miles to parking for the Racetrack, identified by a Park Service interpretive sign on the left side of the road.

THE HIKE After reading about the sliding rocks, begin your sojourn to them by heading due east across the old lakebed. Hiking straight across the valley from the sign is the quickest and most direct route to the rocks, though walking in other directions will also deliver you to the rocks in due time.

A half mile of hiking brings you to the first rock tracks. If you keep hiking toward the mountains on the far side of the lake bed, you'll encounter more and more rocks and accompanying tracks. (These mountains supply the sliding rocks.)

Wander at will among the rocks and return the way you came.

■ TITUS CANYON
Titus Canyon Trail
Through the narrow part of canyon is 4 to 5 miles round trip;
to Klare Spring is 12 miles round trip

In Titus Canyon, gray and white cliffs, red and green hills, and fractured and contorted rocks point to the tremendous geologic forces that shaped the land we call Death Valley National Park.

Titus Canyon offers the hiker—and the motorist (more about vehicles in a moment)—a chance to explore one of Death Valley's scenic gems. Hikers enter a twisting narrows, where a block of the earth's crust has dropped down along fault lines in relation to its mountain walls.

The canyon is named for Morris Titus, who in 1906 left the Nevada boomtown of Rhyolite (now a historic ghost town), near the California border, with a prospecting party. When the prospectors were camped in the canyon, water supplies dwindled. Titus left in search of water and help, but was never seen again.

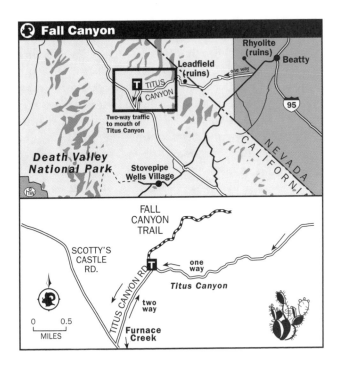

Use care when hiking through Titus Canyon: the road is open to cars.

Winding through the canyon is 28-mile long Titus Canyon Road, a narrow, one-way dirt track. If you're doing the canyon by vehicle, the park suggests using four-wheel drive, though it is open to two-wheel-drive vehicles with good ground clearance. Check on road conditions at the park visitor center in Furnace Creek.

Figure two to three hours for the drive, which takes you through a variety of environments. A historic highlight en route is a stop at the ghost town of Leadfield. The town boomed in 1925 due to the slick efforts of a promoter who controlled a very low-grade deposit of lead ore. A town was built in the narrow canyon; its population soon swelled to 300. A year later, the town was empty.

Today, only a shack or two and some crumbling foundations mark Leadfield, but the road that serviced the mines and miners remains behind, beckoning to those who prospect for scenery.

In theory, vehicles and hikers should not be sharing narrow throughfares, but in practice, in Titus Canyon, the arrangement works. Those few motorists who brave Titus Canyon are a courteous lot—and hikers can hear them coming from a long way off, thus avoiding potential mishaps.

DIRECTIONS TO TRAILHEAD To reach the start of one-way Titus Canyon Road: From Highway 190, a few miles from Stovepipe Wells, head northeast on Highway 374 toward Beatty, Nevada, some 25 miles away. About 4 miles short of Beatty is the signed turnoff for Titus Canyon.

You don't have to drive the 28-mile road to hike Titus Canyon. The lower part of Titus Canyon Road is two-way and takes you to the trailhead. From the junction of highways 374 and 190, head north 14 miles on 190 to Titus Canyon Road.

THE HIKE From the trailhead, it's moderate uphill walking along the gravel floor of the canyon. As you hike along, you'll marvel at the awesome folding and faulting of the canyon's rock walls. For a moderate walk through the rock show, continue a couple miles up-canyon and turn around.

More gung-ho hikers will keep trekking up Titus Canyon, which widens a bit. Nearly 6 miles out is Klare Spring, a waterhole occasionally visited by a herd of bighorn sheep.

See Map
on Page
31

■ FALL CANYON
Fall Canyon Trail
To Narrows is 6.5 miles round trip
with 1,100-foot elevation gain

Walk between the colorful, contorted rock walls of this canyon, and you might just agree with hikers who rank Fall as one of the most magnificent canyons in the park. This is a hike through a dramatic gash in the Grapevine Mountains among soaring walls and the polished rock of the narrows. Depending on the angle of the sun and what it illuminates, the canyon's rock displays hues of red, brown, sepia, and umber.

Fall Canyon shares a trailhead with Titus Canyon, one of Death Valley's marquee canyons, to be sure, but also one that is accessible to vehicles. In the eyes of many hikers, a roadless canyon is automatically more revered than one open to vehicle travel; thus Fall Canyon might rate higher. Few visit Fall Canyon, so you might just find some solitude in its narrow passageways. The canyon floor is the loose soil of a wash and thus can be slow-going.

Fall Canyon gets its name for a 20-foot-high dry waterfall located 3 miles up the canyon. Sure-footed hikers can circumvent the fall with a bit of rock-scrambling and by way of short use trail along the canyon wall. For safety's sake and to avoid a fall into Fall Canyon, the fall bypass route should be undertaken only by confident, experienced hikers. A dramatic segment of canyon lies on the other side of the dry fall.

DIRECTIONS TO TRAILHEAD From its junction with Daylight Pass Road (Highway 374), drive north 14.3 miles to the turnoff for Titus Canyon. Follow Titus Canyon Road (rough but passable for cars with good ground clearance) 2.7 miles east to a parking area at the mouth of Titus Canyon.

THE HIKE From the parking area, head north on an unsigned path (don't trek into Titus Canyon). The trail dips and rises, traveling over low ridges and into shallow washes until it reaches the main Fall Canyon Wash a bit more than 0.5 mile from the trailhead.

Not long after you probe the mouth of the canyon, the trail fades away and the canyon walls, from your hiker's point of view, seem to vault higher and higher. At 1.3 miles, the canyon walls narrow to about 20 feet.

Gaze upward at the colorful walls and continue as the canyon widens and then narrows again at the 2.5-mile mark. This particular narrows is so narrow that its floor is in nearly perpetual shade—a welcome respite on a hot afternoon.

Three miles out, you'll stand face to rock face with the high dry fall. To bypass the fall, retrace your steps 300 feet or so down the wash and look for rock cairns on the canyon's south wall. Carefully ascend the short rock pitch up to the use trail that continues along the canyon wall to the right of the fall.

Just beyond the fall, the canyon is a very narrow world of polished rock. You can wander 0.3 mile or so farther—a dramatic conclusion to this splendid hike.

■ DEATH VALLEY BUTTES
Death Valley Buttes Trail
From Hell's Gate to the top of the buttes is 4 miles round trip with 900-foot elevation gain

Grand views of the central part of the national park are the hiker's reward for a trailless scramble to the top of Death Valley Buttes, three distinct hills at the base of the Grapevine Mountains. The sweeping panorama includes the valley floor, as well as the Funeral and Panamint ranges.

Death Valley Buttes are actually part and parcel of the Grapevine Mountains. Ongoing erosion of the range leaves much rock debris at the base of the mountains; this alluvium gradually buried the lower ridges, leaving behind isolated high points of which the most prominent are the Death Valley Buttes.

The route to the buttes begins at Hell's Gate—named, as the story goes, in 1905 by a teamster who was struck by the contrast between the relative cool of Boundary Canyon and the hotter area near the buttes. The mules would act startled and shake their heads at the sudden searing heat. "They thought they had stuck their noses through the gates of hell," the teamster is reported to have exclaimed.

Hell's Gate may seem an unlikely place in which to build a resort, but that's just what Bob Eichbaum dreamed of doing in the 1920s. In 1905, the young electrical engineer became enchanted with Death Valley when he helped construct an electrical plant in Rhyolite. After 20 years in the tourist business—operating a goat cart concession on Venice Beach and sightseeing tours on Catalina Island—he returned to Death Valley intent on building a grand hotel, what he termed "one of the wonders of the country." He planned to collect customers in Los Angeles and bus them to Hell's Gate, but bad roads doomed his plan and his resort was never built. (Eichbaum, however, did open the original Stovepipe

Wells Hotel in 1926, as well as the Eichbaum Toll Road over Towne Pass into the valley.)

The cross-country route to the buttes is easy enough to accomplish. More difficult is the narrow, rocky ridge that must be traversed—best left to experienced hikers.

DIRECTIONS TO TRAILHEAD From the Furnace Creek Visitor Center, head north on Highway 190 for 11 miles. Veer right toward Beatty on the Beatty Cutoff and travel northeast 10 miles to Hell's Gate, where you'll find a large parking area and picnic tables.

THE HIKE Walk southwest toward the buttes across rocky terrain dotted with creosote and beavertail cactus. Look for the remains of the phone line that crossed this land, connecting Rhyolite to civilization, such as it was, in the southwest.

After 0.5 mile, you leave behind this relatively gentle alluvial fan and strike south toward the ridge of the easternmost butte. Follow the rock crest westward, aided by an intermittent trail, to the 2,725-foot summit. Admire the barren Grapevine Mountains nearby, and the equally austere Funeral Mountains extending southeast.

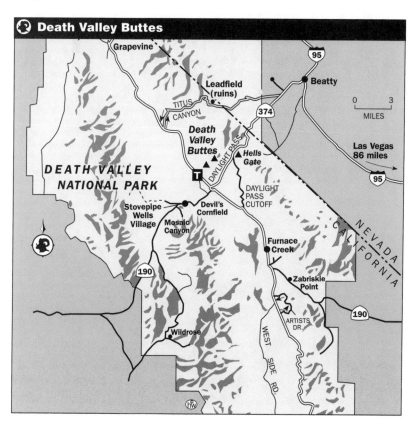

Return the way you came or continue to the next and highest butte. If you press on (only for experienced hikers), you'll descend the steep ridgeline west to a saddle, then ascend the narrow ridge 0.5 mile to Peak 3,017. Enjoy the view across the shimmering valley floor to the Panamint Mountains.

■ KEANE WONDER MINE
Keane Wonder Mine Trail
2 miles round trip with 1,800 feet elevation gain

One of the most noted mines in the Funeral Mountains was Homer Wilson's Keane Wonder, which operated from 1903 to 1916. During its best years, the mine produced a quarter of a million dollars a year in gold.

Even more noteworthy than the mine was "Death Valley's Sky Railroad," a gravity-powered aerial tram that ran for a mile up the precipitous slopes of the Funerals. The half-ton weight of the loaded ore buckets descending to the mill raised the empties back up to the mine.

The tram must have been an energy-saver for the miners who, if they had to hike to work every day, would not have been very productive. The 20-minute

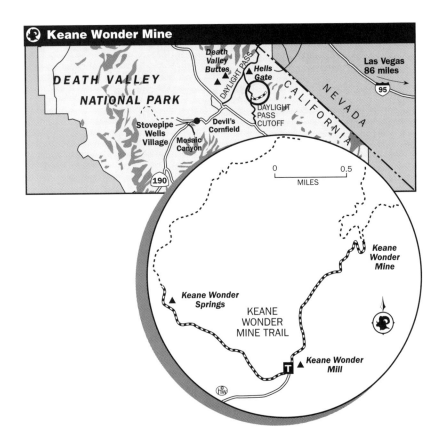

ride was exhilarating for mine visitors, who sat on a little iron bench, legs dangling hundreds of feet above jagged rocks. Few visitors requested a second ride.

While the mine was profitable, most of the money went toward paying off loans, machinery purchase, and searching (unsuccessfully) for more pockets of gold. A failed bank, questionable stock transactions, and insider trading—legal battles for control of the Keane Wonder Mine—outlasted the mine itself.

Hikers can view some old mill ruins and follow a trail along the route of the old tramway, past a series of wooden towers, to the mine. It's a stiff climb; you might wish the rickety tram was still running.

All that remains of the Keane Wonder Mine.

DIRECTIONS TO TRAILHEAD
From Furnace Creek, follow Highway 190 north ten miles, veer right onto the Beatty Cutoff, and drive 5.7 miles to the signed turnoff to Keane Wonder Mine. Turn east and drive 2.8 miles to road's end at the mine.

THE HIKE Follow an old roadbed, then join the footpath and begin an extremely steep ascent. After 0.5 mile, the grade lessens, and another 0.5 mile of more moderate hiking takes you to the top of the aerial tramway. From the ruins of the upper tram station, enjoy the grand valley views.

Stay away from dangerous shafts and tunnels.

■ KEANE WONDER SPRINGS
Keane Wonder Springs Trail
To the springs is 2 miles round trip
with 100-foot elevation gain

Keane Wonder Springs supplied water to the Keane Wonder Mine and mill. The springs is as mineral-laden as the ground itself, a sulfur-rich flow that looks—and smells—like an industrial water supply.

While unappealing, as well as unfit for human consumption, the waters of the Wonder Springs are quite attractive to many bird and insect species. Bighorn sheep wander down from the Funeral Mountains to drink at the springs.

The mostly level path to the springs offers an easy alternative to the challenging ascent to Keane Wonder Mine. Beyond the springs are the ruins of a stamp mill and a miners' cabin.

En route, look for unusually colored rocks, including slick slabs of cream-colored travertine created by the spring's sulfurous waters. Near the spring, the water leaves a kind of gross-looking green-yellow mineral trail.

DIRECTIONS TO TRAILHEAD From Furnace Creek, follow Highway 190 north 10 miles, veer right onto the Beatty Cutoff, and drive 5.7 miles to the signed turnoff to Keane Wonder Mine. Turn east and drive 2.8 miles to road's end at the mine.

THE HIKE The mine trail leads uphill, but you head toward a pair of old rusty water tanks. Below the tanks is a broken pipeline that carried water from Keane Wonder Springs to the mill.

The trail improves as you follow the route of the old pipeline. After crossing a wash, the path passes a couple of mine shafts.

At about the 0.8-mile mark, you'll notice the travertine rock. Follow the white rock uphill to the reed-lined creek and Keane Wonder Springs. A Park Service sign and the malodorous aroma of hydrogen sulfide warn you of the chemical dangers of the spring.

Return to the main trail and continue another 0.2 mile with views of more mining ruins. At trail's end you'll find a rather well-preserved miners' cabin.

■ DEATH VALLEY SAND DUNES
Dunes Cross-country Route
2 to 4 miles round trip

A 14-square-mile field of dunes and some bizarre geology are some of the attractions of walking around the Stovepipe Wells area of Death Valley National Park. Hiking the dunes is most fun in the cooler morning and late afternoon hours. At these hours, the dunes are at their most photogenic, too; the light is softer, the shadows longer.

The Death Valley dunes are formed in much the same way as those megadunes in the Middle East or North Africa. What nature needs to form dunes is fairly simple: a source of sand, wind to separate the sand from gravel, more wind to roll the sand along into drifts, and still more wind, perhaps in the form of a backdraft, to keep the dunes in place.

Death Valley's dunes lie between Towne Pass on the west and Daylight Pass to the east; there's quite a sand-laden draft between the two passes.

"Dune Speak" is a colorful language, a vocabulary of windward and leeward faces, black patches and Chinese walls, blow sand and sand shadows. The slip face of the dunes (away from the wind) is very steep, but never steeper than 34 degrees, which is known as the angle of repose because steeper than this angle a slide occurs, thus reducing the angle a degree or three.

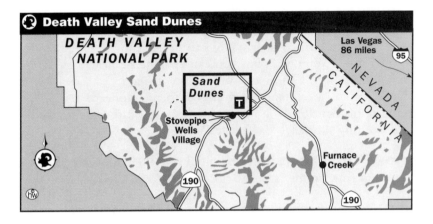

Death Valley Sand Dunes

As you hike the dunes, you'll notice blow sand (loose, very fine particles) piled on the leeward side of plants; these piles are known as sand shadows.

Death Valley's dunes are sub-barchan, or crescent-shaped. The sand dunes are actually tiny pieces of rock, most of them quartz fragments.

Near the dunes are some weird natural features. Those surrealistic-looking corn stalks you see across Highway 190 from the dunes are actually clumps of arrow-weed. The Devil's Cornstalks are perched on wind- and water-eroded pedestals.

Fringing the dunes are expanses of dry mud that have cracked and buckled into interesting patterns. These mud sink areas and the edges of the dunes themselves are good places to look for the tracks of the few desert creatures able to survive in the harsh environment—most notably, rabbits and kangaroo rats.

DIRECTIONS TO TRAILHEAD From the Village of Stovepipe Wells, take Highway 190 east for 2 miles to the interpretive sign for the dunes.

THE HIKE Your hike into the dunes is exactly what you make of it—short or long, a direct or indirect route to the higher sand formations. Figure 4 miles max to climb up, down, and around the taller dunes and return. Remember that doing the dunes means a two-steps-forward-one-step-backward kind of hiking, so pace yourself accordingly. Wear shoes; sand surfaces can be very hot.

■ BURNED WAGONS POINT
Burned Wagons Point Trail
From Highway 190 to Burned Wagons Point
is 4.5 miles round trip

Fearful of the terrible cold and snows of the High Sierra, and mindful of the fate of the Donner Party three years earlier, a group of California-bound pioneers took a more southerly route, ending up hot, hungry, and lost in the autumn of 1849. A splinter group of these pioneers, known as the Jayhawkers, camped in the area of present-day Stovepipe Wells. Here, they slaughtered the last of their oxen and burned their wagons to smoke and preserve the meat.

Today, at Burned Wagons Point, you can imagine the fear these emigrants felt as they looked across the bleak valley floor toward the seemingly insurmountable Panamint Mountains. As you hike to the pioneer's camp, you can also get a taste of their lonely journey—which in this case ended happily with the pioneers exiting the valley via Towne Pass.

DIRECTIONS TO TRAILHEAD From Highway 190 in Stovepipe Wells, drive 6 miles east and park on the opposite side of the closed road.

THE HIKE The trail starts south across the valley floor. A half mile along, the road passes mesquite-covered mounds of sand.

About 1.5 miles from the trailhead, the road enters a cluster of low hills. The main route continues southeast, but you'll join a narrow westbound wash that penetrates a long ridge on your right. This wash soon routes you through the hills. You'll then joint a faint path angling south 0.75 mile to Burned Wagon Point.

Immediately west of Burned Wagon Point, marked with a sign, is McClean Spring, a modest pool of brackish water believed to have been used as a water supply by the '49ers.

Also nearby is pickleweed- and salt grass-lined Salt Creek. (See Salt Creek Interpretive Trail.)

■ GROTTO CANYON
Grotto Canyon Trail
Grotto Canyon Trail
4 miles round trip with 800-foot elevation gain

Grottos carved by floodwaters, dry falls, and narrows of polished rock define Grotto Canyon, which has a remote feeling, considering its close proximity to Stovepipe Wells.

One reason for this isolation is the iffy road leading to the trailhead. The road, such as it is, leads through the soft gravel bed of a wash. A four-wheel drive vehicle with high ground clearance is required to negotiate the road. Most visitors, with and without such vehicles, park alongside Highway 190 and hike a mile up the little-traveled track to the trailhead.

DIRECTIONS TO TRAILHEAD From Highway 190 in the hamlet of Stovepipe Wells, drive 2.5 miles east to the Grotto Canyon Road on the south side of the highway.

THE HIKE Follow the road/wash south on a moderate ascent up the alluvial fan. The best desert views are behind you: Death Valley's shimmering sands and the Grapevine and Cottonwood ranges.

A mile's climb brings you to Grotto Canyon's main wash. Walk the wide wash, which narrows as you continue your ascent. Dramatically eroded walls resembling the stone ruins of some ancient monastery tower above the canyon floor.

At the 1.8-mile mark, you encounter the first grotto, a cool and contemplative place—especially on a hot day. A twisting passageway leads to two dry waterfalls.

These dry falls can be climbed by agile hikers or bypassed by returning 0.1 mile down-canyon to a trail way-marked with cairns. This path leads along the east side of the canyon to leapfrog the falls.

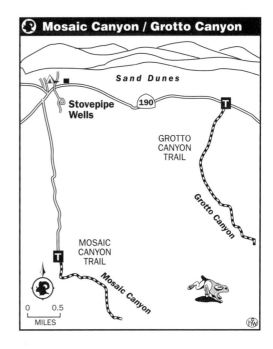

Back in the canyon bottom, continue another 0.2 mile to another dry fall, which marks trail's end.

■ MOSAIC CANYON
Mosaic Canyon Trail
4 miles round trip through the "narrows"

Some Death Valley canyons deliver the scenery promised in their names: Golden, Red Wall, and Corkscrew, to name a few.

Mosaic Canyon is another fine example of truth-in-labeling. The canyon, located near Stovepipe Wells, displays mosaics of water-polished white, gray, and black rock.

Nature has cemented the canyon's stream gravels into mosaics large and small. It's easy to imagine you've entered an art gallery when you view the mosaics on the canyon walls; not only are nature's works of art on display, but the long and narrow white marble walls of the canyon seem quite gallery-like.

Mosaic is one of those desert canyons that's hourglass in shape: a fairly wide head and mouth, with a narrow, deep gorge in between. This shape means that during a storm, rainwater collects on the broad surface area at the head of the canyon then funnels through the narrow canyon midsection at high velocity. The water, laden with rock debris, sculpts the canyon into its photogenic form, and polishes the rock walls.

(By the way, a narrow canyon like Mosaic is the very last place you want to be in a rainstorm! Pay attention to weather reports before considering this hike!)

Mosaic Canyon is an ideal family outing. Rangers lead interpretive walks through the canyon. For schedules of guided walks, check at the main park visitor center in Furnace Creek or the small center at Stovepipe Wells.

Serious hikers can persevere several more miles up ever-steeper slopes toward the head of Mosaic Canyon or enjoy the rock-climbing challenge afforded by rugged tributary canyons.

DIRECTIONS TO TRAILHEAD From the west end of Stovepipe Wells village, turn south on the signed dirt road for Mosaic Canyon. Follow the bumpy road (suitable for passenger cars with good ground clearance) 2.5 miles to its end at a parking lot.

THE HIKE Walk up the sand and gravel canyon bottom. In a short time, you'll round a bend and enter a corridor of polished rock. At the next bend, you'll climb a dry waterfall. The farther you go, the higher the walls get, exposing more and more of the mosaics that gave the canyon its name.

After 0.75 mile, the canyon opens up into a wider wash. As you hike along, marveling at the mosaics, a couple of minor canyons join Mosaic on your right. These can be explored if you have the inclination and determination.

As the wash narrows again about 2 miles from the trailhead, some hikers may get the feeling they're beginning to do more rock climbing than hiking. This is a good turnaround point; stop while you're having a good time and before you exceed your abilities.

The marble walls of Mosaic Canyon resemble those of an art gallery.

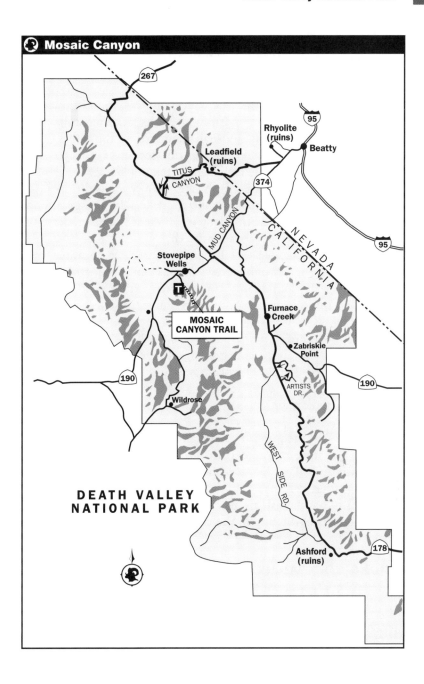

Mosaic Canyon

267

Rhyolite
(ruins)

95

Beatty

Leadfield
(ruins)

TITUS
CANYON

374

MUD CANYON

NEVADA

CALIFORNIA

Stovepipe
Wells

T

MOSAIC
CANYON TRAIL

Furnace
Creek

Zabriskie
Point

95

190

ARTISTS
DR.

Wildrose

190

WEST SIDE RD.

DEATH VALLEY
NATIONAL PARK

Ashford
(ruins)

178

■ SALT CREEK
Salt Creek Interpretive Trail
1 to 2 miles round trip

Salt Creek is the home of the Salt Creek pupfish, found nowhere else on earth. A nature trail along a boardwalk tells its amazing story.

Many desert creatures display unusual adaptation to the rigors of life in arid lands and changes in their environment, but few have had to make more remarkable adjustments than the little Salt Creek pupfish.

Thousands of years ago, a large freshwater lake covered the area. Gradually, this lake shrunk smaller and smaller while the lake's salinity greatly increased. Many plants and animals failed to adapt to an environment radically different from the one in which their forebears existed.

But the pupfish adapted—evolved the ability to filter saltwater, remove the excess salt, and excrete it through kidneys or gills. And the inch-long fish, accustomed to a lot of water and a fairly constant temperature, adapted to life in a relatively tiny amount of water that varies in temperature from near-freezing to nearly 100°F.

Once the pupfish were so numerous that the valley's native peoples harvested them for food. They were still numerous when the *1938 WPA Guide to Death Valley* described them: "Prospectors amuse themselves by holding a pan full of crumbs just below the surface and watching the greedy fish crowd in to eat. They come so rapidly and in such numbers, that they sometimes make small waves."

Alas, by the 1970s, the pupfish was on the endangered species list. The pupfish population has since rebounded thanks to habitat-improvement efforts by wildlife biologists and a Park Service-built boardwalk that reduces the impact of visitors on the soft creek banks.

Best months to see the fish are from mid-February to May. In spring, a million pupfish might be wriggling in the creek; by early summer, just a few thousand remain.

DIRECTIONS TO TRAILHEAD From State Highway 190, some 13 miles north of Furnace Creek, turn west onto a dirt road leading to the Salt Creek parking area.

THE HIKE Interpretive signs line the Park Service's Salt Creek Nature Trail. Begin your walk along the boardwalk. At the northern end of the loop, leave the boardwalk and take the footpath continuing north along the east side of the creek. Walk another 0.5 mile or so along the nearly 30-mile-long creek. You'll see more pupfish, as well as birds ranging from snipes to great blue herons.

■ HARMONY BORAX WORKS
Harmony Borax Works Trail
2.6 miles round trip; to the haystacks is 5 miles round trip

Death Valley National Park. It seems almost a contradiction in terms, particularly when you hike out to the old Harmony Borax Works—a rock salt landscape as tortured as you'll ever find.

A park? Surely if the notion of a park was ever mentioned to one of the rough drivers of the 20-mule-team borax wagons that crossed Death Valley, the response would be unprintable in a family guidebook.

But back to borax. In Death Valley, strangely enough, the borax story and the park story are almost inseparable. Borax super-salesman Stephen T. Mather became the first director of the National Park Service in 1916.

"White gold," Death Valley prospectors called it. Borax is not exactly a glamorous substance, but it has proved to be a profitable one. From 1883 to 1888, more than 20 million pounds of borax were transported from the Harmony Borax Works.

Transport of the borax was the stuff of legends, too. The famous 20-mule teams hauled the huge loaded wagons 165 miles to the rail station at Mojave.

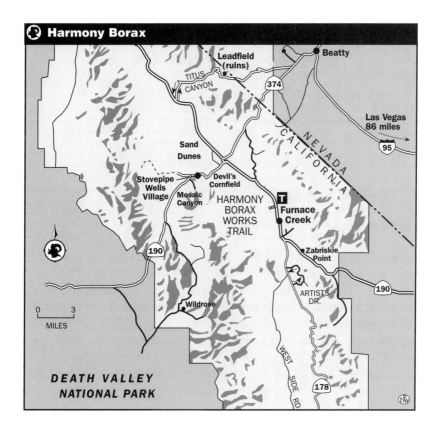

Old-time ad for Borax, the king of clean.

Down-on-his-luck prospector Aaron Winters first discovered borax on the salt flats in Furnace Creek in 1881. He was ecstatic when San Francisco investor William Coleman purchased his rights to the borax field for $20,000. Coleman capitalized construction of the Harmony Borax Works, an endeavor that depended first and foremost on the labors of Chinese-Americans who gathered the fibrous clusters of borate called "cotton-balls."

After purification at the borax works, the substance was loaded into custom 15-foot-long wagons to be hauled by 10 pairs of mules. The animals were controlled by a long jerk line and legendary mule-skinner profanity.

To learn more about this colorful era, visit the Borax Museum at Furnace Creek Ranch and the park visitor center, also located in Furnace Creek.

DIRECTIONS TO TRAILHEAD Reach Harmony Borax Works from Furnace Creek, by following Highway 190 for 1.5 miles to the signed turnoff on the west side of the highway.

THE HIKE A short trail with interpretive signs leads past the ruins of the old borax refinery and some outlying buildings.

The main trail leads 1.3 miles over the salt flats. You'll travel through a wash to trail's end at a wooden post. From here it's less than 200 yards to the edge of the salt marsh where borax was mined.

Adventurous hikers can make the trail-less trek across sometimes spongy terrain to the borax haystacks, 2-foot-high piles of sodium calcium borate balls stacked here in the 1880s by Chinese laborers to prove claim assessment work. The hike—and the photo opportunities—are particularly good early in the morning.

■ GOLDEN CANYON
Golden Canyon Trail
To Red Cathedral is 2.5 miles round trip

The panoramic view of Golden Canyon from Zabriskie Point is magnificent, but don't miss getting right into the canyon itself—only possible by hitting the trail. Sunrise and sunset, when the light is magical and fellow hikers are few, are particularly good times to walk the canyon.

Until the rainy winter of 1976, a road extended through Golden Canyon. A desert deluge washed away the road, and it's been a trail ever since.

The first mile of Golden Canyon Trail is a self-guided interpretive trail. Pick up a copy of the National Park Service's pamphlet, "Trail Guide to Golden Canyon," available at the visitor center or at the trailhead for a small fee. Stops in the guide are keyed to numbers along the trail, and the guide may tell you more about Miocene volcanic activity, Jurassic granitic intrusion, and Precambrian erosion than you ever wanted to know; however, even the most casual student of earth science will gain an appreciation for the complex geology and the millions of years required to sculpt and color Golden Canyon.

At the end of the nature trail, the path branches. One fork heads for Red Cathedral, also called Red Cliffs. The red color is essentially iron oxide—rust—produced by weathering of rocks with a high iron content.

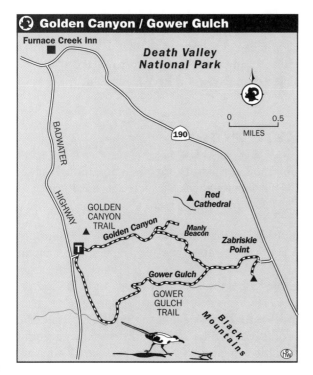

Golden Canyon / Gower Gulch

Furnace Creek Inn

Death Valley National Park

0   0.5
MILES

190

BADWATER

HIGHWAY

GOLDEN CANYON TRAIL

Golden Canyon

Red Cathedral

Manly Beacon

Zabriskie Point

Gower Gulch

GOWER GULCH TRAIL

Black Mountains

DIRECTIONS TO TRAILHEAD From the Furnace Creek Visitor Center, drive south on Highway 190, forking right onto Badwater Road. The signed Golden Canyon Trail is on your left, three miles from the visitor center. The walk through Golden Canyon shares a common trailhead with the longer excursion to Zabriskie Point.

THE HIKE From the parking lot, hike up the alluvial fan into the canyon. Marvel at the tilted, faulted rock walls of the canyon as they close in around you. Notice the ripple marks, created long ago by water lapping at the shore of an ancient lake.

One of the most photographed sights in Death Valley is deeply furrowed Golden Canyon.

Depending on the light, Golden Canyon can seem to glow gold, brass, yellow, or orange. Aptly named Red Cathedral looms over the canyon in colorful contrast.

Deeper and deeper into the badlands you ascend. Watch for white crystalline outcroppings of borax—the same stuff of the 20-mule-team fame.

At the end of the nature trail, you can continue up the main canyon a quarter mile to the old Golden Canyon parking lot. The trail narrows and you continue by squeezing past boulders to the base of Red Cathedral, a colorful natural amphitheater.

See Map on Page 47

■ ZABRISKIE POINT AND GOWER GULCH

Golden Canyon, Zabriskie Point, Gower Gulch Trails

To Zabriskie Point with return via Gower Gulch is 6.5 miles round trip with 900-foot elevation gain

Before sunrise, photographers set up their tripods at Zabriskie Point and point their cameras down at the pale mudstone hills of Golden Canyon and the great valley beyond.

The display of color from purple to gold as sun passes over Golden Canyon is memorable to say the least.

While it's true that you can drive to Zabriskie Point, you'll appreciate the view much more by sweating up those switchbacks on foot. An engaging trail climbs through badlands to the point named for Christian Brevoort Zabriskie, one of the early leaders of Death Valley borax mining operations.

The memorable panorama from Zabriskie Point includes a grand view of the valley, framed by the badlands just below and the Panamint Mountains to the west. A return by way of Gower Gulch offers another perspective on this colorful desert land and enables hikers to make a loop.

DIRECTIONS TO TRAILHEAD From the Furnace Creek Visitor Center, drive south on Highway 190, forking right onto Badwater Road. The signed Golden Canyon Trail is on your left, three miles from the visitor center. The walk to Zabriskie Point shares a common trailhead with the shorter excursion through Golden Canyon.

THE HIKE From stop 10 on the Golden Canyon interpretive trail, take the signed fork toward Zabriskie Point. The path climbs into the badlands toward Manly Beacon, a pinnacle of gold sandstone. The trail crests at the shoulder of the beacon, then descends into the badlands and brings you to a junction. Go left (east) to Zabriskie Point. (The right fork is the return leg of your loop through Gower Gulch.)

Watch for Park Service signs to stay on the trail, which is a bit difficult to follow as it marches up and down the severely eroded silt-stone hills. After a mile, a final steep grade brings you to Zabriskie Point—or, more accurately, the parking lot. Step uphill to the point itself, and savor the vast views of the eroded yellow hills below and the mountains across the valley.

Retrace your steps back to the trail fork. This time you'll descend west into a wash. Wide, gray, and gravelly Gower Gulch definitely has felt the hand of man. The open mouths of tunnels and white smears on the gulch walls are reminders of the borax miners who dug up these hills. Gower Gulch has been altered considerably to protect Furnace Creek developments from flooding.

A bit more than a mile down the trail, the gulch narrows and you'll suddenly encounter a 30-foot-high dry fall. Take the bypass footpath to the right. A final 1.2 miles of trail heads north along the base of the hills, on a route paralleling the highway, and leads back to the trailhead parking area at the mouth of Golden Canyon.

■ DESOLATION CANYON
Desolation Canyon Trail
2.2 miles round trip with 400-foot elevation gain

Deeply eroded hills, a rainbow of color on the lower slopes of the Black Mountains, and a twisted canyon so narrow you can reach out and touch its wall are among the highlights of this walk to and through Desolation Canyon.

The canyon is isolated and austere in places, but no more desolate than any other in the rugged foothills south of Furnace Creek. Desolation, like the better known Black Mountains canyons, offers a marvelous geology lesson.

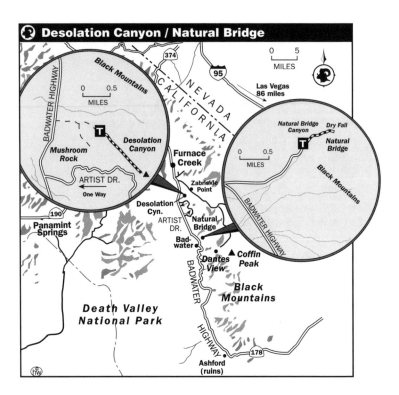

This hike begins by following a broad alluvial fan, then penetrates narrow Desolation Canyon.

DIRECTIONS TO TRAILHEAD From the junction of Highway 190 and the Badwater Road near the Furnace Creek Inn, take the latter road 3.6 miles, then turn left (east) on a dirt road that leads a mile to the trailhead.

THE HIKE Follow the old road (washed out by 2004 storms) east out of the parking area a short distance to where it joins the wash. Walk the wash to the cliffs and turn south with the main canyon toward the canyon narrows. After a quarter mile, the walls of the canyon close in. The soft walls of the canyon, dramatically sculpted by rushing water, soar more than 100 feet above you.

Keep staying right at various forks in the twisted canyon to remain with the main wash. Look for a couple of minor (3 to 5 feet high) dry cascades. Your hike through the canyon will be halted a bit more than a mile from the trailhead. You can continue another 0.5 mile up a narrow right-forking tributary canyon.

■ NATURAL BRIDGE
Natural Bridge Trail
To Natural Bridge is 0.75 mile round trip

An intriguing short path off Badwater Road offers the hiker a little bit of southern Utah—an eroded canyon rim and a large natural bridge formation. Long ago, water surged through a canyon wall, stripping away weaker strata and leaving behind a 50-foot-high rock bridge spanning the canyon.

Beyond the bridge, you can explore other water-cut formations—grottoes and benches, chutes and spillways. A very detailed trailhead display of Death Valley geology will delight those geology buffs fascinated by such topics as slip faults and mud drips.

DIRECTIONS TO TRAILHEAD From Badwater Road, some 15 miles south of Furnace Creek visitor center, follow the signed dirt road 1.5 miles to the Natural Bridge trailhead.

THE HIKE Head up the gravel-floored canyon bottom. Before long, the volcanic walls of the canyon narrow and you'll meet up with the natural bridge.

To extend this sojourn, walk under the bridge and continue up-canyon. Note the textbook examples of slip faults and a couple of fault caves and continue your journey. A dry waterfall, about 0.75 mile from the trailhead can be surmounted, but the 20-foot-high dry fall a mile out halts this hike.

■ COFFIN PEAK
Coffin Peak Trail
From picnic area below Dante's View to Coffin Peak is 2.5 miles with 300-foot elevation gain

Make no mistake: Dante's View offers one of Death Valley's finest panoramas. Trouble is, you can drive to the viewpoint—and thousands of motorists do, meaning your chances for quiet contemplation of the desert below are about as slim as the possibility of rainfall.

For the hiker, there is an alternative: Coffin Peak, offering the same great view as Dante's without the crowds.

The 5,503-foot peak (a smidgen higher than 5,475-foot Dante's View) is situated in the relatively little-traveled Black Mountains that extend along the southeastern boundary of the national park.

In addition to Dante's View, the other major visitor attraction in the Black Mountains is Greenwater, where a few ruins and building foundations are all that remain of a copper mining boomtown. The hype after the 1905 discovery of copper attracted a thousand people, and soon Greenwater had stores, saloons, a post office, and even two newspapers and a men's magazine. What

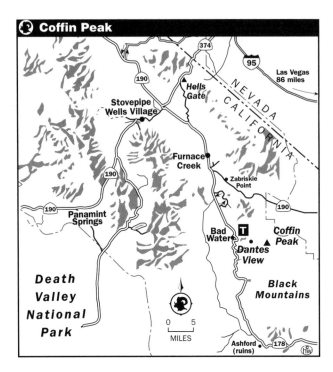

Greenwater lacked, however, was quality ore, and by 1908 Greenwater was a ghost town.

Hikers experienced with cross-country travel will be most comfortable with the trail-less trek to Coffin Peak; however, the less experienced can set out with the assurance that this walk for the most part stays within sight of Dante's View Road.

DIRECTIONS TO TRAILHEAD From Badwater Road, Highway 190 junction just south of the Furnace Creek Visitor Center, drive 10.8 miles on Highway 190 toward Death Valley Junction. Turn right on Dante's View Road and continue 12.6 miles (0.6 mile short of Dante's View). Turn left and park in the wide turnout, which has pit toilets and a picnic table.

THE HIKE From the picnic site, you'll parallel Dante's View Road, ascending a minor hill dotted with Mormon tea. Dodging spiny shrubs, follow the ridgecrest as it bends southeast and climbs to the top of a 5,360-foot hill.

You'll continue east among handsome desert varnish-stained boulders, savoring the valley views. Topping another hill, you descend a short distance northeastward to a saddle, then climb again to Peak 5484.

Now you follow the crest south, then east, toward the conical summit of Coffin Peak. Your view encompasses the Black Mountains, south and north, the Funeral Mountains to the northeast, and the Greenwater Valley, green indeed with creosote, to the southeast. The shimmering valley floor backed by the high Panamint Mountains to the west, completes the panoramic view.

Well, not quite. Just to the northwest is Dante's View, usually swarming with sightseers. After enjoying the view, return the way you came.

■ DANTE'S VIEW
Dante's View Trail
To Dante's View is 1 mile round trip
with 200-foot elevation gain

The short hike to Dante's View, perched more than a mile above the valley floor, offers grand vistas of the lowest and highest points in the continental U.S. Beyond Badwater towers 11,049-foot Telescope Peak, and farther still, 14,494-foot Mt. Whitney.

From the parking area, an unsigned but distinct trail leaves the tourists behind and ascends north toward Dante's Point. A second unsigned little trail (0.25 mile) extends southwest from the parking area to a rocky promontory popular with photographers.

Hellish names to the contrary, Death Valley, as surveyed from Dante's View, appears far from lifeless. The dark splotches on the Panamint Mountains are actually bristlecone pine, pinyon, and juniper. Those small dark spots observed along the west side of the valley are mesquite thickets.

Dante's View—one of Death Valley's first tourist stops.

Directly below Dante's is the vast salt sink. The gleaming white beds of almost pure salt contrast with the brown, gray, tan, and taupe elsewhere on the valley floor.

Dante's View was created during Death Valley's pre-park days in the late 1920s. Local innkeeper Charlie Brown escorted a group of private tour operators high into the Black Mountains to partake of what he considered the best view. All agreed that tourists would be wowed by such vistas. Brown was soon awarded a contract to construct a road to the viewpoint, and within a few months, "Dante's View," as it was dubbed, became the first stop on the Union Pacific's Death Valley bus tours.

I suggest taking the hike in the early morning hours so the sun is at your back when you're savoring the view or composing a photograph. I also suggest taking a light jacket; temperatures at Dante's View average some 25°F less than those on the valley floor.

DIRECTIONS TO TRAILHEAD From Highway 190, 12 miles east of Furnace Creek, turn south on Dante's View Road and follow it 13.2 miles to its end at Dante's View parking area.

THE HIKE Digest the informational signs at the edge of the overlook, enjoy the view, and then walk north along the road 0.1 mile to join the unsigned footpath leading toward Dante's View. The trail climbs briskly and briefly up a hill, then makes a mellow contour along the mountain's west slope. About 0.3 mile from the trailhead, the path meets the summit ridge, then ascends a bit more to reach Dante's View.

■ BADWATER
Badwater Trail
From Badwater Road across Salt Flats
is 1 mile round trip

Badwater—and some of the nearby canyons off Badwater Road—offer object lessons of Death Valley geology in action, as well as shifting patterns of light and iridescent colors that make hikes in this part of the national park unforgettable.

A hike across the barren salt flats to Badwater and beyond may just be the definitive Death Valley experience. It's an excursion into extremes—the lowest land in North America and one of the hottest places on earth. Because temperature increases as elevation decreases, Badwater is no place to linger in the summer when temperatures of 120°F. are regularly recorded.

While Badwater is not the planet's lowest land (that distinction belongs to the Dead Sea, located some 1,290 feet below sea level in Israel), its proximity to adjacent high country makes its lowness seem quite pronounced. The

National Park highpoint, Telescope Peak (11,048 feet), is located fewer than 20 miles west of Badwater.

A sea level sign posted high on the cliffs above Badwater helps visitors imagine just what a depression 279.6 feet represents (actually the low point is now measured as -282 feet). These cliffs thrust skyward all the way up to Dante's View, 5,475 feet above sea level.

As the story goes, an early mapmaker named the briny pools "Badwater" when his mule refused to partake of the water. Badwater's water is indeed bad—as is most surface water in Death Valley—because of an extremely high concentration of salts; undrinkable it is, but not poisonous.

Badwater, circa 1939. Styles may have changed, but little else has in this ancient, amazing land.

While Badwater's environmental conditions are hostile to life, some plants and animals manage to survive. Patches of grass and clumps of pickleweed edge the shallow pools, where water beetles and the larvae of insects can be observed.

DIRECTIONS TO TRAILHEAD From the junction of highways 190 and 178, head south on the latter (Badwater Road) for 16.5 miles to the signed Badwater parking area on the west side of the road.

THE HIKE A causeway leads out onto the salt flats. To really get a feel for the enormity of the valley floor, continue past the well-beaten pathway a bit farther out onto the salt flats.

■ PANAMINT DUNES
Dunes Cross-Country Route
To top of highest dunes is 9 miles round trip
with 1,100-foot elevation gain

They're not the California desert's highest, longest, or largest, but the Panamint Dunes are often adjudged the most pristine by dune connoisseurs. This pristine quality is likely one of the happy results of the lack of easy access to this dune complex.

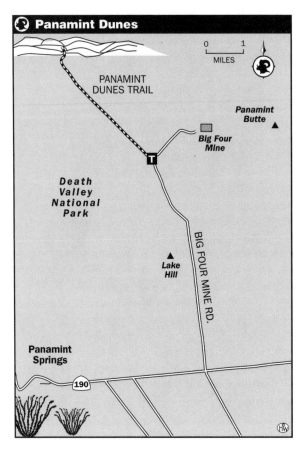

In fact, the dunes look rather easy to access from the road head; however, a 4-mile ascent over the desert floor is required just to reach the base of the most attractive taller dunes.

After reaching the top of this inspiring sandscape, most hikers think their effort time well spent. The Panamint Dunes are star-shaped and, in the right light, hikers might conclude they have captured a fallen star.

The Panamints, like dune ecosystems elsewhere, appear devoid of life but actually offer habitat for a number of plants and animals. The most obviously successful flora is dune grass, which thrives on the north side of the dunes. Look for the tracks of such denizens of the dunes as the Mojave fringe-toed lizard, the kangaroo rat, and kit fox.

DIRECTIONS TO TRAILHEAD From Highway 190 at Panamint Springs, head 5 miles east to Panamint Dunes Road, also called Big Four Mine Road. Turn north and travel 6 miles on the rough gravel road (suitable for passenger cars with high ground clearance). When the road begins to swing steeply right (up to the mine), park.

THE HIKE From the parking area, take aim at the dunes and begin hiking across a rock-strewn alluvial fan, which, fortunately for the feet, soon gives way to compacted sand. Some 2.5 miles of trail-less tramping over the sand brings you to the very base of the dunes.

Keeping company with creosote bushes, you ascend onward, your progress slowed by softer sand. After another mile-plus of slow hiking, you'll gain the lower edges of the highest dunes.

Improvise an upward trajectory over the ridges and around the hollows of the ever-changing dunes. Gain the rather narrow dune ridgeline and savor the panorama.

From atop the dunes, the vista is a dreamy one of the heat-shimmering Panamint Valley extending far south, the bordering Cottonwood Mountains to the east, colorful Panamint Butte to the southeast, and civilization in the form of Panamint Spring to the southwest.

Pay particular attention to Telescope Peak to the far southeast. If you navigate straight toward the peak on your return route, you'll be on the right course for the trailhead.

■ PANAMINT CITY
Surprise Canyon Trail
From Novak (Chris Wicht) Camp to Panamint City is 13 miles round trip with 3,400-foot elevation gain

T he cry of prospectors who swarmed into these mountains after silver was discovered in 1873 lingers on to this day: "Pan a mint." By 1875, once tranquil Surprise Canyon was the locale of Panamint City boasting a population of 2,000. More than 200 stone stores and homes lined a one-mile-long Main Street; in fact, Main was the only street because the narrowness of the canyon precluded any side streets.

With a multitude of saloons, a house of ill fame in Little Chief Canyon, a Boot Hill in Sourdough Canyon, and a homicide rate that would be high in a big city, the town had a reputation nearly as bad as Bodie. To its credit, however, Panamint City also had a newspaper—Death Valley's first—and enough ore (silver and copper) to keep the dream of riches alive for a couple of years.

In the days before conflict-of-interest laws were on the books, Nevada's senators—John P. Jones and William Stewart (nouveau riche from the Comstock Lode)—bought out the Panamint City claims and dominated the scene with their Surprise Valley Mill and Water Company. More than two million dollars in ore was produced during the brief boom; considering the capital investment involved, most historians believe Panamint City was about a break-even enterprise for the two senators.

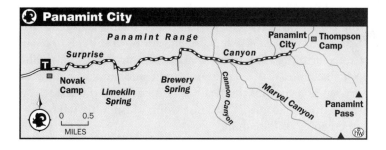

Much of the ore was reduced right in Panamint by the company's huge 20-stamp mill, built of a half-million bricks at a cost of $210,000. The mill was a testament to the faith the miners had in the riches hidden below ground. It was, by one account, "the closest thing to a church Panamint ever had."

Transporting the silver was a problem. Wells Fargo, the usual carrier in such circumstances, determined that the risk of robbery was far too great, and refused. To thwart any would-be thieves, the mining company cast the silver into 450-pound squares—far too heavy for a highwayman to carry off on horseback.

Nature's fickleness (the ore veins were hard to work and did not live up to their intial promise) and nature's fury (two 1876 flash floods killed 200 people and wiped out the town) finished Panamint City. Periodic small-scale attempts (the latest in 1982) were made to coax more precious metals from the earth, but they failed.

Today, about all that's left of Panamint City's glory days are some stone foundations and the ore smelter's tall brick chimney.

A 6-mile road, now a footpath (though very skilled drivers with four-wheel-drive, winch-equipped vehicles once used the route) leads to Panamint City. The road/trail frequently crosses the creek in the lower canyon as it probes a very rough, rocky (and sometimes very wet) narrows. You'll pass occasional springs trickling from the canyon walls and feeding the year-round creek in Surprise Canyon.

A variety of environments from bare cliffs to barrel cactus to juniper woodland add surprises to the canyon trek. Lucky hikers sometimes spot bighorn sheep gamboling high on the canyon walls.

DIRECTIONS TO TRAILHEAD From Highway 190, some 34 miles west of Stovepipe Wells and just 2.5 miles east of the hamlet of Panamint Springs, head south on Panamint Valley Road for 14 miles to Trona-Wildrose Road. Turn south (right) and proceed 9.5 miles to Ballarat Road. Turn left and head 3.5 miles into the tiny Ballarat. Turn north on Indian Canyon Road and travel 2 miles to Surprise Canyon Road, turn right and continue 4 miles to road's end at Novak Camp. Park alongside the road and stay off adjoining private property.

THE HIKE The path (washed-out road) meanders creekside with occasional crossings through sometimes narrow, sometimes wide Surprise Canyon. Early on, the trail establishes a pattern that continues for 3.5 wet miles.

Finally, the route leaves the creek behind as it begins an aggressive 1.5 miles of ascent. After gaining 1,000 feet in elevation, you'll glimpse the first of Panamint City's far-flung mining ruins about 5 miles from the trailhead.

You'll spot Panamint City's enormous brick smokestack as the road emerges from the narrows and reaches the head of Surprise Canyon, a bowl surrounded by pinyon pine-dotted slopes. Continue your journey to what is—or at least once was—the center of Panamint.

■ DARWIN FALLS

Darwin Falls Trail

2 miles round trip

Tucked away in (what appears to be) a forlorn range of mountains on the east side of the Panamint Valley is a year-round creek and waterfall. Darwin Falls and the mini oasis surrounding it are small reminders of the surprises found off the main roads.

When Congress passed the landmark California Desert Protection Act of 1994, Death Valley National Park gained considerable acreage on its western frontier, including Darwin Falls, centerpiece of this wilderness area. It's well worth a stop, particularly for the visitor entering the national park from the west via U.S. Highway 395 and California State Highway 190.

Darwin Falls is fed by an underground spring bubbling to the surface of the volcanic rock floor of Darwin Canyon. Wildlife and more than 80 species of birds find water and shelter at the cottonwood- and willow-fringed oasis.

During the nineteenth-century boomtown days of Darwin, a Chinese-American farmer grew vegetables in a rich patch of earth below the falls and sold his produce to the miners. For more than 100 years, visitors have enjoyed bathing in the stone basins in the canyon bottom.

Every Eden has its serpent and, in the case of Darwin Falls, evil incarnate is the salt cedar tamarisk, an aggressive weed that prevents animals from reaching the water. Not only is the tamarisk fast-growing, it's a huge water consumer. Worse yet, the plant drops salty leaves that kill surrounding native vegetation. Thanks to the efforts of conservation groups, much of the invasive tamarisk has been removed from the Darwin Falls area.

Best times for a visit are the cooler months, and in spring when the creek flow is the greatest, the falls at their fullest. Forget hiking in the summer. At 3,100 feet in elevation, Darwin Falls is far from the hottest place in the Mojave, but because of the presence of the water, it's miserably humid.

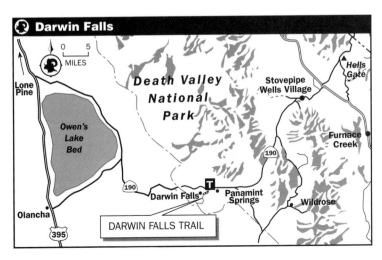

DIRECTIONS TO TRAILHEAD The turnoff for Darwin Falls is located off Highway 190, 1 mile west of Panamint Springs. Turn right on Darwin Canyon Road and drive 2.5 miles to the parking area.

THE HIKE It's dry-going when you first walk the canyon bottom. Soon you'll notice some wet sand, then spot a trickle of water. A quarter-mile along, the canyon narrows and you'll begin walking alongside a little creek. Ferns, reeds and monkeyflowers line the creek. The path ends at a 30-foot waterfall.

■ WILDROSE PEAK
Wildrose Peak Trail
8.4 miles round trip with 2,300-foot elevation gain

Death Valley and Panamint Valley views are awesome from the summit of Wildrose Peak. The 9,064-foot peak in the middle of the Panamint Mountains beckons the hiker with a well-maintained trail and glorious views coming and going.

The Panamint Mountains are known as the wettest range in Death Valley— a small claim to fame to be sure in the midst of one of America's most arid lands; nevertheless, there's enough precipitation in the form of rain and snow to nurture stands of pinyon pine and juniper, and water the "wildrose," the spring-blooming cliffrose that brightens the mountain.

In summer, when temperatures climb to more than 110°F. on the floor of Death Valley, Wildrose Peak remains a pleasant place to walk. The peak and upper parts of the trail are snowbound in winter; however, Wildrose can be hiked a bit earlier in spring than neighboring Telescope Peak (11,049 feet), which typically remains mantled in snow well into May.

The trailhead alone is worth the trip. Here you'll find 10 charcoal kilns, built in the 1870s to make charcoal from the trees growing in Wildrose Canyon. Charcoal was carried from the giant beehive-shaped stone kilns by mules to the Modock Mine, located in the Argus Range, 25 miles away.

DIRECTIONS TO TRAILHEAD From Highway 178 some 52 miles from Highway 395, turn right at the signed paved road for Wildrose and proceed 9.5 miles northwest to a junction with Mahogany Flat Road. Turn right, soon passing Wildrose Campground, and travel 6 miles (the last 2 miles on dirt road) to a wide turnout for the kilns and parking for Wildrose Peak-bound hikers.

If you're journeying from the "main" part of Death Valley, travel 9 miles from Stovepipe Wells south on Highway 190 to Wildrose Road. Turn left and drive south 21 miles to Mahogany Flat Road.

THE HIKE Join the signed trail northwest of the charcoal kilns and begin your ascent above Wildrose Canyon. As you pass in and out of a pinyon and juniper woodland, enjoy the great views of High Sierra peaks, including mighty Mt. Whitney. The path descends briefly into a wooded canyon, then climbs northeast.

About 2 miles out, the path reaches a saddle at the crest of the Panamints. Following the crest, the trail serves up great vistas of Death Valley shimmering in the heat 8,000 feet below, as well as over-the-shoulder views of Telescope Peak.

Vigorous switchbacks lead past wind-bent pinyon pine to the small, flat summit. The fantastic view takes in most of 90-mile-long Death Valley with the Amargosa Range beyond and Furnace Creek appearing as a green island on the vast salt flats. To the west are the sawtooth summits of the Sierra Nevada.

■ TELESCOPE PEAK
Telescope Peak Trail
To Rogers and Bennett Peaks is 7 miles round trip with 1,800-foot elevation gain; to Telescope Peak is 14 miles round trip with 3,000-foot gain

Most park visitors are content to stop their cars at Badwater, 282 feet below sea level, and look up at Telescope Peak, the greatest vertical rise in the lower 48 states. For the serious hiker, however, the challenge of climbing 11,049-foot Telescope Peak and looking down at Death Valley will prove irresistible. The views from Telescope Peak Trail include Badwater, low point of

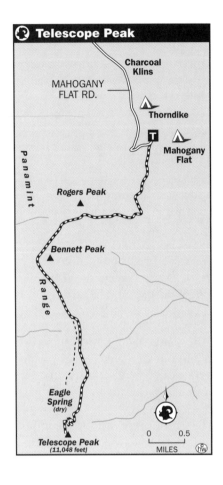

the continental U.S., and Mt. Whitney, the continental high point.

The trail starts where most trails end—a mile and a half in the sky—and climbs a sagebrush- and pinyon pine-dotted hogback ridge to the pinnacle that is Telescope Peak. The well-maintained trails up Telescope and Wildrose peaks offer a distinctly different hiking experience than other park trails, which, for the most part, are of two types: nature/interpretive trails or cross-country routes through canyons or washes.

Magnificent vistas from the below-sea level salt pans to the snowy summits of the Sierra Nevada reward the hardy hiker who makes the ascent of Telescope Peak. The 360-degree panorama inspired W.T. Henderson, the first to ascend the great mountain in 1860, to declare: "You can see so far, it's just like looking through a telescope."

Best times to make the climb are from about mid-May to November. During the colder months, Telescope Peak and much of the trail is covered in snow. Try to begin your hike at dawn, both to savor the sunrise and to allow sufficient time for the long journey.

DIRECTIONS TO TRAILHEAD From Highway 178, some 50 miles northeast of Highway 395 and Ridgecrest, turn right on Wildrose Canyon Road and follow it 9 miles to road's end at Mahogany Flat Campground. Park at the campground.

THE HIKE The path climbs over pinyon pine-forested slopes and soon offers dramatic views of Death Valley and the Furnace Creek area. After 2 miles, the trail gains the spine of a ridge and soon a second valley, Panamint, comes into view.

Three miles of moderate climbing brings you to a saddle between Rogers Peak and Bennett Peak. You can strike cross-country to reach the antennae-crowned summit, which stands about 400-feet higher than the trail. To reach Bennett Peak, continue on the main trail to a second saddle, then ascend cross-country past stands of limber pine to the top.

Telescope Peak Trail's final third is steep and remarkable. The path zigzags up the peak's steep east side, ascending through a stunted forest of limber and bristlecone pine.

From atop the peak, the far-reaching views include the White Mountains to the north and the High Sierra to the northeast. Off in those two patches of purple haze are Las Vegas far to the east and the San Gabriel Mountains above Los Angeles to the southwest.

It's 7 miles to the summit of Telescope Peak, and the views are worth the trip.

The gnarled limbs of the bristlecone pine are a unique art form.

CHAPTER 2

WEST MOJAVE AND THE GREAT BASIN

Topographically, the East and West Mojave are quite different. The West presents great sandscapes, with many flat areas and some isolated ridges and buttes. The East Mojave is more mountainous.

On the fringe of the L.A. metropolis is the deep rock-walled gorge of Soledad Canyon, where the legendary bandit Tiburcio Vasquez fled the law, finding refuge amid rocks known as Robber's Roost. Because Vasquez hid here before his capture in the Santa Monica Mountains (he was hung in San Jose in 1875), the sandstone crags were named after him.

Situated south of the Tehachapi Mountains and northwest of the San Gabriel Mountains, the Antelope Valley makes up the western frontier of the Mojave Desert. The rapidly expanding cities of Palmdale, Lancaster, and Victorville are located here.

The Antelope Valley's natural attractions include a reserve for the state's official flower—the California poppy—and another reserve for the endangered desert tortoise. Other parks preserve a Joshua tree woodland (Saddleback Butte State Park) and display the remarkable earthquake-fractured geology of this desert (Devil's Punchbowl County Park).

Joshua trees thrive in the valley. Palmdale, established in 1886 was actually named for the Joshuas; settlers mistakenly believed the spiky trees were palms. Saddleback Butte was originally named Joshua Tree State Park when it was created in 1960, but the name was changed to avoid confusion with Joshua Tree National Monument, which is now a national park.

When the Los Angeles-to-San Francisco rail line was constructed through the valley in the 1870s, it completely changed the ecology of the West Mojave. Because the Antelope Valley, a natural reservoir, had extensive ground water, farmers grew alfalfa. Hay was supplied to dairy farmers in Los Angeles until well into the 1920s.

The Spartan-looking valley once supported thousands of pronghorn antelope—hence the name Antelope Valley—and the numerous Indian tribes who hunted them. The railroad tracks interrupted the antelope's migration, thus dooming the animals.

The California poppy blooms on many a grassy slope in the Southland, but only in the Antelope Valley does the showy flower blanket entire hillsides in such brilliant orange sheets. Surely the finest concentration of California's state flower is preserved at the California State Poppy Reserve west of Lancaster.

North of the Antelope Valley are more wonders of the West Mojave: the Ancient Bristlecone Pine Forest on the slopes of the White Mountains, the lava flows of Fossil Falls, the bizarre science-fiction landscape of Trona Pinnacles.

■ BODIE STATE HISTORIC PARK
Bodie Trail
1 mile or more round trip

Bodie State Historic Park preserves a one-time gold rush boomtown of the 1870s and 1880s, in a state of "arrested decay." A park brochure details a lengthy walking tour of Bodie, which has a remarkably diverse collection of buildings in various states of decrepitude.

Bodie is a step back in time; it is a boomtown gone bust, a curious, isolated world that at first glance appears to be far removed from the present. But there is also a perceptible sense of peace, a comfortable familiarity about the place that was once home to nearly 10,000 people.

Access to the abandoned town, located in the high desert southeast of the small town of Bridgeport, can be tricky; only one of the roads leading to Bodie is paved, and even that ends up as 3 miles of dirt and rocks. The rugged, time-consuming drive up to town is quite fitting; one could hardly expect to approach it via a superhighway off-ramp.

Nearly 90 percent of the visitors to Bodie arrive during the summer months. The weather from October through April is unpredictable; although the park is open year-round, once the winter snows hit, the roads are not plowed, leaving Bodie (elevation 8,400 feet) virtually inaccessible during the notoriously long and brutal winters. Intrepid souls still manage to get through—on mountain bikes, cross-country skis, and four-wheel drive vehicles.

The remote location, the ramshackle buildings, the cemetery at the edge of town—the entire place appears to be constructed like a Hollywood film set. But there's no fakery here; part of Bodie's appeal is the dignity with which it's been allowed to age without insensitive restoration or commercialism. The Old Miners' Union Hall is today the park museum for Bodie, considered by many to be the very best ghost town in the West.

DIRECTIONS TO TRAILHEAD From U.S. 395, some 15 miles north of Lee Vining and 7 miles south of Bridgeport, turn east on Highway 270 (Bodie Road). Travel 13 miles (the few on dirt road) to Bodie State Historic Park. If you're traveling during the off-season, call the park about current road conditions.

THE HIKE This hike is strictly improvisational. Be sure to pick up the park brochure and map.

■ MONO LAKE TUFA STATE RESERVE

South Tufa Trail

1 to 2 miles round trip

It's one of the grand landscapes of the American West—an ancient lake cradled by volcanoes, glacier-carved canyons, and snowy peaks. Visitors marvel at the 8-mile-long (north to south) and 13-mile-wide (east to west) lake and its unusual tufa towers, remarkable limestone creations that rise from the lake in magnificent knobs and spires.

Mono Lake has been called "California's Dead Sea," but it's actually a life-support system for great numbers of birds. California gulls fly in from the coast to nest on the lake's isles. An estimated 90 percent of the state's population of this gull is born on Mono Lake.

Some 800,000 eared grebes, duck-like diving birds, have been tallied at the lake. Mono's summertime winged visitors include Wilson's and red-necked phalaropes, species that commute from wintering grounds in South America.

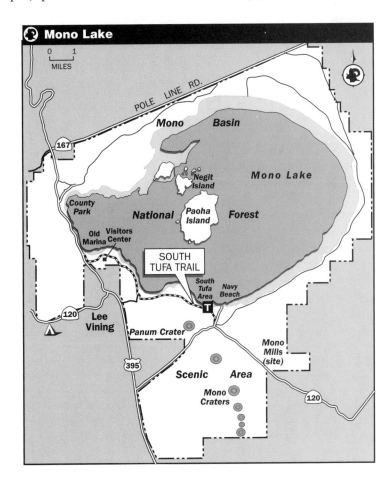

Tufa towers and winged visitors enhance the views at Mono Lake.

Primary bird food is the brine shrimp, which, like other organisms dependent on Mono's waters, has evolved over the last million years or so to adapt to an extremely saline habitat.

While Mono is anything but a dead sea, it was, until recently, a dying lake. Beginning in 1941 and continuing for more than a half century, the Los Angeles Department of Water and Power diverted most of the major creeks and rivers that had sustained Mono Lake for centuries. Such diversions caused the lake level to drop 40 feet and its waters to double in salinity.

The resultant damage to the lake's ecological integrity and to Mono Basin's wildlife habitat prompted the Mono Lake Committee and National Audubon Society to take legal action to stop this drastic drain. "Save Mono Lake" was the rallying cry for environmentalists from around the state. Finally, after 16 years of conservation efforts and legal challenges by citizen activists in numerous courts and forums, the State Water Resources Control Board agreed to raise the lake level in 1994.

Theoretically and legally at least, Mono Lake has been saved; however, much shoreline and wildlife habitat restoration will be necessary to return the lake to ideal environmental health.

You can learn more about the lake and conservation efforts at the Mono Basin National Forest Scenic Area Visitor Center located on the outskirts of Lee Vining. The Mono Lake Committee maintains an information center and attractive gift/bookstore in "downtown" Lee Vining.

Travelers with limited time can get a quick look at the lake and some tufa formations with the help of two boardwalk trails located at Old Marina on the west shore and Mono Lake County Park on the northwest shore.

DIRECTIONS TO TRAILHEAD From Highway 395, about 5 miles south of the hamlet of Lee Vining, turn east on Highway 120 and drive 5 miles to the signed turnoff for the South Tufa Area/Mono Lake Tufa State Reserve. Turn left and proceed a mile on good gravel road to a parking area near the trailhead.

THE HIKE The best place to observe Mono's most compelling natural attraction—its tufa towers—is the South Tufa Area, explored by a short interpretive trail. The trail's shoreline segments will no doubt need to be relocated periodically as the lake rises and reclaims its ancient bed.

Tufa towers are formed when calcium-rich freshwater springs bubble up into the carbonate-saturated alkaline lake water. This calcium-carbonate co-mingling results in limestone formations—the magnificent tufa spires.

Trailside interpretive signs explain more than most hikers will want to know about the lake's food chain of algae, billions of brine flies, trillions of shrimp, as well as gulls, grebes, and other migratory birds. Some visitors, overwhelmed by the lake's majesty, might be disappointed to learn that Mono is the native Yokut word for "brine fly."

South Tufa Trail leads past some landlocked tufa formations, then skirts the lakeshore for a look out at those protruding from the midst of Mono.

Loop back to the parking area if you wish, or extend your hike by continuing on to Navy Beach, the lake's best swimming area.

■ HOT CREEK GEOLOGICAL SITE
Hot Creek Trail
2 miles round trip with 100-foot elevation gain

A soothing soak, fabulous fly-fishing, and an up-close look at one of California's most intriguing geothermal areas are highlights of a hike along Hot Creek. If hot springs, hiking, and trout weren't reasons enough for a visit, Hot Creek has one more attraction: a long hiking season.

Hot Creek Trail is the very last Mammoth-area path to be snow-covered in winter and the very first to be snow-free in the spring. In fact, for several months the trail provides the only passable hike for many miles around.

While Hot Creek might suggest a place for cooking fish, not catching them, fly-fishers revere the creek, which consistently ranks among the top-five watercourses in California. It seems Hot Creek's open-to-the-sunlight setting and unusually warm waters create optimal conditions for the growth of the kind of underwater vegetation (read fish food and habitat) preferred by trout. The terrific fly-fishing here is strictly for sport and of the catch-and-release variety.

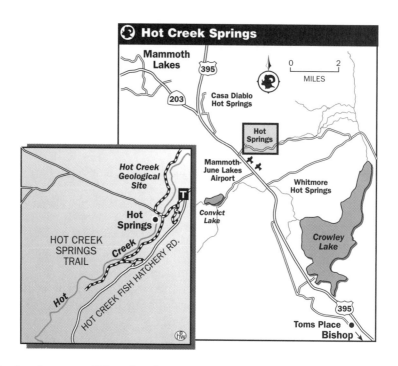

The headwaters of Hot Creek are anything but hot; its waters arise as Mammoth Creek, high in the High Sierra by Mammoth Lakes Basin. After descending to the high desert floor, it's joined by a large hot spring that gushes into the cool Sierra stream and transforms it into Hot Creek.

After percolating through a geothermal area, Hot Creek flows a few more miles east through the wide-open, sagebrushy spaces to empty into the Owens River near Crowley Lake.

The U.S. Forest Service (Inyo National Forest) has done a fine job of providing trailside amenities: restrooms, a picnic area, plus interpretive signs that explain how volcanic action of long ago and underground forces of today put the "hot" in Hot Creek. Just in case anyone leaves all good sense behind in the parking lot, the Forest Service has built lots of fencing and posted lots of signs to discourage you from plopping into those sections of Hot Creek where the water is boiling.

Observing a few simple precautions will make your Hot Creek outing memorable for all the right reasons. Stay on the trail and remember that the footbridge is the only place to cross Hot Creek. Bathe only in the big, open, warm-but-not-scalding areas in mid-creek.

You'll likely lose all motivation and momentum for a hike if you slip into the soothing waters right away. I recommend hiking first, soaking second.

DIRECTIONS TO TRAILHEAD From Highway 395, some 35 miles north of Bishop, and just 3 miles south of Highway 203 (the road to Mammoth), turn east on Hot Creek Hatchery Road and travel 3 miles to the parking area for Hot Creek Geological Site.

THE HIKE Stairs and 0.1 mile of paved path aid your descent to the creek. Your nose will confirm that you're proceeding in the right direction as the characteristic sulfur smell wafts your way.

Take the footbridge over to the north bank of Hot Creek and head west (left) on the trail. You'll likely spot groups of semi-submerged soakers, as well as fly-fishers on the south side of the creek.

Travel a mile or so up-creek through the narrow Hot Creek Gorge and savor the view of those snow-capped, 2-mile-high Sierra peaks to the west. Ambitious hikers can walk almost all the way to Hot Creek Fish Hatchery, but most will find the prospect of relaxing in Hot Creek more compelling.

■ ANCIENT BRISTLECONE PINE FOREST
Methuselah Trail
4.5 miles round trip

High on the stony, storm-battered crests of the White Mountains, east of Bishop, grow the oldest trees on earth. These 4,000-year old trees are bristlecone pine, which survive—in fact, thrive—in conditions that doom most other life.

The bristlecones are protected by the 28,000-acre Ancient Bristlecone Pine Forest, set aside in 1958. The forest, which crowns the White Mountains, is under the jurisdiction of the Inyo National Forest. Bristlecone pines are found in other parts of the Great Basin, in eastern California, Nevada, and Utah, but the pines in the White Mountains are by far the oldest.

Bristlecones are old, but they're not very tall—only 25 feet or so. And they're slow growers, sometimes expanding only an inch in diameter every 100 years. Some sapling-sized specimens are actually hundreds of years old.

The pines are wonderfully gnarled and contorted—a photographer's delight. Some assume a sumo-wrestler's stance, others grow nearly parallel to the ground. Their trunks and limbs have been sanded and polished by windblown pebbles and ice.

The name bristlecone comes from the foxtail-like branches with short needles. The cones themselves are purple when young, turning to a chocolate color when mature.

Oddly enough, the trees thrive where climatic conditions are most severe, where they are most exposed to the fury of winter storms. Bristlecones clinging to the high peaks live longer than those growing in lower, more sheltered places. The most ancient *Pinus longaeva* manage to gather nutrients from the poorest limestone soil.

The oldest of the tribe is Methuselah, about 4,700 years old. Many trees in both Schulman and Patriarch groves are 4,000 years old and still growing.

For many years, bristlecones were thought to be not only the oldest living trees, but the oldest living things in the world. More recently, botanists have come to believe that the oldest flora award should go to some of the creosote bushes growing in the Soggy Dry Lake area of the Mojave Desert. Dubbed "King Clone," the creosote are estimated to be more than 10,000 years old.

Geologists categorize the White Mountains, where the bristlecone grow, as basin-and-range-type terrain. The mountains rise quickly and dramatically nearly

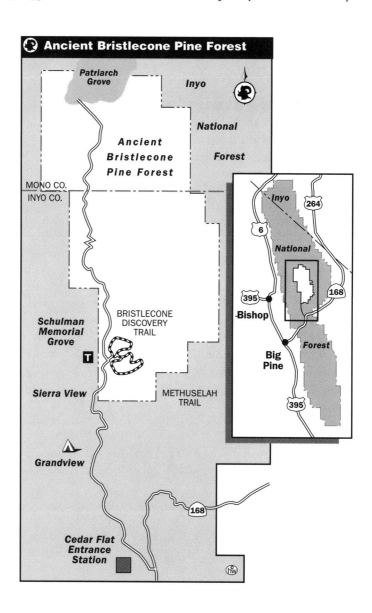

2 miles above the desert floor. Summit views of the surrounding desert are superb.

Two trails explore Schulman Grove, named in honor of Dr. Edward Schulman, the scientist who in the 1950s first figured the advanced age of the bristlecones. Methuselah Trail is a 4.5-mile loop through the Bristlecone Forest, while Discovery Trail is an easier 1-mile walk.

The best time to pay a visit to the ancient pines is June through October. Summertime is more like springtime in the White Mountains. Patches of snow linger in shady crevices. Wildflowers, such as lupine and Indian paintbrush, do not bloom until August, or even September.

Allow yourself at least half a day to hike both Discovery and Methuselah Trails. At Schulman Grove, where the trails begin, is a small visitor center and some inter-

Bristlecone detail.

pretive displays. With the displays and pamphlets, you can learn more about the emerging science of dendrochronology—from Leonardo DaVinci's discovery of tree-ring dating to modern radiocarbon methodology—than you ever wanted to know. During summer months, naturalists sometimes staff the visitor center and give talks about the bristlecone ecology.

DIRECTIONS TO TRAILHEAD This is one hike where getting there really is half the fun—a most scenic drive.

From U.S. 395 in Big Pine (south of Bishop) turn east on California 168 (Westgard Pass Road) and drive 13 miles to the signed turnoff for the Bristlecone Pines. About 5.5 miles from the highway, you'll spot Grandview Campground and a few miles later come to a glorious viewpoint. Sierra View lives up to the promise of its name and delivers a panorama of eastern High Sierra peaks.

At the end of the paved road is Schulman Grove, where there's plenty of parking. Both Discovery and Methuselah trails are well signed.

THE HIKE An interpretive brochure for the Methuselah Trail is available at the trailhead. Methuselah Trail features close-up views of the trees and far-reaching panoramas of mountains and desert.

As 4.5-mile hikes go, this one seems longer, both because of the shortness of breath caused by high altitude and the many photo opportunities en route. The trail winds through some of the most beautiful parts of Schulman Grove, and then climbs to a ridge offering views of the Inyo and Last Chance Mountains.

See Map on Page 72

■ ANCIENT BRISTLECONE PINE FOREST
Discovery Trail
1 mile loop

This walk is a good introduction to the White Mountains, the highest range in the Great Basin. Parallel to the High Sierra, the mountains extend some 60 miles north from Westgard Pass back to the community of Big Pine northward into Nevada. The White Mountains lie in the considerable rain shadow of the High Sierra and thus receive but 6 to 12 inches or so of rain per year.

When regarded from afar, the White Mountains look austere, even desolate. Upon closer examination, it's obvious the range supports a variety of flora: pinyon-juniper woodland, great amounts of sage, scrub, and the ecological community botanists call Great Basin montane.

With such harsh weather conditions and poor soil, the White Mountains seem unlikely habitat for a long-lived tree. Yet the bristlecone pine survives— even thrives—here, a testament to a Nature that can be as enduring as it is surprising.

DIRECTIONS TO TRAILHEAD The scenic drive on 395 is one of the finest in the state, especially in the fall when the autumn colors are spectacular.

From U.S. 395 in Big Pine (south of Bishop), turn east on California 168 (Westgard Pass Road) and drive 13 miles to the signed turnoff for the Bristlecone Pines. About 5.5 miles from the highway, you'll spot Grandview Campground and a few miles later come to a glorious viewpoint. Sierra View lives up to the promise of its name and delivers a panorama of eastern High Sierra peaks.

At the end of the paved road is Schulman Grove, where there's plenty of parking. Both Discovery and Methuselah trails are well signed.

THE HIKE Bristlecone Discovery Trail is a 1-mile, self-guided loop trip suitable for the whole family. Numbered posts correspond to descriptions in a pamphlet available at the trailhead. Along the trail is Pine Alpha, the first 4,000-year old bristlecone discovered by Dr. Edward Schulman.

■ INYO MOUNTAINS WILDERNESS
Lonesome Miner Trail
From Hunter Canyon to Tent Platform (Miners Camp) is 6 miles round trip with 2,100-foot elevation gain

Lonesome Miner Trail is every bit as lonely as its name suggests—an old prospectors' route through some of the most rugged and remote backcountry in California.

No doubt most of the many old miners' trails in the Inyo Mountains could be categorized as lonesome, but this particular path was named by volunteer trail builders and the BLM, who worked very hard to discover—and uncover—the trail. It traverses the Inyo Mountain Wilderness, established in 1994.

Forty-mile-long Lonesome Miner Trail, strenuous and difficult to follow, extends from Hunter Canyon in the Saline Valley to Reward Canyon in the Owens Valley. It's a patchwork of historic trails built by miners from 1867 to 1941. The path descends into and climbs out of several steep canyons on the east side of the Inyo Mountains and passes several historic mining sites. Vistas from trail high points include the High Sierra and Death Valley National Park.

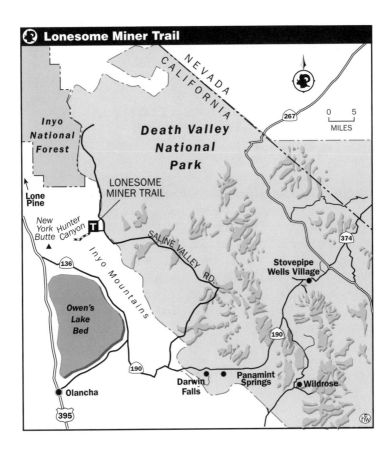

One of the more accessible and easier to follow stretches of trail, and a good introduction to the east side of the Inyo Mountains, is through Hunter Canyon, sometimes called the Hunter Canyon Trail. A good destination for a day hike is what I've called Miners Camp, where prospectors hewed out a 20-foot by 80-foot campsite out of a rock ledge, then built three wooden tent platforms. The ledge and platforms make intriguing picnic sites or campsites, and they offer a commanding view of the Saline Valley below.

DIRECTIONS TO TRAILHEAD From Highway 190, about 35 miles east of Lone Pine, turn north on Saline Valley Road and drive some 38 miles to Saline Valley Marsh. A half mile north of the entrance to this historic site, turn west and drive a mile to road's end and the signed trailhead for Hunter Canyon Trail.

THE HIKE From the old mine equipment in Little Hunter Canyon, the path follows the creekbed past some mesquite thickets up the canyon for a quarter mile. The trail then leaves the canyon, switchbacking up to the ridge on the south side.

The ridge route continues ascending, offering grand views eastward of Saline Valley, the Last Chance Range, and the northwestern reaches of Death Valley National Park. Enjoy the excellent view from Miners Camp, as well.

From Miners Camp, Lonesome Miner Trail continues climbing more than 3,000 feet in elevation, steeply up the ridge. After topping the ridge, the path descends steeply to Bighorn Spring, about another 3 miles past the camp.

■ MANZANAR NATIONAL HISTORIC SITE
Manzanar Trail
0.5 to 2 miles round trip

For some 60 years, stone guardhouses, cement foundations, a cemetery, and remnant orchards located on this lonely, bleak edge of the Owens Valley at the base of eastern Sierra Nevada were all that remained to remind passersby of Manzanar, a sad chapter in American history.

Manzanar, the land was called, from the Spanish word meaning "apple orchards." From 1910 to 1932 a farming community by that name grew apples and peaches—said to be among the sweetest in the state—before water rights were lost to Los Angeles and its aqueduct and the orchards and hamlet were abandoned.

As a farming community, Manzanar was little noted; as a site of the first World War II Japanese-American Relocation Camp, it will be long remembered. Some 10,000 Americans of Japanese heritage (the majority of whom were U.S. citizens) were uprooted from their homes and businesses and confined here from 1942 to 1945.

Manzanar in modern times has become synonymous with America's darker impulses, with the country's highly emotional state after that "day of infamy," the Japanese bombing of Pearl Harbor, Hawaii, on December 7, 1941. As a plaque near the entrance to the historic site reads: "May the injustice and humiliation suffered here as a result of hysteria, racism, and economic exploitation never emerge again."

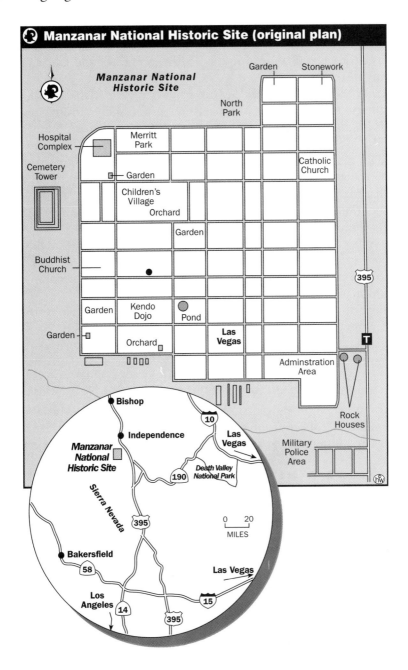

Manzanar National Historic Site (original plan)

Two months after the bombing, President Franklin Roosevelt signed Executive Order 90060, which required all those of Japanese descent living on the West Coast to be sent to relocation camps. The U.S. Supreme Court upheld the executive order with the rationale that in time of war, military judgment (concern about spies and saboteurs) superseded the civil rights of citizens.

During its more than three years of operation, greater Manzanar spread out over 6,000 acres, and included schools, housing, a sewage-treatment plant, cultivated fields, and an airport. A 550-acre core complex that included housing and administrative offices was ringed by barbed wire and under surveillance by guards posted in eight 50-foot towers; it's this center section that's preserved today in the historic site.

Historians and National Park Service experts regard Manzanar as offering the best interpretive opportunity of the 10 relocation sites scattered around the West. This is a primary reason why Manzanar National Historic Site was established in 1992.

As budget permits, the National Park Service intends to increase interpretation at Manzanar. Even with the passage of so much time, it remains an emotionally charged task. In addition, the Manzanar story would not be complete without mention of the farming community that preceded the relocation center and the centuries of use by native Paiute and Shoshone.

Begin your visit to Manzanar with a 3.3-mile auto tour that follows roads around the camp's perimter. The tour is keyed to signs and a pamphlet that identify where the camouflage netting factory, Buddhist temple, Catholic church, and many other structures once stood.

This historic Manzanar High School auditorium has been restored and adapted for use as the site's interpretive center, which opened in 2004. At the center, there's a theater and some 8,000 feet of exhibit space. It's open from 9:00 AM until 4:30 PM daily. The National Park Service is currently restoring a mess hall, relocated to Manzanar from the Bishop Airport. The mess hall is of the same type as the three dozen used by the Japanese who were interned here.

To learn more about Manzanar, visit the Eastern California Museum, which holds a significant collection of photographs and artifacts from the relocation camp era. The museum is located at 155 N. Grant Street in Independence.

DIRECTIONS TO TRAILHEAD Manzanar National Historic Site is located on the west side of Highway 395, 12 miles north of Lone Pine and 6 miles south of Independence.

THE HIKE The walking is strictly free-form, wander-at-will. You can drive up and down most of the site's dirt roads, but walking here seems more respectful and in character.

As you walk the dusty lanes, most of what you'll see—rock gardens, traces of an irrigation aqueduct, concrete foundations—offer only small clues to what was, at the time, the Owens Valley's largest community. This is a ghost town where there are more ghosts than town.

Among Manzanar's most intriguing ruins are the twin sentry stations located near the turnoff from Highway 395. The stone creations are designed in a unique pagoda style.

You'll spot the historic site's only building, Manzanar's auditorium (now a maintenance station for Inyo County), 0.25 mile north of the entrance station.

■ FOSSIL FALLS
Fossil Falls Trail
0.5 mile round trip

S ome 20,000 years ago, molten lava flowed into the bed of the Owens River. The river waters have since sculpted and polished the lava rock into some stunning forms—among them, the lava cascade known as Fossil Falls.

At the very least, a visitor can't help but be impressed by the two mighty forces, volcanism and running water, that created and shaped the scenery in this corner of the West Mojave.

The second sterling example of volcanism in the vicinity is the red cinder cone just north of the lava flow. Red Hill, as the locals call the cone-shaped hill, is quarried for its cinders, used for roads, running tracks, and decorative purposes.

Archeologists have found evidence of native American habitation in the Fossil Falls area dating from 4,000 BC to the nineteenth century. Rock rings supported brush and tule shelters that served the Shoshone.

DIRECTIONS TO TRAILHEAD From Highway 14, some 20 miles north of its junction with Highway 395 (and 3 miles north of the all but abandoned hamlet of Little Lake), turn east on signed Cinder Road. Travel a half mile on the road, which soon turns from pavement to gravel, to the BLM-signed turnoff on your right for Fossil Falls. Follow this gravel road south, then east for 1.5 miles to a parking lot and day-use area.

THE HIKE Splotches of orange paint on the rocks help you stay on the short trail to Fossil Falls, where the cliffs are quite impressive. Be very careful. Rock climbers and local search-and-rescue teams practice their skills at Fossil Falls.

■ WALKER PASS

Pacific Crest Trail

From Walker Pass to Crest Overlook is 4 miles round trip with 1,000-foot elevation gain

Think Pacific Crest Trail, and dry lands do not come to mind. My vision of the 2,600-mile PCT is a trailside landscape of forests and alpine lakes, as well as the snow-capped summits of the High Sierra and Cascade Range.

Lest we hikers forget, however, the West's premiere long-distance trail crosses both the Colorado and Mojave deserts on its way from Baja, Mexico, to the southern Sierra. At Walker Pass, the northbound PCT ascends from the desert floor for the last time and offers grand vistas of both the mighty High Sierra to the north and the vast desert to the south.

The walker near Walker Pass encounters a transition zone between desert and mountains, highlighted by Joshua trees giving way to pinyon pines. This is high and dry country, and those northbound PCT hikers crossing it must hike more than a dozen miles to find the next water source.

While exploring the vast territory from Utah west to California, U.S. Army Lieutenant Joseph Walker led an expedition over the crest of the High Sierra in the autumn of 1833. On his return route east in the spring of 1834, Walker skirted the south end of the Sierra by way of a route known today as Walker Pass. Historians credit Walker with discovering the Owens Valley and finding a

Walker Pass: a passageway from the desert to the High Sierra.

route (the California Trail) from the Great Salt Lake all the way to California's far north coast.

The Walker Pass region is part of the 74,640-acre Owens Peak Wilderness, set aside in 1994 under provisions of the California Desert Protection Act. It's one of a dozen such desert wilderness areas located west of Death Valley National Park.

DIRECTIONS TO TRAILHEAD From Highway 14, some 41 miles north of the town of Mojave, turn west on Highway 178 (the road to Lake Isabella) and travel 8 miles to Walker Pass. Look for a historical marker on the south side of the road and the beginning of the trail opposite it on the north side of the road.

Parking is available in a dirt pullout on the north side of the road. Upon departure, be very careful when you rejoin Highway 178 because visibility is poor and cars speed very quickly over the pass.

THE HIKE The sandy track ascends northeast over sage-scented slopes dotted with yucca, pinyon pine, and Joshua trees. After a short (0.2 mile) climb, the trail gentles and offers over-the-shoulder desert views of pine-cloaked Scodie Mountain (toured by the PCT south of Walker Pass) and the Indian Wells Valley shimmering below to the southeast.

The Joshua trees, whose presence clearly defines the limits of the Mojave Desert, seem to fall away like tired hikers as you ascend. For a half mile or so, the path passes through a kind of no-man's zone without trees before the pinyon pine appear in force about a mile from the trailhead.

Now in the company of pines, the trail switchbacks among granite outcroppings to reach a saddle at the 1.7-mile mark. Here, you'll get the first trailside views of the High Sierra.

Continue briefly along the ridgeline, and then make a 0.3-mile ascent to a second saddle. Amidst a dense population of pinyon pine, you can spread out a picnic and savor vistas of two worlds—the Sierra Nevada peaks and forests to the north and the austere basins and ranges of the desert to the south.

■ LITTLE PETROGLYPH CANYON
Petroglyph Trail
2.4 miles round trip

Many of us admire petroglyphs as an art form. The ancient representations of humans and animals found on rocks throughout the desert Southwest are reproduced on clothing, tiles, jewelry, crockery, and many more items.

Once dismissed by some critics as whimsical doodling, petroglyphs are now increasingly recognized as having important ritual significance and to embody the religious beliefs of the Native American artists who made them.

One of the largest concentrations of rock art in North America is located in what has become known as "Little Petroglyph Canyon" in the Coso Mountains. The petroglyphs have been protected from the outside world by their location in remote and rugged badlands and, in recent times, by the strict security of the China Lake Naval Air Weapons Station. You can visit Little Petroglyph Canyon by joining a guided walking tour.

Shoshone, Southern Paiute and Northern Paiute, shamans made the petroglyphs in the Coso Mountains region. Shamans pecked out their art with a hammerstone—often just after emerging from a trance.

One reason for the sheer number of petroglyphs—some 11,000 in two canyons—is the nearly perfect medium for the message: a multitude of flat basaltic rocks, with a surface that's ideal for scratching out an image. The dark rocks accumulated a cover of oxidized minerals called desert varnish. As the artists of old scratched and pecked the varnish, the underlying lighter color of the rock emerged in distinct dramatic relief.

Scientists say some petroglyphs may be several thousand years old, but the vast majority are less than a thousand years old and some were made only a few hundred years ago.

By far the most common motif is the bighorn sheep; the powerful animals were highly prized by Native Americans who hunted them as game and revered them as spirit helpers with rain-making powers. About 25 percent of the petroglyphs found here are geometric shapes—spirals, dot patterns, zigzags, and more. Such images are puzzling and could have many interpretations including clan identification, religious symbols, and record-keeping.

DIRECTIONS TO TRAILHEAD Guided hikes only are available for this trip. Contact the Maturango Museum in Ridgecrest at (760) 375-6900 to arrange a visit and get directions to this site.

Thousands of petroglyphs: the bighorn sheep is the most common motif.

THE HIKE The Navy allows escorted tour groups to visit Little Petroglyph Canyon by reservation only during the spring and autumn months. Best bets are the tours conducted by docents from the Maturango Museum in Ridgecrest. The popular petroglyph tours are often booked weeks, even months in advance.

You'll get an excellent introduction from the museum docents, but once you're in the canyon, you can walk at your own pace. (However, you are required to return to the trailhead at the appointed time.)

From the parking area, you'll walk down-canyon on an arroyo bottom that alternates between sandy and rocky surfaces. Many of the best groupings of petroglyphs are located within a short walk of the trailhead. The array of images includes rattlesnakes, bighorn sheep, two men shooting arrows at each other, and self-portraits of the shaman artists themselves.

A bit more than a mile from the parking area, the canyon ends at a dramatic drop-off. Enjoy the vistas of the Indian Wells Valley and distant Ridgecrest.

■ RIDGECREST'S RADEMACHER HILLS

Rademacher Hills Trail

Loop to Overlook is 1.1 mile round trip with
300-foot elevation gain; longer options possible

Nineteenth-century prospectors scratched trails and poked tunnels in the ridges around Ridgecrest in a (mostly futile) search for gold. Twentieth-century miners continued the tradition of tunnel- and trail-building in what became known as the Rademacher Hills for the Rademacher Mine.

Today, these old mining trails, realigned and restored, are part of the Rademacher Hills Trail system that traverses the desert flatlands and rocky ridges south of Ridgecrest. The hiker's reward for climbing to the top of these hills is a marvelous desert panorama that takes in the town, China Lake, Indian Wells Valley, as well as the Panamint Mountains and Telescope Peak in Death Valley National Park.

Now the Rademacher Hills comprise a 500-acre BLM recreation area attractive to joggers, hikers, and horseback riders, but not so long ago the area was a post-industrial mess. Locals were in the habit of using the hills as a dumpsite for everything from autos to construction debris and as terrain to tear up with motorcycles and off-road vehicles.

Beginning in the early 1990s, the BLM halted illegal off-highway vehicle activity and coordinated volunteers from the local high school, scout troops,

Rademacher Hills: walk on the wild side of Ridgecrest.

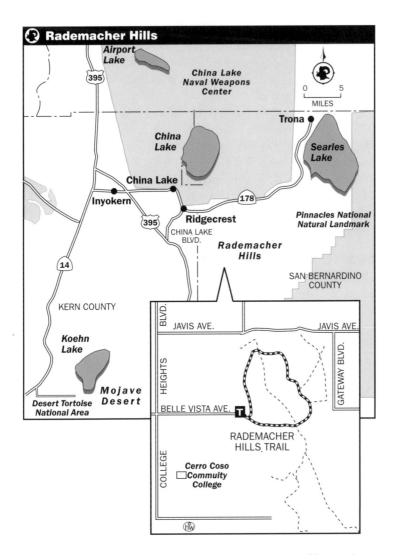

and Sierra Club in efforts to haul away trash, remove graffiti, and restore eroded slopes. Old trails were rehabilitated and new ones constructed.

Thanks to this good work, the Rademacher Hills have been transformed from a civic eyesore into community asset and handsome backdrop for Ridgecrest. A tip of the hiker's cap goes to rangers and employees of the BLM's Ridgecrest office who oversee millions of acres of remote Mojave Desert, but spent considerable time and effort in demonstrating desert conservation right on the outskirts of Ridgecrest.

The core of the trail system is a rough figure-8 of footpaths that contour around and cross over a 2,997-foot peak. This peak and its 3 miles of trail is a good place to start for first-time Rademacher Hills ramblers.

Sunland Trailhead, one of 11(!) offering access to the hills, is the best place to start and puts two destinations within easy reach—a summit viewpoint and the Ron Henry Interpretive Site, where there's a modest-sized desert plant display. Ambitious hikers can get oriented from the viewpoint then choose to wander any of the 11 miles of trail.

Make the Maturango Museum part of your post-hike plans. Museum exhibits highlight the cultural and natural history of the western Mojave Desert. An adjoining visitor center offers maps and publications—particularly helpful for those desert travelers headed for Death Valley National Park. The Museum store offers some unique desert-themed items and a good selection of books about the Mojave. You'll drive past the museum, located at the corner of China Lake Boulevard and Las Flores Avenue in downtown Ridgecrest, on the way to the Rademacher Hills Sunland Trailhead.

DIRECTIONS TO TRAILHEAD From Highway 14, some 44 miles north of the town of Mojave, turn east on Highway 178 and travel 14 miles to Ridgecrest. In Ridgecrest, the highway turns south and travels through Ridgecrest as China Lake Boulevard.

At Ridgecrest Boulevard, Highway 178 heads eastward again, but you continue traveling south another mile on China Lake Boulevard to the south end of town. Turn left on College Heights Boulevard and travel 2 miles. As Cerro Coso Community College comes into view on the hill ahead of you, look left for the BLM sign directing you to the Rademacher Hills Sunland Trailhead. Follow dirt Belle Vista Road 0.5 mile to its end at a small parking area.

THE HIKE From Sunland Trailhead, the trail makes a contouring ascent north, gaining better and better views of Ridgecrest. After surmounting a very rocky stretch, you'll come to a junction. If you want to quickly gain the summit, bear right and hike up a short but steep section of pathway to the top of the hill.

A bench perched strategically on the flat-topped summit offers a place to contemplate the desert scene. The path then descends past a fenced mine shaft to a four-way trail junction and the Ron Henry Interpretive Site, honoring Ronald H. Henry (1916-1994), "acclaimed China Lake chemist and outstanding public lands volunteer."

If all desert bushes look more or less the same to you, interpretive signs at the site positively identify indigo bush, wishbone bush, cheese bush, thorn bush, burro bush, and creosote bush.

From the interpretive site, it's an easy 0.25-mile descent to the trailhead.

■ TRONA PINNACLES
Trona Trail
To and through Tufa Monoliths
is approximately 1 mile round trip

On the way to Death Valley, off a road that seems to lead to nowhere, are the Trona Pinnacles, among the most unusual sights in the Mojave Desert. Five hundred tufa towers, many more than 100 feet high, rise from Searles Dry Lake basin.

From a distance, the pinnacles appear to be the ruins of some ancient, other-worldly civilization. Trekkies and movie buffs will recognize the Trona Pinnacles as one of the out-of-this-world locations in the Star Trek adventure *The Final Frontier.*

Scientists believe the tufa (calcium carbonate) rock formations developed some 10,000 to 100,000 years ago, when Searles Lake was a substantial body of water, fed by rainfall and by runoff from retreating Sierra Nevada glaciers.

The pinnacles formed underwater in the mineral-rich lake. Highly concentrated calcium carbonate brine bonded with algae to make reef-like formations of hollow tubes, and then the spires we see exposed today.

Once-deep Searles Lake, now a vast alkali basin, has long attracted the mining industry. Beginning in the 1870s, borax was extracted from the lake surface. Trona is the name of the predominant mineral (a double salt—sodium carbonate/bicarbonate) found in the lake. Trona minerals are used in the manufacture of baking powder, soaps, glass, and cleaning solvents.

The tufa formations are similar to the ones rising above Mono Lake; in fact, Trona's tufas, known officially as Pinnacles National Natural Landmark, are the best in the United States.

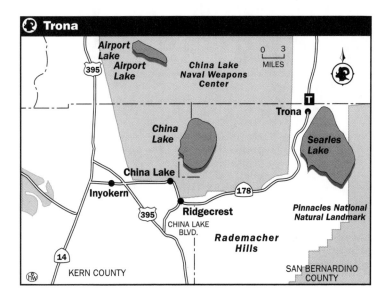

DIRECTIONS TO TRAILHEAD From California 14, take the Highway 178–Ridgecrest exit and drive 15 miles into Ridgecrest. Continue east another 11 miles. Turn right on the BLM-signed Pinnacles Road. Proceed 7 miles over the rutted dirt road (suitable for passenger cars with good ground clearance) to the Trona Pinnacles.

THE HIKE The pinnacles are spread over a 4-mile-long, 3-mile-wide area, but the main concentration of spires can be reached by an easy walk from the parking area. Wander at will from tufa tower to tufa tower as far as time and imagination permit. Wear sturdy footwear and pay attention to your footing on this walk; tufa cuts like coral.

■ RED ROCK CANYON
Hagen, Red Cliffs Trails
1 to 2 miles round trip; Season: October to May

The view of Red Rock Canyon may very well seem like déjà vu. Cliffs and canyons in these parts have appeared in the background of many a Western movie.

A black-and-white movie of Red Rock Canyon would be dramatic: shadow and light playing over the canyon walls. Technicolor, however, might more

Red Rock Canyon is both movie backdrop and desert park.

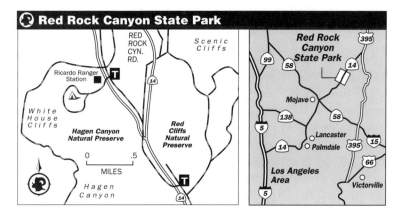

vividly capture the aptly named red rock, along with the chocolate brown, black, white, and pink hues of the pleated cliffs.

The Kawai'isu, lived in the Red Rock Canyon area more than 10,000 years ago. They occupied the land several hundred years before Europeans arrived.

Gold fever in the 1890s prompted exploration of almost all the canyons in the El Paso Mountains. During this era, Rudolph Hagen acquired much land in the Red Rock area. He named the little mining community-stage stop Ricardo after his son Richard. The Ricardo Ranger Station is located at the site of the once-thriving hamlet.

Red Rock Canyon became a state recreation area in 1969; when it became obvious off-road vehicles were damaging the hills and canyons, Red Rock was upgraded to a park in 1982.

DIRECTIONS TO TRAILHEAD Red Rock Canyon State Park is located 25 miles north of the town of Mojave off Highway 14. Turn northwest off 14 onto the signed road for the park campground. Follow this road a short mile to Ricardo Ranger Station. The station has a small visitor center with nature exhibits.

THE HIKE The best places to hike are in the park's two preserves, which are closed to vehicles. You'll find some trails to hike, but this park lends itself to improvisation.

Hagen Canyon Natural Preserve is a striking badlands, the dramatic cliffs capped by a layer of dark basalt.

The park's 0.75-mile nature trail tells the geologic story of the area, and points out typical desert flora. It's keyed to an interpretive pamphlet available at the trailhead. Join the nature trail at the south end of the park campground.

■ RED CLIFFS NATURAL PRESERVE
Red Cliffs Trail
To Scenic Cliffs is 2 to 3 miles round trip

R ed Cliffs is my favorite of the park's natural preserves, set aside to protect the unique canyons, cliff faces, plants, and wildlife.

Motorists get a brief but good view of the pink- and red-hued cliffs as they speed by on Highway 14. Those who drive to the parking area on the east side of the highway get even better views of the Red Cliffs. Hikers who venture into the preserve get the best views of all.

In moviemaking terminology, the highway view is the "establishing shot," the parking lot view the "long shot," and the trailside view the "close-up." Certainly the "hiker's POV" is a spectacular one indeed.

It's natural to take a cinematographer's view of this land because it has been featured in so many films. From 1920's Western serials to *Beneath the Planet of the Apes* to *Jurassic Park*, the cliffs have proved to be supremely photogenic in both shadowy black and white and rich, saturated color.

Note that hiking is not permitted in the Scenic Cliffs area from February 1 through July 1 in order to allow birds of prey to nest on the cliffs. Signs along the Scenic Cliffs near Iron Canyon delineate where you can wander and where you can't.

DIRECTIONS TO TRAILHEAD Red Rock Canyon State Park is located 25 miles north of the town of Mojave off Highway 14. Begin your exploration of Red Cliffs Natural Preserve at the parking area on the east side of the highway.

THE HIKE The route, which employs old dirt roads and some wash walking, starts out parallel to the cliffs and ascends 0.25 mile to a low rise. Behold the Red Cliffs and their bands of brown, red, pink, and white.

Cross a Joshua tree-dotted basin and head directly toward the Scenic Cliffs. At the 0.75-mile mark, you can climb one of the nearby high points for vistas of the cliffs, the South El Paso Mountains, and the wide desert floor shimmering in the distance.

Walk the dirt road to the Scenic Cliffs and remember to look down as well as up. The natural preserve's towering, banded cliffs are so compelling a sight that it's easy to overlook such special plant life as desert holly, fishhook cactus, and the rare Red Rock tar plant.

■ DESERT TORTOISE NATURAL AREA
Main Loop Trail, Discovery Trail
0.5 to 5 miles round trip; season: October-June

Everything a desert tortoise is—patient, quiet, slow, a homebody—we fast-paced urbanites are not. Perhaps that's why we Californians so admire our official state reptile.

One of the best places to glimpse a *Gopherus agassazi* is at the Desert Tortoise Natural Area in the West Mojave Desert near California City. March through mid-June is the best time to glimpse a tortoise; it is also the prime time to view the desert wildflowers blooming around their burrows.

Ancestors of the present-day desert tortoise roamed the earth with dinosaurs and, until recently, managed to adapt to changing environmental conditions. Then came grazing animals that squashed them and collapsed their burrows, and off-road vehicles that did likewise, as well as residential and commercial development that obliterated their habitat. Tortoises have been illegally collected, shot at in perverse fun, and were even sold as dog food in Los Angeles during the 1890s.

Once, the western Mojave desert supported as many as 2,000 tortoises per square mile. Today the tortoise population is a fraction of that, and the creature is considered a "threatened" species by state and federal governments.

One of the densest populations of tortoises remaining can be found in the 21,000-acre Desert Tortoise Natural Area set aside by conservation groups and the U.S. Bureau of Land Management to give the venerable reptiles a fighting chance for survival. The tortoises inside their fenced preserve seem to be doing better than their fellows out in the open desert, though the preserve population has suffered from the diseases brought in by unthinking people who release captive tortoises in the natural area. As a result, the tortoises become afflicted with a difficult-to-cure upper respiratory condition that spreads rapidly through the population.

In springtime, the tortoises emerge from their burrows to feed. Tortoises stay very close to their burrows,

A chance to see a desert tortoise in a special preserve.

wandering off only for a little eating, basking, or mating. They grow to 14 inches long and live a very slow 50 to 100 years.

During one visit to the preserve, it occurred to me that somewhere out in the Mojave there is an old tortoise that has witnessed both a Model T passing and the space shuttle landing.

First stop for visitors should be the colorfully painted motorhome that is the Desert Tortoise Natural Area headquarters during the March through June "tortoise season."

DIRECTIONS TO TRAILHEAD From Highway 14 (Antelope Valley Freeway), 5 miles north of the town of Mojave, exit on California City Boulevard. Drive some 10 miles east (through California City). Turn left (northeast) on 20 Mule Team Parkway and in 1.4 miles reach Randsburg-Mojave Road. Turn left at this junction, where you'll find a shaded picnic area and information panels about the desert tortoise. Proceed 4.5 more miles on the dirt road (usually in good shape, but almost impassable after a hard rain) to the Desert Tortoise Natural Area parking lot.

THE HIKE Several trails crisscross the Desert Tortoise Natural Area. The Main Loop Trail makes a short circle from the parking area and connects to Plant Trail and Animal Trail, self-guided nature trails with interpretive pamphlets that explain, respectively, the local flora and fauna.

More ambitious is the 1.8-mile Discovery Loop Trail that follows strategically placed brown posts emblazoned with a hiker's logo across the open and (in spring) blooming desert. In the shelter of the spreading creosote bushes are phacelia, fiddleneck, goldfields, and evening snow. Near the headquarters is the stunning desert candle.

Look for tortoise burrows—and tortoises—near creosote bushes. The best time to spot a tortoise is in the morning hours and in the late afternoon. You are more likely to spot one away from the nature trails than right next to the paths. Ask the naturalist, on duty during the spring visitor season, for help in locating a tortoise.

■ TOMO-KAHNI
Tomo-Kahni Trail
2-mile guided tour

Explore the ancient land of the Kawai'isu, an intriguing preserve of wind-sculpted rock formations, pictographs, and a pinyon pine forest located east of the town of Tehachapi. Tomo-Kahni, an intriguing blend of High Desert and High Sierra environments, is a state park in the making and can be visited by joining special ranger- and docent-led walking tours.

The park was created in 1993 in order to protect and interpret a village site used during the winter months by the Kawai'isu. Tribal elders suggested the name Tomo-Kahni which, in the Kawai'isu language, means "winter village."

The Kawai'isu were hunter-gatherers who inhabited a very large territory ranging from the Southern Sierra to the Tehachapi Range to the western Mojave Desert. Such a diverse environment required the Kawai'isu to master the use of a multitude of plants.

According to Yale University anthropologist Maurice Zigmond, who studied the Kawai'isu and their land from the 1930s and 1970s, these Native Americans used more than 200 plants for foods, beverages, and medicine. Zigmond documented a great deal of the Kawai'isu language and culture in his writings.

The Kawai'isu, of Shoshonean lineage, call themselves *Nuooah*, which, in their language, means "the People." Kawai'isu forebears may have lived in the desert-mountains environment some 3,000 years ago. The tribe has long been known for its creation of colorful and intricately designed baskets.

Visitors to the Tomo-Kahni site learn more about the Kawai'isu as they walk the pinyon pine woodland and discover how these people used pinyon pine nuts, as well as many other nuts, berries, and plants for food. One sandstone rock outcropping has more than 400 mortar holes where the Kawai'isu ground acorns.

DIRECTIONS TO TRAILHEAD Guided tours only are available to this site. Call the California State Parks office (number below) to schedule a tour and get directions to the meeting point.

THE HIKE Tours of Tomo-Kahni are offered on spring and fall weekends (weather permitting) only by reservation. The slow to moderately paced walking tour (with some steep trail sections) lasts two to three hours. Wear sturdy boots and a hat for sun protection, and bring water.

Tours begin with an orientation held at the Tehachapi Museum Annex, located just across the street from the main Tehachapi Museum, at 311 South Green Street. After the orientation, visitors drive about 12 miles to the park. (High-clearance vehicles are recommended.)

Tour costs are $5 per adult and $3 for children. Call the California State Parks office in Lancaster for more information and reservations: (661) 942-0662.

■ CALIFORNIA POPPY RESERVE
Antelope Loop Trail
From the visitor center to Antelope Butte Vista
Point is 2.5 miles round trip with 300-foot elevation
gain; season: March-May

The California poppy blooms on many a grassy slope in the Southland, but only in the Antelope Valley does the showy flower blanket whole hillsides in such brilliant orange sheets. Surely, the finest concentration of California's state flower (during a good wildflower year) is preserved at the Antelope Valley California Poppy Reserve in the Mojave Desert west of Lancaster.

The poppy is the star of the flower show, which includes a supporting cast of fiddlenecks, cream cups, tidy tips, and goldfields. March through Memorial Day is the time to saunter through this wondrous display of desert wildflowers.

The poppy has always been recognized as something special. Early Spanish Californians called it *Dormidera*, "the drowsy one," because the petals curl up at night. They fashioned a hair tonic/restorer by frying the blossoms in olive oil and adding perfume.

At the reserve, you can pick up a map at the Jane S. Pineiro Interpretive Center, named for the painter who was instrumental in setting aside an area where California's state flower could be preserved for future generations to admire. Some of Pineiro's watercolors are on display in the center, which also has wildflower interpretive displays and a slide show.

Built into the side of a hill, the center boast an award-winning solar design, windmill power, and "natural" air conditioning.

DIRECTIONS TO TRAILHEAD From the Antelope Valley Freeway (California 14) in Lancaster, exit on Avenue I and drive west 15 miles. Avenue I

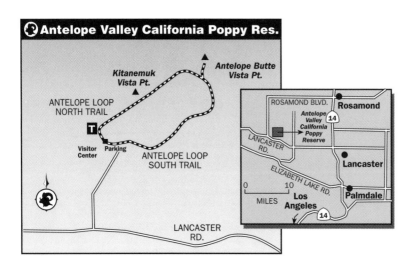

The flowers that bloom in the spring attract admirers to see the colorful show.

becomes Lancaster Road a few miles before the Poppy Reserve. The reserve (day use fee) is open 9 AM to 4 PM daily.

Spring wildflower displays are always unpredictable. To check on what's blooming where, call the park at (661) 942-0662 before making the trip.

THE HIKE Antelope Loop Trail—and all trails in the reserve—are easy walking and suitable for the whole family. Seven miles of gentle trails crisscross the 1,760-acre reserve; many hikers take every trail in the park without getting too tired.

Begin on the signed Antelope Loop Trail to the left of the visitor center. The trail passes through an orange sea of poppies and fiddlenecks, then climbs briefly to Kitanemuk Vista Point, 0.75 mile from the visitor center. Atop Vista Point are those flowery symbols of faithfulness and friendship, forget-me-nots, and an unforgettable view of the Mojave Desert and the snow-covered Tehachapis.

After enjoying the view, continue on to Antelope Butte Vista Point, where another lookout offers fine desert panoramas. From here, join the south loop of the Antelope Loop Trail and return to the visitor center.

After you've circled the "upper west side" of the Poppy Reserve, you may wish to extend your hike by joining the Poppy Loop Trail and exploring the "lower east side."

■ ARTHUR RIPLEY DESERT WOODLAND STATE PARK

Ripley Nature Trail

0.5 mile interpretive trail plus a few miles of freeform walking

Believe it or not, Arthur Ripley Desert Woodland State Park hosts one of the last virgin Joshua tree forests in the Antelope Valley.

With its thriving Joshuas and junipers, accompanied by a thick undergrowth of buckwheat, beavertail cactus, sage and Mormon tea, the preserve is a reminder of how most of the Antelope Valley may have appeared to early travelers such as missionary Father Garcés in 1776, or explorer John C. Frémont in 1848.

Located in far northern Los Angeles County, about three miles as the raven flies from the Kern County line, the park has yet to be plotted on most maps, and is all but unknown to most desert travelers. Poppy-lovers sometimes happen upon the park because it's located just seven miles down the road from the famed Antelope Valley California Poppy Reserve.

The Tehachapi Range, which separates the Antelope Valley from the San Joaquin Valley, forms the park's impressive mountain backdrop to the north. Mile-high Sawmill Mountain in the nearby Angeles National Forest, rises dramatically to the south.

The State Department of Parks and Recreation seems content to leave well enough alone at Ripley. A single roadside sign (blink and you'll miss it) identifies

Give thanks to Arthur Ripley for preserving this special woodland.

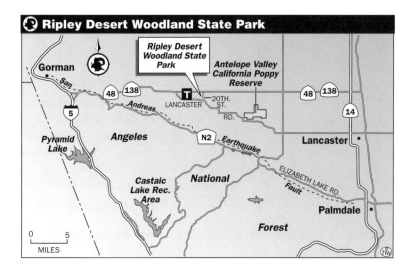

the preserve, whose only visitor amenity is a rustic outhouse (very attractively situated, by the way, amidst the desert flora).

The park provides habitat for abundant Antelope Valley wildlife (except for the long-gone antelope, of course). Quail, roadrunners, king snakes, rattlesnakes, kangaroo rats, coyotes and ground squirrels are commonly sighted within the park's boundaries. Lots of black-tailed rabbits and the occasional cottontail hop down the numerous bunny trails that crisscross the preserve.

The park's Joshuas are smaller than most; these *Yucca brevifolia* belong to the smaller-than-average subspecies *Herbertii*. Struggling for nutrients in the preserve's sandy soil, these Joshuas rarely exceed 14 feet in height.

Joshuas have a well-deserved reputation for assuming grotesque shapes and the trees at the preserve are no exception; in fact, their twisted limbs and torsos appear all the more weird because of their bordering-on-dwarf stature.

Farmer Arthur Ripley (1901-1988) willed 560 acres of his property to the state. He and many other farmers and developers cleared hundreds of thousands of acres in the western Antelope Valley for crops and subdivisions. Ripley, however, cared enough about this particular pristine desert woodland to protect it for future generations.

The park's spring wildflowers in a good year include fiddleneck, scarlet bugler, coreopsis, goldfields, chia, blue dicks and filaree. Ripley's bigger plants are generally more dependable bloomers. In spring, the beavertail cactus produces attention-getting magenta-hued flowers while goldenbush puts forth yellow daisy-like blooms. Greeting hikers is the fragrant blue sage, which raises long spikey arms covered with blue flowers. Star of the spring show, though, is the Joshua tree with creamy white blossoms festooning its uplifted arms.

DIRECTIONS TO TRAILHEAD From Interstate 5, about 6 miles south of Gorman and 27 miles north of Valencia, exit on Highway 138 and head east

15 miles to Lancaster Road. Turn right (south). Follow Lancaster Road, which soon bends east, a bit more than 4 miles to the signed Arthur Ripley Desert Woodland State Park on the left (north) side of the road. Park carefully along the road.

If you're traveling from the Antelope Valley, you'll exit the Antelope Valley Freeway (14) in Lancaster on Highway 138 (Avenue D) and travel about 19 miles west to 210th Street. Turn south a mile to Lancaster Road.

From the Antelope Valley California Poppy Reserve, continue another 7 miles west on Lancaster Road to the state park.

The Mojave Desert State Parks Visitor Center, located in a small shopping center in Lancaster, has desert information and a small bookstore. From the Antelope Valley Freeway (14), take the Avenue K exit and follow the signs.

THE HIKE A twelve-stop interpretive trail, keyed to a pamphlet available from the state parks visitor center in Lancaster, leads past some of the preserve's featured flora. (A brochure is by no means necessary to enjoy the trail.)

Ripley's other rambles are of the do-it-yourself variety. Wander at will amongst the juniper and Joshua trees, inhale the sage-scented fresh air, and rejoice at the beauty of this wooded island on the land.

■ SADDLEBACK BUTTE
Saddleback Butte Trail
From campground to Saddleback Peak is 4 miles round trip
with 1,000-foot elevation gain; season: October-May

Rarely visited Saddleback Butte State Park, located on the eastern fringe of Antelope Valley, is high-desert country, a land of creosote bush and Joshua trees. The park takes the name of its most prominent feature—3,651-foot Saddleback Butte, a granite mountaintop that stands head and shoulders above Antelope Valley.

The Richard Dowen Nature Trail is a good introduction to the Joshua tree and other plant life found in this corner of the desert. The trail to the boulder-strewn summit of Saddleback Peak takes a straight-line course, with most of the elevation gain occurring in the last half mile. From atop the peak, enjoy far-reaching desert views.

DIRECTIONS TO TRAILHEAD From Highway 14 (Antelope Valley Freeway) in Lancaster, take the 20th Street exit. Head north on 20th and turn right (east) on Avenue J. Drive 18 miles to Saddleback Butte State Park. Follow the dirt park road to the campground, where the trail begins. Park (day-use fee) near the trail sign.

THE HIKE The signed trail heads straight for the saddle. The soft, sandy track, marked with yellow posts, leads through an impressive Joshua tree woodland.

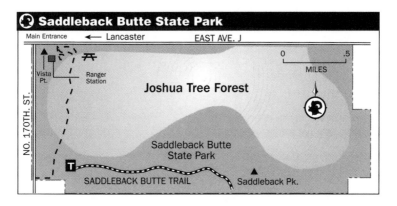

After 1.5 miles, the trail switchbacks steeply up the rocky slope of the butte. An invigorating climb brings you to the saddle of Saddleback Butte. To reach the peak, follow the steep leftward trail to the summit.

From the top, you can look south to the San Gabriel Mountains. At the base of the mountains, keen eyes will discern the California Aqueduct, which carries water to the Southland from the Sacramento Delta. To the east is the vast Mojave Desert, and to the north is Edwards Air Force Base. To the west are the cities of Lancaster and Palmdale, and farther west are the rugged Tehachapi Mountains.

■ ANTELOPE VALLEY INDIAN MUSEUM
Antelope Valley Nature Trail
Nature Trail loop is 0.5 mile, plus another optional 0.5 mile or so off trail

Antelope Valley Indian Museum offers an intriguing look at the indigenous people of the Mojave Desert, California, and the Southwest. A museum tour and interpretive trail combine to help visitors learn of the special cultural adaptations these Native Americans made to living in dry lands.

Artist Howard Arden Edwards found inspiration in the Antelope Valley in the 1920s and built a house atop the bedrock of Piute Butte. The unique house, which presents a Swiss chalet-style look on the outside, makes use of natural rock formations in its interior design and features the artist's large, brightly painted American Indian murals and motifs.

Grace Oliver purchased the property in 1938, combined her Indian artifacts collection with that of the Edwards family, and operated a museum intermittently for 40 years. The state purchased the museum in 1979.

Today, the musum interprets and exhibits important collections from three American Indian cultural regions: the American Southwest, the western Great Basin, and California. These three regions are linked by the Antelope Valley, an easy-access corridor with water en route and an important trade route for some 4,000 years.

After your museum tour, step outside to the nature trail, highlighted by big boulders and Joshua trees. The 14-stop interpretive path is keyed to a brochure available in the museum.

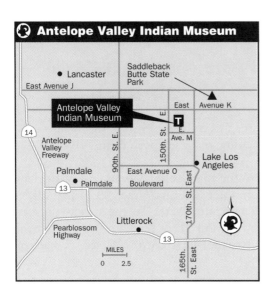

The museum is open on weekends only, from 11 AM to 4 PM, mid-September to mid-June.

DIRECTIONS TO TRAIL-HEAD Antelope Valley Indian Museum is located some 20 miles east of Highway 14 (Antelope Valley Freeway), between 150th and 170 streets, on Avenue M.

From Highway 14 in Lancaster, exit on Avenue K and drive 17 miles east to 150th Street East. Turn south and drive 2 miles to Avenue M. Turn

Take time to tour the remarkable Antelope Valley Indian Museum.

east and drive 0.7 mile to the turnoff for the museum on the north side of the road.

You can also choose to exit Highway 14 in Lancaster and head east on Pearblossom Highway (138). Turn left (north) on 165th Street East (which becomes 170th Street East), then turn left (west) on Avenue M.

THE HIKE The path offers an overview of the Antelope Valley. Observe the San Gabriel Mountains bordering the valley to the south and the handsome buttes rising on the eastern part of the valley. To the immediate south are Lovejoy Buttes (3,342 feet) and to the northeast is Saddleback Butte (3,651 feet), while the museum rests on Piute Butte (3,175 feet).

You'll pass the old Edwards barn and corral, meander among the creosote, cholla, and Joshua trees and perhaps be lucky enough to sight some of the local inhabitants—the desert tortoise, Antelope ground squirrel, or roadrunner.

■ VASQUEZ ROCKS
Geology Trail, Pacific Crest Trail
1 to 3 miles round trip

Chances are, you've seen the rocks on television and the big screen many times—from old westerns to modern sci-fi films. And you've probably seen Vasquez Rocks while motoring along the Antelope Valley Freeway; the famed formations are but a couple of miles from California Highway 14.

But the best place to see the Southland's most famous geological silhouette is Vasquez Rocks County Park Natural Area in Agua Dulce. Hiking trails circle the rocks, which are not only enjoyable to view, but fun to climb upon.

Through a camera lens, and from a distance, the rocks look insurmountable; actually, they're rather easy to climb. The rocks are only about 100 to 150 feet high, and you can find safe and mellow routes to the top of the sandstone outcrops.

The rocks themselves are tilted and worn sandstone, the result of years of earthquake action and erosion by elements. The big beds of sedimentary rock known as the Mint Canyon Formation were laid down some 8 to 15 million years ago. The Vasquez Rocks Formation is composed of coarser, redder layers underneath.

Tataviam Indians occupied the area until the late 1700s, when their culture was overwhelmed and eventually extinguished by the soldiers, settlers, and missionaries of the San Fernando Mission.

During the 1850s and 1860s, notorious highwayman Tiburcio Vasquez used the rocks and canyons as a hideout from the Los Angeles lawmen who were pursuing him. Even before he was hung for his crimes in 1875, the area was known as Vasquez Rocks.

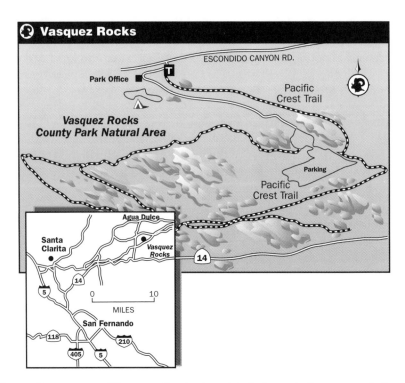

The trail system at Vasquez Rocks is a bit informal. Because of the open nature of the terrain, hikers can—and do—tend to wander where their rock fancy takes them. If you remember that the park entrance/office is more or less to the north, and the Antelope Valley Freeway is to the south, you'll stay fairly well-oriented.

A favorite route of mine, a clockwise tour of three miles or so, is described below; however, part of the fun of Vasquez Rocks is going your own way.

DIRECTIONS TO TRAILHEAD From Highway14 (Antelope Valley Freeway), a few miles northeast of the outskirts of Canyon Country, exit on Agua Dulce Canyon Road. Head north 1.5 miles. Agua Dulce Canyon Road swings west and you join Escondido Canyon Road, proceeding a quarter mile to the signed Vasquez Rocks County Park entrance on your right. You can park just inside the entrance at the small parking area near the park office, or you can continue to the main lot near the largest of the rock formations.

THE HIKE Begin at the signed trailhead for Geology Trail just across the park road from the parking lot. (Pick up an interpretive brochure, as well as a trail map, from the office.) Soon after you begin your trailside study of strata, Geology Trail intersects Pacific Crest Trail and you'll head right.

The mile-long stretch of PCT through the park is part of a segment that connects the San Gabriel Mountains to the south with the Sierra Pelona area of

Angeles National Forest to the north. The path parallels the park road. To your left are some scattered residence and the open desert beyond; to your right are some of the most famous of the Vasquez Rocks.

Pacific Crest Trail joins a dirt road at the edge of the picnic area and continues west atop the north wall of Escondido Canyon. Very few park visitors, it seems, hike here, though the rock formations are stunning and a seasonal creek flows through the canyon. Only the annoying hum of the nearby Antelope Valley Freeway disturbs the natural beauty of the area.

You can cross the creek with the PCT, double back along the other side of Escondido Canyon, and continue your exploration of the little-known southern part of the park. But to continue to the main rock formations, stay west with the dirt road and you'll soon reach a junction with the park's horse trail. You can take this trail if you wish, or continue a short distance farther and join the foot trail.

The Vasquez Rocks area is a transition zone between mountain and desert environments. Yucca, buckwheat, sage and California juniper are among the plants you'll pass en route.

The footpath drops northwestward then heads east to visit the most dramatic of the Vasquez Rocks.

■ DEVIL'S PUNCHBOWL NATURAL AREA COUNTY PARK
Devil's Punchbowl Loop Trail
1 mile loop from visitor center

Devil's Punchbowl Trail is an ideal, family-friendly introduction to a strange wonderland of rock that sits astride the San Andreas Fault. Along with earthquakes, the erosive forces of wind and water have carved the sharply angled sandstone formations.

Devil's Punchbowl itself may have been the work of the devil, or more likely, it was a deep canyon cut by streams running out of the San Gabriel Mountains. Over millions of years, the streams tore at the sedimentary rock and eroded the steep and cockeyed rock layers of the Punchbowl formation. Originally horizontal,

Earthquake-fractured Devil's Punchbowl.

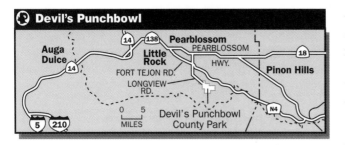

these layers of siltstone and sandstone were folded into a syncline (U-shaped fold), by the pinching action of earthly forces.

DIRECTIONS TO TRAILHEAD From Highway 138 on the east edge of Pearblossom, exit on County Road N6 (Longview Road) and proceed south 7.5 miles to the entrance of Devil's Punchbowl Natural Area County Park.

THE HIKE A 0.3-mile nature trail, Pinyon Pathway, introduces visitors to park geology and plant life, and the 1-mile loop trail offers grand views of the Punchbowl. A picnic area is perched on the rim of the Punchbowl.

The more intrepid may wish to explore lower Punchbowl Canyon, located below Devil's Punchbowl Loop Trail. Access this canyon from Big Rock Creek Road.

■ DEVIL'S CHAIR
Punchbowl Trail
From South Fork Campground to Devil's Chair is 6 miles round trip with 1,000-foot elevation gain; to park headquarters is 12 miles round trip

Southern California has many faults, and the mightiest of these is the San Andreas. Nowhere is the presence of this fault more obvious than in Devil's Punchbowl County Park. The dun-colored rocks have been tilted every which way and weathered by wind and rain. They are a bizarre sight to behold.

Punchbowl Trail takes you into the Devil's domain, a satanically landscaped rock garden on the desert side of the San Gabriel Mountains. The trip offers views of the Punchbowl Fault and the San Jacinto Fault—part of what seismologists call the San Andreas Rift Zone. If you're superstitious, you'll want to carry a good-luck charm in your day pack when you hike to the monstrous mass of white rock known as the Devil's Chair.

Winter is a fine time to visit the Punchbowl. Winds scour the desert clean, and from the Devil's Chair, you can get superb views of this land, as well as the seemingly infinite sandscape of the Mojave.

Note that the 6-mile Punchbowl Trail may be hiked from two directions. For aesthetic and logistical reasons, I prefer the route from the Forest Service's South Fork Campground to Devil's Chair.

The leg-weary or families with small children may wish to proceed directly to Devil's Punchbowl County Park. A 0.3-mile nature trail, Pinyon Pathway, introduces visitors to park geology and plant life, and a 1-mile loop trail offers grand views of the Punchbowl.

DIRECTIONS TO TRAILHEAD From Pearblossom Highway (Highway 138) in Pearblossom, turn south onto Longview Road, then briefly left on Fort Tejon Road and right on Valyermo Road. Continue 3 miles to Big Rock Creek Road. Two-and-a-half miles past this junction, turn right on a signed dirt road to South Fork Campground and proceed 1 mile to the special day use/hiker's parking lot below the campground. The road is suitable for passenger cars, but on occasion, Big Rock Creek may be too high for a low-slung car to ford; you may have to walk an extra mile to the trailhead. The signed trail departs from the parking area.

If you want to go directly to Devil's Punchbowl County Park, turn south on County Road N6 from Highway 138 in Pearblossom and follow it to the county park. Punchbowl Trail begins near the picnic area.

THE HIKE From the parking area below South Fork Campground, join the signed trail. Almost immediately, you'll reach a trail junction. (Steep South Fork Trail ascends the canyon cut by the South Fork of Big Rock Creek up to the Angeles Crest Highway at Islip Saddle.) Stay on Punchbowl Trail and boulder-hop across the creek.

The trail climbs through manzanita- and heat-stunted pinyon pine to a saddle where there's a view of the park and its faults. Descend from the saddle, down chaparral-covered slopes and over to Holcomb Canyon. Along the way, notice the strange dovetailing of three plant communities: yucca-covered hills, oak woodland, and juniper and piney woods.

You may wish to take a break near Holcomb Creek crossing. Oaks and big cone spruce shade the creek.

From Holcomb Creek, the trail ascends steeply up another ridge through a pinyon pine forest to the Devil's Chair. From a distance, those with fanciful imaginations can picture the devil himself ruling over this kingdom of fractured rock. Below the chair, there's an awesome panorama of the Punchbowl and its jumbled sedimentary strata. The somersaulted sandstone formation resembles pulled taffy. If you look west to the canyon wall, you can see the vertical crush zone of the fault, marked by white rocks.

While visiting the Devil's Chair, stay behind the protective fence; people have taken an accidental plunge into the Punchbowl. Return to the trailhead the way you came or continue on the Punchbowl Trail to county park headquarters.

Above Devil's Chair, the trail contours west and offers close-up views of the Punchbowl. About 1.5 mile from the Chair, your route crosses Punchbowl Creek, briefly joins a dirt road, and then bears right on the trail leading to the Punchbowl parking area.

■ BIG ROCK CANYON
South Fork Trail
From South Fork Campground to Islip Saddle is 10.4 miles
round trip with 2,100-foot elevation gain

For purposes of geographical orientation, Southland hikers often divide the San Gabriel Mountains into a front country, backcountry, foothills, high country, east end, west end, urban interface, and alpine wilderness. Rarely, however, does the north (desert) side of the range come up for discussion.

The San Gabriels thrust abruptly up from the desert floor, stopping much of the Mojave's heat and hot air from reaching the Los Angeles Basin. From vista points near the crest of Angeles Crest Highway at Dawson Saddle (7,901 feet), travelers get grand panoramas of the Mojave Desert, which, from this vantage point, seems mighty close to the metropolis. Clear-day vistas are quintessential West Mojave: dry lake beds and isolated buttes.

At the base of the mountains lie the communities of Pearblossom and Little Rock. In earlier times, farmers tapped the intermittent creeks cascading from the north shoulders of the range and planted orchards of pears, peaches, cherries, and almonds.

The desert side of the San Gabriels is characterized by deep V-shaped gorges. Perhaps the most dramatic of these gorges is the South Fork of Big Rock Creek, a steep canyon that extends from the northern crest of the range down to the San Andreas Fault Zone and the intensively fractured Devil's Punchbowl.

South Fork Trail climbs from the high desert to the highway, from pinyon pine to ponderosa pine. The path traces the South Fork of Big Rock Creek Canyon adjacent to Devil's Punchbowl and ascends to Islip Saddle (6,685 feet), located on Angeles Crest Highway. With changes in elevation come changes in vegetation—from sage and cactus to manzanita and ceanothus to incense cedar and spruce.

Long ago, before Angeles Crest Highway was constructed and the San Gabriel Mountains became easy to cross by car, South Fork Trail was a major passageway into the mountains. These days, the path is little used, and you might just find yourself the only one enjoying this connection between desert and alpine environments.

DIRECTIONS TO TRAILHEAD From Pearblossom Highway (Highway 138) in Pearblossom, turn south onto Longview Road, then briefly left on Fort Tejon Road and right on Valyermo Road. Continue 3 miles to Big Rock Creek Road. Some 2.5 miles past this junction, turn right on the signed dirt road to South Fork Campground and proceed 1 mile to the special day use/hiker's parking lot below the campground. The road is suitable for passenger cars, but on occasion, Big Rock Creek may be too high for a low-slung car to ford; you may have to walk an extra mile to the trailhead. The signed trail departs from the parking area.

Those hikers wishing to make a one-way descent on South Fork Trail will find the upper trailhead at Islip Saddle parking area, located at mile 64.1 on Angles Crest Highway.

THE HIKE From the parking area below South Fork Campground, join the signed trail heading south. Almost immediately, you'll reach a trail junction with the path leading to Devil's Punchbowl. Stay left and you'll soon pass South Fork Campground on your left.

After 0.25 mile, cross to the other side of Big Rock Creek and switchback up the canyon wall. The trail continues its ascent, sometimes at quite a height above Big Rock Creek. With your ascent, the environment changes from desert to forest, though not all at once, and the hiker will note some intriguing combinations of desert and woodland plant life in the transition zone.

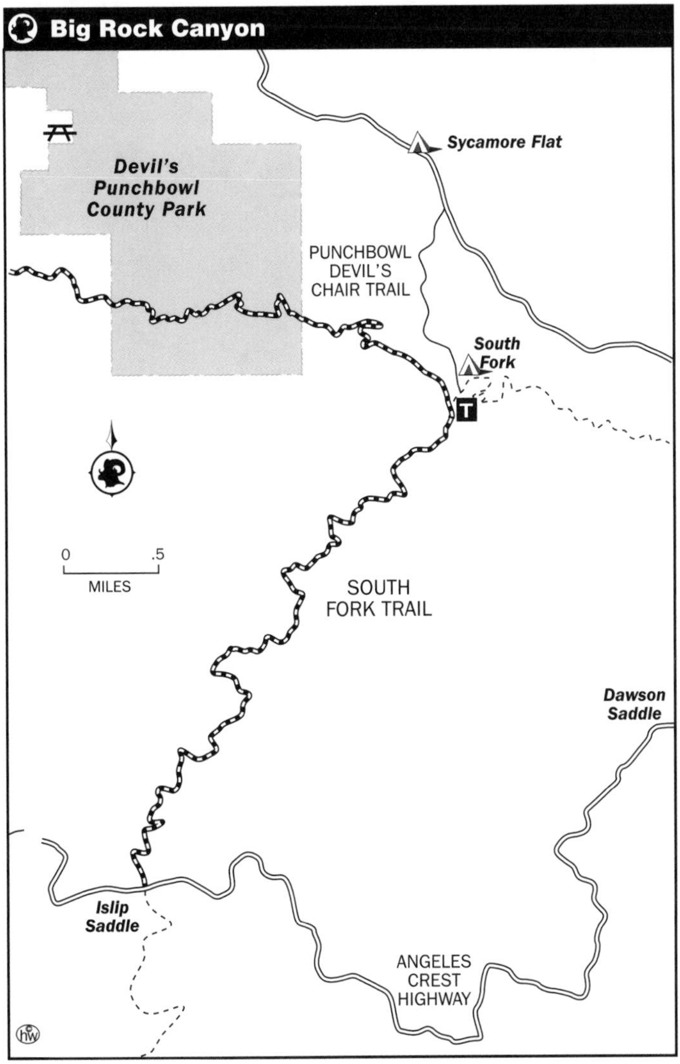

South Fork Trail meets Angeles Crest Highway at a point where the Pacific Crest Trail climbs northward toward Mt. Williamson.

Big Rock Canyon

Devil's Punchbowl County Park

Sycamore Flat

PUNCHBOWL DEVIL'S CHAIR TRAIL

South Fork

0   .5
MILES

SOUTH FORK TRAIL

Dawson Saddle

Islip Saddle

ANGELES CREST HIGHWAY

Contemplate the wonders of the East Mojave.

CHAPTER 3

MOJAVE NATIONAL PRESERVE AND EAST MOJAVE

As you hike up to the top of Kelso Dunes, you might just find that the dunes sha-boom, sha-boom, sha-boom for you. Geologists speculate that the extreme dryness of the East Mojave Desert, combined with the wind-polished, rounded nature of the individual sand grains, has something to do with their musical ability.

Except for the sha-booming dunes, the Kelso Dunes are absolutely quiet. Often hikers find they have a 45-square-mile formation of magnificently sculpted sand, the most extensive dune field in the West, all to themselves.

Two decades of park politicking finally ended in October 1994 when Congress passed the California Desert Protection Act, which transferred the East Mojave National Scenic Area, administered by the BLM, to the National Park Service and established the new Mojave National Preserve. The Mojave's elevated national profile has not yet attracted hordes of sightseers, although some 17 million people live within a four-hour drive.

To many travelers, though, the East Mojave is that vast, bleak, interminable stretch of desert to be crossed as quickly as possible while driving Interstate 15 from Barstow to Las Vegas. Few realize that I-15 is the northern boundary of what desert rats have long called "the Crown Jewel of the California Desert"—so close to Glitter City, but truly a world apart.

Although virtually unknown, Mojave National Preserve is quite accessible; it's bounded north and south by two major interstates, I-15 and I-40, and on the east by U.S. Highway 95. Just south of I-40 is one of the longest remaining stretches of old Route 66. Still, the area bounded by these three highways long has been dubbed "The Lonesome Triangle" and will probably keep this nickname for many years to come.

With few campgrounds and even fewer motels or other amenities, this land is a hard one to get to know—but an easy one to get to like: 1.6 million acres that includes such wonders as canyons sculpted by the Mojave River, the vast caves of Mitchell Caverns, and the world's largest Joshua tree forest. Mojave National Preserve offers the chance to relive history by hiking traditional paths to Fort Piute and Hole-in-the-Wall and by driving the old Mojave Road and fabled Route 66. The preserve is a wonderful concentration of mining history, back roads and footpaths, tabletop mesas, cinder cones, and a dozen mountain ranges. This diversity, everything that makes a desert a desert, draws us to experience its silent places. It's a call of the wild that can't be heard, only felt and experienced.

It's a grand view from atop the Kelso Dunes: the Kelso Mountains to the north, the Bristol Mountains to the southwest, the Granite Mountains to the south, the Providence Mountains to the east. Everywhere are mountain ranges, small and large, from the jagged, red-colored spire-like Castle Peaks to the flat-topped Table Mountain. In fact, despite evidence to the contrary—most notably the stunning Kelso Dunes—the East Mojave is really a desert of mountains not sand.

From the park's Kelso Depot Visitor Center, lonesome backroads lead toward Cima Dome a 75-square-mile chunk of uplifted volcanic rock. A geological rarity, Cima has been called the most symmetrical natural dome in the United States. Another distinctive feature of the dome is its handsome rock outcroppings—the same type found in Joshua Tree National Park to the south. Rock climbers, rock scramblers, and hikers love Cima's rock show.

On and around Cima Dome is the world's largest and densest Joshua tree forest. Botanists say Cima's Joshuas are more symmetrical than their cousins elsewhere in the Mojave, though, to me, every tree is a rugged individualist with branches that seem like handfuls of daggers.

Hole-in-the-Wall and Mid Hills are the centerpieces of Mojave National Preserve. Both locales offer diverse desert scenery, fine campgrounds, and the feeling of being in the middle of nowhere though, in fact, located right in the middle of the preserve.

Linking Mid Hills to Hole-in-the-Wall is an 8-mile trail, my favorite hike in the East Mojave; nearby is the preserve's best drive. In 1989, Wildhorse Canyon Road, which loops from Mid Hills Campground to Hole-in-the-Wall Campground, was declared the nation's first official "Back Country Byway," an honor bestowed upon America's most scenic backroads.

Hole-in-the-Wall is the kind of place Butch Cassidy and the Sundance Kid would have chosen for a hideout. Geologists call this twisted maze of red rock rhyolite, a kind of lava that existed as hot liquid far below the earth's surface, then crystallized. A series of iron rings aids descent into Hole-in-the-Wall; they're not particularly difficult for those who are reasonably agile and take their time.

Kelso Dunes, the Joshua trees, Hole-in-the-Wall, and Mid Hills—the heart of the preserve can be viewed in a weekend. But you'll need a week just to see all the major sights, and maybe a lifetime to really get to know the preserve. Return for a meander through a "botanical island," the pinyon pine and juniper woodland in Caruthers Canyon; tour Ivanpah Valley, which supports the largest desert tortoise population in the California Desert, and see if you can spot one of the elusive, seldom seen creatures; climb atop enormous volcanic cinder cones, then with flashlights crawl through narrow lava tubes. Return to explore the ruins of Fort Piute, wonder about the lonely life of the soldiers stationed there, marvel at the ruts carved into rock by the wheels of pioneer wagon trains; guess at the meaning of the petroglyphs left behind by the Native Americans who roamed this land long ago.

Mojave National Preserve is a worthy addition to the National Park System and a great place to explore on foot.

■ CALICO EARLY MAN SITE
Early Man Trail
0.25 mile round trip

Prehistoric stone tools found at the Calico Early Man Archaeological Site— scrapers, hand picks, choppers, and the like—may be up to 200,000 years old. So say a tiny minority of scientists who have studied the artifacts. The site's authenticity is highly controversial among anthropologists and archaeologists, who heatedly debate the topic of Early Arrivals vs. Late Arrivals.

Nearly all present-day scientists fall into the Late Arrivals camp and estimate that humans arrived in this part of the Mojave Desert no more than 10,000 to 12,000 years ago.

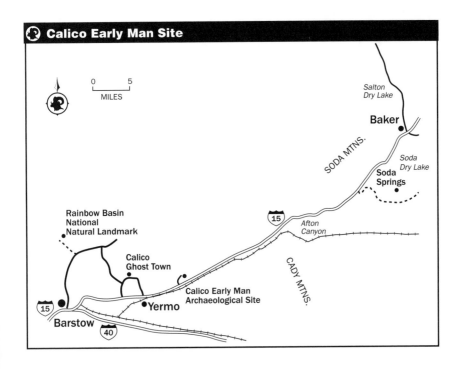

Nevertheless, Calico was the only place in North America where the famed archaeologist-paleontologist, Dr. Louis S. B. Leakey, chose to work. Known primarily for his work in Olduvai Gorge in East Africa, Leakey directed the excavation of the site from 1963 until his death in 1972. The National Geographic Society funded the project.

A visit to this site is an introduction to the tedious, methodical work of archaeologists, a process unknown to many of us. Working with awls and hand tools no bigger than toothbrushes, archaeologists have recovered many thousands of artifacts, moved uncounted tons of earth, kept meticulous records, and dug some 26 feet into the earth—3 inches at a time.

A tour of the site is guaranteed to raise incomprehensible questions about the origins of human life and the passage of an unfathomably long period of time. It's an experience that is simultaneously enlightening and disturbing, inspiring and profound.

DIRECTIONS TO TRAILHEAD From Interstate 15, some 15 miles north of Barstow, take the Minneola Road exit and follow the signs north 2.5 miles along graded dirt roads to the site.

THE HIKE Begin your tour at the visitor center and museum (formerly a Camp Leakey structure where archaeological work was done). Friends of Calico offer guided tours of the site (open Wednesday through Sunday from 8 AM to 4:30 PM). Tours are conducted every hour, beginning at 8:30 AM This tour schedule is subject to change.

You can also pick up interpretive information at the visitor center and join the self-guided trail. Signed walkways lead you around the digs.

■ RAINBOW BASIN
Owl Canyon Trail
From Owl Canyon Campground to Velvet Peak is 5 miles
round trip with 500-foot elevation gain

The designation on the map of "National Natural Landmark" is a tip-off, but nothing can prepare you for the sight of the spectacular series of colorful hills that comprise Rainbow Basin. Pink, white, orange, brown, red, black, and green sediments form the basin's rainbow-colored walls.

Rainbow Basin is administered by the U.S. Bureau of Land Management. It's located just north of I-15 in Barstow, and just outside Mojave National Preserve. It is, to say the least, extremely scenic. This geologically fascinating destination in the Calico Mountains is ideal for on-foot exploration.

Some 15 million years ago, grasslands filled Rainbow Basin, which was populated by saber-toothed tigers, mastodons, camels, three-toed horses and even rhinoceros. Their fossil remains are encased in sedimentary rock that once formed a lake bed. As a result of intense geologic activity over the millennia,

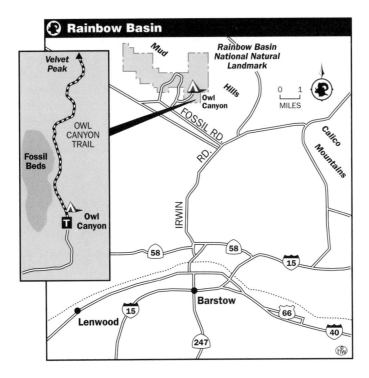

what was once at the bottom of the lake is now a series of folded, faulted, colorful hills.

Owl Canyon is one of three moderate walks in Rainbow Basin. This canyon takes its name from the barn owls who live there. Hikers should be reasonably agile in order to tackle Owl Canyon Trail, because getting through the canyon means scrambling over some boulders.

You could spend a pleasant weekend camping and hiking in Rainbow Basin. Stationed at Owl Canyon Campground is a campground host, who can provide hiking and touring tips.

DIRECTIONS TO TRAILHEAD Follow Interstate 15 to Barstow, then join Highway 58 to Fort Irwin Road, following it 5 miles. Turn west on dirt Fossil Road and proceed 3 miles to Owl Canyon Campground. The trail begins at the north end of the campground.

THE HIKE Follow the marked trail into Owl Canyon. Half a mile up-canyon look for a small cave on your right.

Sandstone, siltstone, shale, and volcanic debris are among the exposed rock visible to the hiker. The geologic formations en route are not only rainbow-colored but dramatic in shape. Particularly evident are massive downfolds geologists call "synclines."

The canyon narrows for a time, then opens up at its end into a multicolored amphitheater. Velvet Peak is the high spot above the rocky bowl. Experienced hikers can scramble up the bowl's rocky ridges for fine views of Rainbow Basin and the vast East Mojave.

■ AFTON CANYON
Afton Canyon Trail
6.5 miles round trip or longer

Afton Canyon Natural Area, 42,000 acres under the administration of the U.S. Bureau of Land Management, borders Mojave National Preserve on the northwest, and is one of the most conveniently located sites in the eastern Mojave.

The narrow, corridor-like Afton Canyon has been referred to as the "Grand Canyon of the Mojave." It is an 8-mile-long, narrow gorge with sheer walls that rise 600 feet above the canyon floor.

Afton Canyon is one of the few places where the Mojave River runs year round. The dependable source of water supports a variety of plants, including cottonwoods, willows, rabbit bush, smoke trees, and grasses. For more than a decade, botanists and hard-working volunteers have waged war against the invasive tamarisk, which threatens to choke out native species. The labor-intensive program, which requires cutting the tamarisk with a chain saw and immediately applying herbicide, will eventually result in a more oasis-like streamside community.

The plants that grow in the canyon provide shelter for many species of wildlife. Migratory birds are attracted to the site, as are several other species of birds, including stream-frequenting herons, egrets, killdeer, and ibis. California mud turtles, frogs, minnows, and the Mohave chub live in the river or along the shore.

The Mojave Road in Afton Canyon has been re-routed in order to protect the sensitive riparian environment, and off-highway vehicles have been prohibited in the area due to significant damage that has been caused by irresponsible riders in such places as "Competition Hill," which can be seen on the approach to the canyon.

Railroad aficionados will delight in the number of freight trains that regularly pass through on the tracks that run the length of the canyon. The sight and sound of a mighty locomotive powering across gleaming trestles are practically unforgettable.

There are two main hikes in Afton Canyon Natural Area: the walk up Pyramid Canyon (3.5 miles round trip), the major side canyon, and the hike through large Afton Canyon (6.5 miles round trip or longer and shorter jaunts). You may also explore the side canyons to the north and south of Afton Canyon.

Afton Canyon is the Grand Canyon of the Mojave.

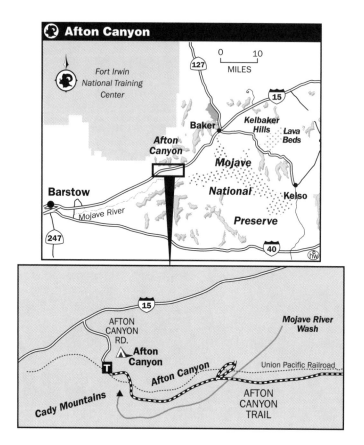

The water-cut 8 miles of Afton Canyon is an intriguing out-and-back hike; if you follow it to its end, it's a 16-mile round trip and full-day hike, but most hikers prefer sampling the canyon with a more modest 5- to 6-mile jaunt. The short walk along the riverbed from the campground to the railroad trestle is a favorite exploration suitable for the whole family.

DIRECTIONS TO TRAILHEAD Take the Afton exit off Interstate 15, 33 miles east of Barstow; the graded 3-mile road leads to the campground in Afton Canyon. Park at the campground, being careful not to take a campsite.

THE HIKE As you walk through the canyon, you'll view an old mine on the south wall of Afton Canyon. Although it appears to be an abandoned gold mine, it never produced as promised. Years ago, the unscrupulous owner of the mine simply salted it with gold in order to sell worthless shares to unwitting investors.

Continuing east, you'll notice a number of side canyons situated on the north wall of Afton Canyon. These side canyons are most obvious when you look for the manmade culverts that have been placed to prevent further water erosion. At the culvert marked 192.99 is another canyon that features magnificently eroded shapes caused by thousands of years of wind and water. At the culvert marked 194.65, take a flashlight to explore a fascinating cave/canyon that twists and turns; just when you think it ends, it turns once again and keeps going.

Beyond this point, the canyon widens and holds less interest for the hiker. Afton Canyon extends a few more miles to a double-trestle bridge near Cave Mountain. For a different perspective of the canyon, consider returning via the river bottom.

■ PYRAMID CANYON
Pyramid Canyon Trail
To Pyramid Canyon is 3.5 miles round trip

Pyramid Canyon, the deepest and largest of the side canyons in the Afton Canyon Natural Area, can easily be located and hiked. The scenic water-eroded formations of this canyon make it especially enjoyable.

Raptors, including golden eagles and red-tailed hawks, can often be seen circling in this area. The canyon is a rich site to see agates, geodes, and Mexican sapphires.

DIRECTIONS TO TRAILHEAD Take the Afton exit off Interstate 15, 33 miles east of Barstow; the graded 3-mile road leads to the campground in Afton Canyon. Park at the campground, being careful not to take a campsite.

THE HIKE Cross the river under the first set of railroad trestles, just south of the campground. Although there's no real trail up Pyramid Canyon, simply follow it to its rocky end, a bit less than 2 miles from Afton Canyon. Improvise your route; the canyon is so wide that you may walk up one side and return to the trailhead on the opposite side.

■ CLARK MOUNTAIN
Clark Mountain Trail
To the summit is 5 miles round trip

At 7,929 feet, Clark Mountain is the tallest peak in Mojave National Preserve. Because the peak is a bit geographically isolated from the main part of the Clark Mountain Range situated to the northeast, it's a distinct landmark, easy to recognize even when viewed from many miles away.

Clark Mountain is also just a bit isolated from the main part of the preserve—the only section located north of Interstate 15. The rugged mountain is one of the few places in the Mojave that is covered with a relict stand of white fir trees.

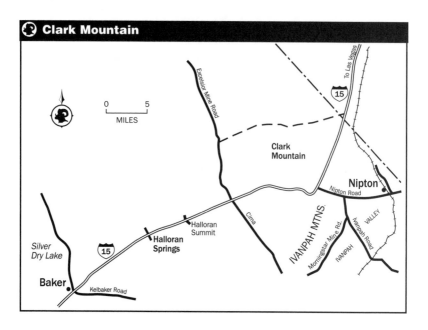

This handsome environment has been inhabited for thousands of years. Chemehuevi, Piute, and Mohaves lived here. Archeologists have discovered a number of artifacts, including petroglyphs, rock shelters, and rock alignments in the Clark Mountains. They also have found a number of large ash-filled pits where native people once roasted agave for food. Some experts speculate that native people may have considered the mountain a spiritually significant site.

Clark Mountain has been mined for more than a century; in nineteenth-century currency, it produced more than 4 million dollars worth of silver, along with significant amounts of gold, copper, and several other rare, precious, and semi-precious materials.

The town of Ivanpah was established on the the slopes of Clark Mountain soon after three lucky prospectors discovered a rich vein of silver in the mountain. A short-lived boomtown, the eastern Mojave's first, was founded in 1869; in 1875, its population was 500, mostly miners. By the end of the century, the town was abandoned. Only a few ruins of the fifteen buildings that once stood here still can be seen today.

Clark Mountain is the subject of one of the more colorful and enticing Mojave mining tales—the Lost River of Gold. A 1920s miner, Earl Dorr, tried to convince investors to finance his discovery in Crystal Cave—a 3,000-foot-deep river through the mountain, its sands filled with gold.

Dorr managed to gain the backing of several wealthy Los Angeles speculators. He struck a rich vein, all right, but it was zinc, not gold. The Lost River has never been found, and today the mine is privately owned. The notion, however, of a Lost River of Gold continues to fascinate and inspire imaginations to this day.

These days, most of the area's mining is concentrated near Mountain Pass, located at the southern base of Clark Mountain. Long-established rare-earth mines operated by the Molybdenum Corporation of America (also known as Molycorp) produce elements useful in high-tech manufacturing.

As for the slopes of the mountain itself, some prospecting for turquoise and copper took place in the 1990s. Nowadays, the bulk of Clark Mountain is official preserve wilderness, as mandated by the California Desert Protection Act of 1994.

Clark Mountain has much to offer today's visitor in the way of scenic value and a diverse environment, but it presents access difficulties. Roads to the mountain are dirt; road conditions can be quite variable and it should not be attempted in any vehicle except one suited to traveling on questionable roads; four-wheel drive is best in these parts.

DIRECTIONS TO TRAILHEAD One access to Clark Mountain is off I-15 at Mountain Pass. There you'll view the Molycorp Mine. The dirt road just past the one-room elementary school is the main access to Clark Mountain. It leads through a land of Joshuas and rises into a landscape of junipers and pinyon pine.

At the end of the road, you'll find a handsome picnic area, complete with barbecue pits, picnic tables, and a volleyball court, all nestled in a pinyon pine forest. The facilities were established here by Molycorp many years ago. The company formerly held its annual family picnic at the Clark Mountain site.

Today, the spot is a lovely place to picnic, or to use as a jumping-off spot for more exploration of Clark Mountain. The area supports a number of plant communities, offering habitat for several animal species. Bighorn sheep thrive here, as do raptors and several snakes and lizards.

Another way to reach Clark Mountain is by way of the powerline road that extends east-west along the far northern boundary of the preserve. Access this road by exiting Interstate 15 on paved Excelsor Mine Road and traveling 7.7 miles to the graded powerline road. Turn right and travel 6 miles to a rougher road leading south toward Clark Mountain.

You can also join the powerline road from Primm, Nevada. Exit I-15 and head over to the west side of the highway. Drive 0.5 mile west, away from the casinos and Ivanpah Dry Lake, which spreads south and east. At a junction, bear north 0.9 mile to intersect the powerline road. The good gravel road leads some 10 miles as it ascends 4,906-foot Keany Pass. On clear days, enjoy far-reaching views over Nevada. Continue west on the powerline road and past a right-forking road that leads to Mesquite Pass and down the Mesquite Mountains to Mesquite Dry Lake. About 0.8 mile past Mesquite Pass Road, you'll reach a junction with a rough road leading south toward Clark Mountain.

Ascend amidst Joshua trees, pinyon pine, juniper, and scores of cacti. About 3.4 miles from the powerline road, bear left at a junction and drive 2 miles to Coliseum Gorge, where you'll get a great close-up view of Clark Mountain's upper slopes to the south.

THE HIKE Hikers can utilize a number of rough dirt roads ascending the mountain. Be sure to stay on preserve lands and heed the various private property/no trespassing signs posted along these roads.

■ NIPTON
Nipton Interpretive Trail
Around town is 0.25 mile round trip

Located just 2 miles from the California/Nevada border, Nipton is the kind of desert town that often appears on television or newspapers as a human interest spot. The town's motto is "Where the past is present." It's perfectly appropriate, especially when the midnight freight train rumbles through.

Nipton was founded in 1904 with the coming of the San Pedro, Los Angeles, and Salt Lake Railroad. A small community sprang up at the Nipton railhead to serve the local mining, ranching, and railroad workers.

These days, Nipton is growing under the leadership of geologist Jerry Freeman, who purchased the town in 1984 and restored the hamlet's hotel and store. Hotel Nipton, where silent film star and former "it girl" Clara Bow was a frequent guest, is a pleasant Southwestern-style bed-and-breakfast. For a hedonistic desert treat, the hotel even offers outdoor hot tubs.

Nipton also boasts a small campground that includes four overnight hookups for RVs, plus several more sites with fire rings and picnic tables. Nippeno Camp, as it's known, can also accommodate overnight guests in a couple of "eco-shelters"—platform cabin tents.

Hotel Nipton is the best B&B for 100 miles around!

Purchase provisions and mementos—even lottery tickets—and catch up on all the local news at the Nipton Trading Post. The creation of Mojave National Preserve has put little Nipton back on the map, and the town is evolving into a kind of gateway community for Mojave visitors, complete with a Park Service information kiosk.

DIRECTIONS TO TRAILHEAD From Interstate 15, some 40 miles east of Baker and some 10 miles west of the California/Nevada border, exit on Nipton Road and travel 10 miles east to the hamlet of Nipton.

THE HIKE Ask for an interpretive pamphlet at the store, and take a stroll through Nipton history past the old buildings.

■ KELBAKER HILLS
Kelbaker Hills Trail
2 miles round trip with 300-foot elevation gain

If Mojave National Preserve had a "Main Street," Kelbaker Road would be it. The road is the preserve's busiest, and it provides access to several of its most popular attractions, including Kelso Depot and Kelso Dunes.

The National Park Service recently installed a large Mojave National Preserve entry sign just outside of Baker on Kelbaker Road. The entry monument, one of the grand granite proclamations characteristic of other western national parks, emphasizes Kelbaker's status as the major Mojave road.

Most preserve visitors remain in the vehicles while driving Kelbaker Road from Baker to Kelso Depot and thus miss a couple of interesting sites en route. One of my favorite leg-stretcher jaunts is up to into Kelbaker Hills.

Here's your chance to name one of the preserve's geographic features. I call them the Kelbaker Hills because of their proximity to Kelbaker Road, as well as for their location a dozen miles southeast of Baker and two dozen miles northwest of Kelso; however, they don't really have a name on the map or one in common usage. Others have suggested the "Baker Hills" due to their close-to-town position or the "Rhyolite Hills" because of their volcanic composition.

By whatever name, these hills offer a close-to-the-paved-road wilderness experience, as well as a short (though moderately strenuous) hike.

DIRECTIONS TO TRAILHEAD From Interstate 15 in Baker, drive 11 miles east on Kelbaker Road. Just as the road makes a pronounced bend right (south) turn left (north) on the unsigned dirt road. Drive 0.8 mile along the preserve's signed wilderness boundary. Look east of the road for a distinct gap in the Kelbaker Hills and scarce parking just east off the road.

THE HIKE If you locate a sketchy old road extending east up the wash leading to the hills, take it; otherwise, simply walk up the wash toward the obvious gap

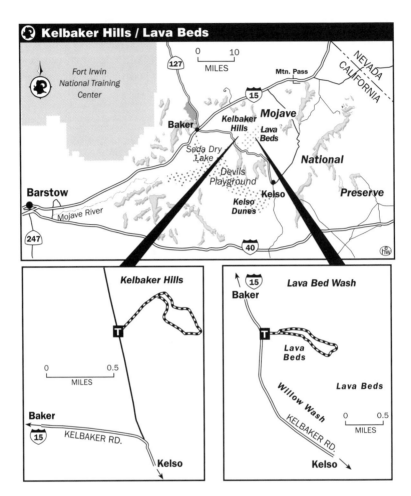

in the hills. Your route will angle toward the base of the tallest hills, and just to the left of them.

A bit more than 0.5 mile out, you'll observe a couple of narrow ravines (favorite burro routes, judging by the tracks) that lead to the top of the hills. Climb (careful, it's loose footing) any one of these ravines for good views of this part of the preserve.

Experienced rock scramblers can make their way to the top of the highest hills. Those determined to make a loop hike out of this jaunt can do so by descending a ravine southeasterly and junctioning the main wash that leads back to the gap in the hills, and then returning to the trailhead.

■ LAVA BEDS
Lava Beds Trail
1.2-mile loop

Another Kelbaker roadside attraction is the preserve's northern lava beds. A wash extending alongside the lava formation gives the hiker a convenient thoroughfare as well as a close-up view of the volcanic cliff face.

This look at the lava resembles those hillside cuts made by highway-makers, though it was nature, not a road crew, that revealed the lava beds. Green, gray, and red lichen color the north side of the lava outcroppings.

DIRECTIONS TO TRAILHEAD From Baker and I-15, head 14.2 miles south on Kelbaker Road to the Lava Beds and an unsigned turnout on your left. The turnout is just south of the long, narrow beds and just north of a wash. (Hint: if Kelbaker Road takes you through a major gap in the Lava Beds, you ventured about 0.4 mile too far south of the trailhead for this little exploration.)

THE HIKE Head east on a faint but visible trail at the base of the lava beds. Marvel at the odd geology as you walk 0.6 mile to trail's end.

Scramble to the top of the lava beds and a miniature plateau paved with a mosaic of lava talus that resembles the ruins of an ancient Roman Empire road. Make your way west cross-country over the plateau. Just short of Kelbaker Road, descend from the plateau by scrambling down the rocks to the trailhead.

■ CIMA DOME
Teutonia Peak Trail
To Teutonia Peak is 4 miles round trip

Cima Dome is certainly one of the easiest Mojave National Preserve sites to reach, but when you reach it, you may wonder why you did. It's not a geologic formation you can view close up: the dome slopes so gently, it's best viewed from a distance. What Gertrude Stein said of Oakland comes to mind: "There's no there there."

Two places to get "the big picture" of Cima Dome are from Mid Hills Campground and from I-15 as you drive southeast of Baker and crest a low rise.

The dome is a mass of once-molten monzonite, a granite-like rock. Over thousands of years it's been extensively eroded and now sprawls over some 75 square miles. It's more than 10 miles in diameter.

Another distinctive feature of the dome is its handsome rock outcroppings— the same type found in Joshua Tree National Park to the south. Rock climbers, rock scramblers, and hikers love Cima's rock show.

The word to remember around Cima Dome is symmetry. A geological rarity, the formation has been called the most symmetrical natural dome in the United States. If you take a look at the area's USGS topographical map and

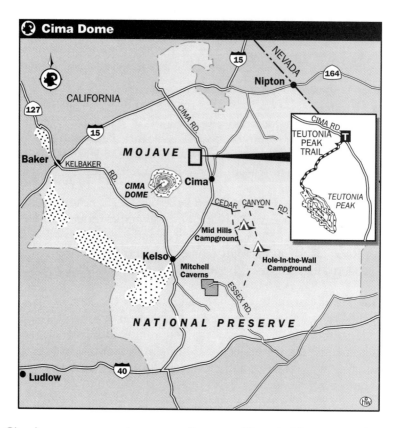

study Cima's near-concentric contour lines, you'll probably agree with this symmetry claim.

Symmetry is also a word used in conjunction with the area's other natural attraction: the Joshua tree. Botanists say Cima's Joshuas are more symmetrical than their cousins elsewhere in the Mojave.

Cima's Joshua trees are tall—some more than 25 feet high—and several hundred years old. Collectively, they form the world's largest and densest Joshua tree forest.

Here at an elevation of about 4,000 feet, this distinct symbol of the Mojave Desert truly thrives. Bring your camera!

This hike travels the famed Joshua tree forest, and then visits Cima Dome, which rises 1,500 feet above the surrounding desert playas.

DIRECTIONS TO TRAILHEAD The beginning of the trail is just off Cima Road, a scenic byway that stretches 17 miles from the Cima Road exit on Interstate 15 south to Cima. The signed trailhead is about 9 miles from I-15.

THE HIKE The mellow, 2-mile Teutonia Peak Trail meanders through the Joshua tree forest and ascends to a lookout over Cima Dome. From the lookout, its a 0.25-mile moderately strenuous scramble over rocks to the top of Teutonia Peak (elevation 5,755 feet).

■ KEYSTONE CANYON AND NEW YORK PEAK

Keystone Canyon Trail

From Keystone Canyon to road's end is 3 miles round trip with a 700-foot elevation gain; to New York Peak is 4.5 miles round trip with a 2,000-foot elevation gain

Thrusting high above Lanfair Valley, the impressive, granite-crowned New York Mountains are among the preserve's highest peaks. New York Peak, the range's 7,463-foot signature summit, offers commanding views of the preserve and far beyond—to the Panamint Mountains of Death Valley National Park, the San Jacinto Mountains behind Palm Springs, and the mountains of Nevada and western Arizona.

Keystone Canyon shares botanical similarities with Caruthers Canyon, located a few miles to the south. Both canyons cradle relict stands of white fir—arboreal survivors from a time of much cooler and wetter climatic conditions. Yerba santa, ceanothus, and other shrubs more common to California's coastal slopes grow in the upper reaches of the New York Mountains.

Although the last Ice Age evaporated some 10,000 years ago, and the Mojave has become a considerably drier landscape, the firs and "coastal" flora still flourish. The survival of these moist-environment plants in the New York Mountains is due to the range's height; the high peaks snag moisture from passing storms and clouds.

The high-elevation-dwelling firs are by no means the only attraction for tree lovers along the Keystone Canyon Trail. Lower Keystone Canyon hosts pinyon pine, juniper, and turbinella oak. More typical preserve vegetation such as Mojave yucca, sagebrush, and prickly pear are also a strong presence in the canyon.

Seasoned hikers with good map-reading and route-finding skills will most enjoy the steep and challenging ascent to New York Peak. (Experienced desert peak baggers ascend via a couple different routes, including a scramble by way of Keystone Spring.) Those hikers seeking an easier outing can traverse fascinating Keystone Canyon and turn around at road's end.

While the view from atop New York Peak is unsurpassed, hikers be warned that some serious rock scrambling is required to reach the summit. However, nearly the same glorious panorama is available from the ridgecrest below the peak.

DIRECTIONS TO TRAILHEAD (The Park Service recommends four-wheel drive.) From Interstate 15, exit on Nipton Road and travel 3.5 miles to Ivanpah

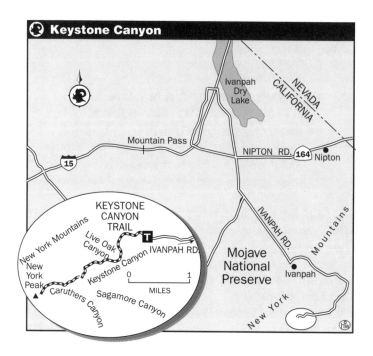

Road. Turn right (south) and head toward the New York Mountains. Twelve miles along, the road crosses railroad tracks, bends east, and turns to dirt. After 6 more miles, just as dirt Ivanpah Road bends southeast, turn right on the narrow, unsigned road leading to Keystone Canyon. Avoid a couple left-forking, narrower roads, and travel 2.5 miles from Ivanpah Road to a junction just before the road descends into Keystone Canyon. Briefly follow the left fork to a parking area.

THE HIKE Walk up the deteriorating road into Keystone Canyon. The wide range of trailside flora includes pinyon pine and juniper, yerba santa and cliffrose.

Keystone Canyon bends south and you'll stick with it. A half mile out, ignore a right-forking road that leads into Live Oak Canyon, and just after another 0.1 mile, ignore a left-forking road; this one leads 0.25 mile to Keystone Spring.

Continue your ascent through Keystone Canyon as the views of granite-topped mountains improve and the road you're following gets worse. At road's end, about 1.5 miles from the trailhead, you'll find a small abandoned copper mine. It's colorful in an odd sort of way, with green and blue copper ore debris scattered around ore car tracks that protrude from the mine shaft.

Above you to the southwest are two gullies leading toward the crest. Choose one of them and begin a brutal 0.25-mile ascent, gaining 500 feet in elevation, and catch your breath at a narrow saddle.

From this saddle, repeat this exercise, with another 0.25-mile ascent and 500-foot gain to reach the ridgecrest just south of New York Peak. Scramble southwest among the boulders, keeping your eye out for a stand of white fir that grows in the company of pinyon pine.

If time, energy, and your abilities permit, continue along the rugged ridge to the summit. Otherwise, enjoy the marvelous view from the ridge. Broad Ivanpah Valley lies straight down to the north, and you'll be able to identify several prominent preserve features, including Cima Dome to the west and Clark Mountain to the northwest. On particularly clear days, look for the high peaks of the San Bernardino and San Gabriel mountains on the eastern border of the Los Angeles metropolitan area. The Virgin Mountains of far southwestern Utah are located more than 100 miles to the northeast.

With caution, and a careful eye for loose rock, retrace your route back to the trailhead.

■ CARUTHERS CANYON
Caruthers Canyon Trail
From Caruthers Canyon to the old mine is 3 miles round trip
with 400-foot elevation gain

Botanists call them disjuncts. Bureaucrats call them UPAs (Unusual Plant Assemblages). The more lyrical naturalists among us call them islands on the land.

By whatever name, the isolated communities of pinyon pine and white fir in the New York Mountains are very special places. Nearly 300 plant species have been counted on the slopes of this range and in its colorfully named canyons—Cottonwood and Caruthers, Butcher Knife and Fourth of July.

Perhaps the most botanically unique area in the mountains, indeed in the whole Mojave National Preserve, is Caruthers Canyon. A cool, inviting pinyon pine-juniper woodland stands in marked contrast to the sparsely vegetated sandscape common in other parts of the desert. The conifers are joined by oaks and a variety of coastal chaparral plants including manzanita, yerba santa, ceanothus, and coffee berry. The canyon is one of the few locales in the park boasting free-flowing water for much of the year.

What is a coastal ecosystem doing in the middle of the desert?

Botanists believe that during wetter times such coastal scrub vegetation was quite widespread. As the climate became more arid, coastal ecosystems were "stranded" atop high and moist slopes. The botanical islands high in the New York Mountains are outposts of Rocky Mountains and coastal California flora.

Caruthers Canyon is a treat for the hiker. An abandoned dirt road leads through a rocky basin and into a historic gold mining region. Prospectors began digging in the New York Mountains in the 1860s and continued well into the twentieth century. At trail's end are a couple of gold mine shafts.

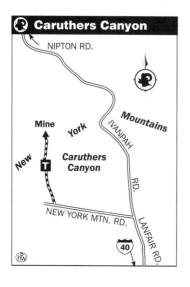

The canyon's woodland offers great bird-watching. The western tanager, gray-headed junco, yellow-breasted chat, and many more species are found here. Circling high in the sky are the raptors—golden eagles, prairie falcons, and red-tailed hawks.

DIRECTIONS TO TRAILHEAD From I-40, 28 miles west of Needles, and some 117 miles east of Barstow, exit on Mt. Springs Road (not maintained, and the pavement is very rough and crumbling). You'll pass the hamlet of Goffs and head north 27.5 miles on the main road, known as Lanfair Road, then Ivanpah Road, to New York Mountains Road. (Part of Ivanpah Road and New York Mountains Road are dirt; they are suitable for vehicles with good ground clearance.) Turn left (west) on New York Mountains Road. A couple OX Cattle Ranch buildings stand near this road's intersection with Ivanpah Road. Drive 5.5 miles to an unsigned junction with a dirt road and turn north. Proceed 2 miles to a woodland laced with turnouts that serve as primitive campsites. Leave your car here; farther along, the road dips into a wash and gets very rough. From the Caruthers Canyon "campground" follow the main dirt road up the

A remnant of the mining days in Caruthers Canyon.

canyon. As you ascend, look behind you for a great view of Table Mountain, the most dominant peak of the central part of Mojave.

Caution: After heavy rains, Lanfair/Ivanpah Road is often impassable for several days.

THE HIKE Handsome boulders line the trail and frame views of the tall peak before you, New York Mountain. The range's 7,532-foot signature peak is crowned with a botanical island of its own—a relict stand of Rocky Mountain white fir.

A half mile along, you'll come to a fork in the road. The rightward road climbs 0.25 mile to an old mining shack. Take the left fork, dipping in and out of a wash and gaining a great view of the canyon and its castellated walls.

If it's rained recently, you might find some water collected in pools on the rocky canyon bottom. Enjoy the tranquility of the gold mine area, but don't stray into the dark and dangerous shafts.

■ PIUTE CANYON
Piute Canyon Trail
To Fort Piute is 6.5 miles round trip
with 600-foot elevation gain

In 1865, Fort Piute was described by a visitor as "a Godforsaken place—the meanest I ever saw for a military station." It's doubtful that many would disagree; however, the ruins of the fort, along with pretty Piute Valley and Piute Creek add up to an intriguing, way-off-the-beaten-path tour for the adventurous.

Fort Piute, located east of Lanfair Valley, at the southern end of the Piute Mountains, was established to provide a military presence in the desert, and to protect mail delivery out West, as well as pioneer travelers on their westward journeys.

Indians resisted the intrusion of settlers on tribal lands; there were frequent attacks on westbound sellers and mail wagons traveling the route from Prescott, Arizona, to Los Angeles.

Subsequent military escorts protected travelers, but conditions at the outpost were intolerable for many soldiers stationed at Fort Piute. Desertion was a regular occurrence, and the outpost was officially staffed by just 18 men of the Company "D" 9th Infantry Division from 1867 to 1868.

Today, the small, primitive installation lies in ruins; its thick rock and mortar walls have been weathered and crumbled to a height of just 2 or 3 feet. The stone outlines of the original buildings delineate three connecting rooms that served as a tiny living quarters, corral, and cookhouse. A park service crew restored the walls to their current height in 2002, and further work on the Fort Piute site, including parking and picnic areas, is planned.

The walk along Piute Creek is of more than military interest. The only perennial stream in the preserve, Piute Creek is an oasis-like area where cottonwoods, willows, and sedges flourish. Bighorn sheep frequently visit this watering site, as do a large number of birds. (This is a fragile ecosystem, not a recreation area. Please treat the creek gently.)

The hike to Fort Piute explores Piute Creek and gorge and gives you a chance to walk a portion of the historic Mojave Road. Following the Mojave Road Trail, as it's called, lets you walk back into time and get a glimpse of the hardships faced by early pioneers.

This is not an adventure for the inexperienced or for first-time visitors to Mojave National Preserve; the roads and paths are unsigned and sometimes hard to follow. Experienced hikers and repeat visitors, however, will thoroughly enjoy their exploration of Fort Piute.

DIRECTIONS TO TRAILHEAD Head west on Interstate 40 and take the turnoff for the road leading to the hamlet of Goffs. Pass through Goffs and drive some 16 miles along Lanfair Road to a point about 100 feet beyond its junction with Cedar Canyon Road. Turn right (east) on a road that goes by four names: Cedar Canyon Road, the utility road, Cable Road, Pole Road. The latter three names arise from the fact that the road follows a buried telephone cable. Drive east, staying right at a junction 3.7 miles out, and sticking with the cable road about 6 more miles to another junction where there's a cattle guard. Turn left before the cattle guard on another dirt road and proceed 0.5 mile to an abandoned section of the Mojave Road

From the intersection of Lanfair and Cedar Canyon roads, drive east on the utility road 9.5 miles. Turn north on the small dirt road that leads 0.5 mile to the old Mojave Road.

THE HIKE Begin your trek at Piute Hill and a meeting with the old Mojave Road just over the crest of the hill. From atop the hill, pause to take in the view. Table Mountain can be seen directly to the west, and in the north are Castle Peaks.

Happily for hikers, the route leads down the difficult grade that challenged early pioneers. No doubt, the volcanic rock on the road really rattled the settlers' wagons. On the 2 miles of travel on Mojave Road, you'll pass along loose, sandy trail near Piute Creek, where there's nice picnicking. (The water is not safe to drink.) To avoid trampling the creekbed, try taking the trail on the north side of the creek.

About 0.5 mile from the fort, you'll cross the creek. The Mojave Road narrows. Look sharply for the Piute Canyon Trail coming in from the west. (This will be your optional return route.) Continue on a slight descent to the fort.

An interpretive marker provides some historic information about the history of "Fort Pah Ute, 1867-68." Don't sit on the walls or disturb the ruins; like all cultural resources in the desert, the fort is protected by federal law.

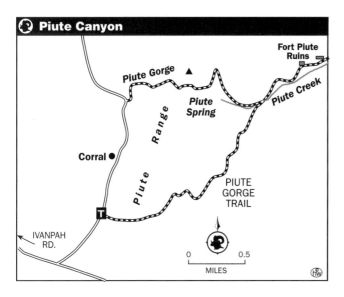

Head back along the Mojave Road 0.5 mile, bearing right on unsigned Piute Canyon Trail. This narrow path stays high on the canyon wall, heading west at first, then north. A half mile along, you can see prominent Piute Gorge to the west; you'll be following this gorge back to the trailhead.

This trail is very faint; if you lose the path, keep heading west and descending to the floor of Piute Gorge. Expect a steep scramble to reach the bottom of the gorge.

At the bottom, you'll proceed west up Piute Gorge; stay on the gorge bottom. After 0.5 mile you'll come to an intersection where another canyon comes in from the left. Don't take this route; continue up the gorge to the right.

At littler farther, a trail leading out of the gorge takes off from the left. (Keep a sharp eye out for this one.) Take this trail up to the rim of the gorge, where there's a scenic overlook. From here, follow the dirt road south past a corral back to the trailhead.

■ TABLE MOUNTAIN
Table Mountain Trail
To summit is 7 miles round trip with 1,000-foot elevation gain

Driving to the region on Black Canyon Road, you'll note the magnificent Providence Mountains to the west, and, in the distance, the smaller Kelso and Marl ranges. To the east are the steep Woods Mountains and one of the preserve's most distinctive landmarks, Table Mountain, a 6,176-foot mesa that juts up from the desert floor. It can be seen from many vantage points throughout Mojave, despite its close proximity to other great mountains—the Providence Range to the southwest and the New York Mountains to the north. As your drive closer, the mountain's white granite base topped by dark lava cliffs is an impressive sight.

This is open country, reminiscent of the Old West, complete with barbed wire fences, sagebrush, range cattle, occasional windmills, and views that go on forever.

Hikers can ascend to the summit of steep-sided Table Mountain via a route that's about one-third dirt road and two-thirds cross-country travel. Reward for the 3.5-mile one-way climb (with 1,000-foot elevation gain) to the top of the flat-topped mesa is a 360-degree panoramic view of much of the preserve.

DIRECTIONS TO TRAILHEAD To reach the trailhead for the Table Mountain climb, head 6.4 miles south on Black Canyon Road from its junction with Cedar Canyon Road. Park on the east side of the road and look for the trail (an old dirt road) that begins on the northeast side of the parking area.

THE HIKE The path leads east a mile, then north to a windmill and water tank. Then you head for the mountain by way of two eastward approaches—either by way of a ridge or by hiking along the base of the ridge.

■ MID HILLS AND HOLE-IN-THE-WALL
Mid Hills to Hole-in-the-Wall Trail
From Mid Hills Campground to Hole-in-the-Wall Campground is 8 miles one way with 1,000-foot elevation loss

Hole-in-the-Wall and Mid Hills are the centerpieces of Mojave National Preserve. Both locales offer diverse desert scenery and fine campgrounds. Doubling the pleasure of these special places is an 8-mile trail that links them together.

Mile-high Mid Hills recalls the Great Basin Desert topography of Nevada and Utah. It's 1,000 or so feet higher than Hole-in-the-Wall, and thus, as a starting point, offers the hiker an easier way to go.

Mid Hills, so named because of its location halfway between the Providence and New York mountains, offers a grand observation point from which to gaze out at the East Mojave's dominant mountain ranges: the coffee-with-cream-colored Pinto Mountains to the north, and the rolling Kelso Dunes shining on the western horizon. Looking north-west, you'll also get a superb view of Cima Dome, the 75-square-mile chunk of uplifted volcanic rock.

Hole-in-the-Wall is a twisted maze of red rock. Geologists call this rhyolite, a kind of lava that existed as hot liquid far below the earth's surface, and later crystal-ized.

A series of iron rings aids descent into Banshee Canyon. They're not particularly difficult for those who are reasonably agile and take their time.

If you're not up for a daylong hike, the 0.75-mile trip from Hole-in-the-Wall Campground to Banshee Canyon and the 5-mile jaunt to Wild Horse Canyon offer some easier alternatives.

A word about desert hiking in general and this desert hike in particular: you'll often travel in the bottom of sandy washes

Hikers on the eight-mile, mostly downhill route between Mid Hills and Hole-in-the-Wall.

instead of over more clearly defined trails found in forest locales. This means the hiker must rely on maps, a sense of direction, rock cairns, and signs.

This is an adventurous excursion through a diverse desert environment. You'll see basin-and-range tabletop mesas, and you'll encounter large pinyon trees, an array of colorful cactus, and lichen-covered granite rocks. East Mojave views—Table Mountain, Wild Horse Mesa, the Providence Range—are unparalleled.

DIRECTIONS TO TRAILHEAD From Interstate 40, approximately 42 miles west of Needles and nearly 100 miles east of Barstow, exit on Essex Road. Head north 9.5 miles to the junction of Essex Road and Black Canyon Road. Bear right on the latter road, which soon turns to dirt. (Well-graded Black Canyon Road is suitable for passenger cars.) After 8.5 miles of travel you'll spot Hole-in-the-Wall Campground on your left.

Another 5 or so miles of travel on Black Canyon Road brings you to the signed turnoff for Mid Hills Campground. You'll turn left and travel 2 miles to the campground. The Mid Hills Trailhead is located adjacent to a windmill immediately opposite the entrance road to the campground.

THE HIKE In a short distance, the path ascends to a saddle which offers splendid views of the Pinto Valley to the northeast. (The saddle is the high point.)

From the saddle, the path angles south, descending into and then climbing out of a wash. (Keep a close eye on the trail; it's easy to lose here.)

The trail reaches a dirt road, follows it for a mere 100 feet, then turns sharply left to join a wash for a time, exits it, and crosses a road. You encounter another wash, enter it, and exit it.

After a modest ascent, the trail joins a road, passes through a gate, and joins another road for a little more than a mile. This road serves up spectacular views to the south of the Providence Mountains and Wild Horse Mesa.

Adjacent to a group of large boulders, a road veers left, but you bear right, soon turning sharp left with the road. The route passes through another gate, then works its way through a dense thicket of cholla cactus.

After following another wash, the trail crosses a dirt road, then soon joins a second road, which follows a wash to a dead-end at an abandoned dam. The trail ascends through some rocks, levels for a time, then descends. A quarter mile before trail's end, you'll spy the Hole-in-the-Wall spur trail leading off to the left.

Alternatively, continue south another quarter mile to the Hole-in-the-Wall Trailhead on Wildhorse Canyon Road.

■ HOLE-IN-THE-WALL
Hole-in-the-Wall Trail
To Hole-in-the-Wall is 2 miles round trip

H ole-in-the-Wall is an inviting locale, the kind of place Butch Cassidy and the Sundance Kid might have chosen as a hideout. You can imagine them hiding out in this maze of rocks.

In fact, Bob Hollimon, a former member of Butch Cassidy's gang who became a Mojave cattle rancher, claimed Banshee Canyon reminded him of the Hole-in-the-Wall gang hideout in Wyoming.

The fine camping area, outstanding views of the surrounding mountains, and unforgettable scenery attract visitors to this out-of-the-way place.

Directly east of the campground are the Woods Mountains. The range features appropriately named Rustlers Canyon, a remote spot where cattle rustlers and various outlaws once hid from lawmen.

Although the location of the small campground at Hole-in-the-Wall (elevation 4,200 feet) is pleasant enough to attract campers, bird-watchers, and others who just want to "stay-put," more adventurous types find the highlight of a trip to Hole-in-the-Wall is exploring the wondrous volcanic formations that form its backdrop. Visit the information center (staffing hours vary) located here.

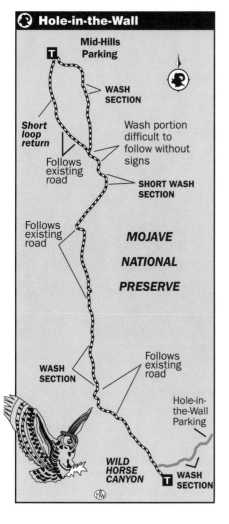

Hole-in-the-Wall

Mid-Hills Parking

WASH SECTION

Wash portion difficult to follow without signs

Short loop return

Follows existing road

SHORT WASH SECTION

Follows existing road

MOJAVE

NATIONAL

PRESERVE

WASH SECTION

Follows existing road

Hole-in-the-Wall Parking

WILD HORSE CANYON

WASH SECTION

Immediately west of the campground is a maze of volcanic rocks that descend first into Banshee Canyon, then into a large, open desert box canyon named Wildhorse Canyon. The two canyons couldn't be more dissimilar, and they provide the visitor with a glimpse of the diversity of the Mojave National Preserve.

Hikers once used ropes and ladders to descend into Banshee Canyon from the campground area; today, the descent is accomplished by negotiating two sets of iron rings that have been set into the rock. Maneuvering through the rings is not particularly difficult for those who are reasonably agile and take their time. But acrophobes or claustrophobes may want to pass on this adventure.

The story about the naming of Hole-in-the-Wall is easy to envision as you encounter the twisted maze of red rock. As the legend goes, in the 1880s, a couple of ranch hands from nearby Dominguez Ranch were searching for some stray cattle, and they came upon a pair of Indians who were leading a few cattle. Suspecting them of stealing their stock, the ranch hands chased the Indians into a canyon, which they thought was a dead-end. To their amazement, the Indians scrambled up the rocks in the lower canyon and then disappeared—seemingly right into the blank wall. The men concluded the Indians must have found or created a hole in the wall.

Enjoy exploring the volcanic rock formations known as rhyolite, a crystallized form of lava. The holes provide frames for taking silly photographs. You might spot any number of raptors circling overhead: golden eagles, hawks, and owls.

Hole-in-the-Wall rocks have a violent past—geologically speaking, that is. Some 18 million years ago, a volcano in the Woods Mountains erupted and spewed ash and rocks (some 60 feet across—among the largest ever documented!). Hot ashes cremated every living thing in the area; countless plant and animal fossils lie entombed beneath the volcanic tuff of Hole-in-the-Wall's cliffs.

DIRECTIONS TO TRAILHEAD

From Interstate 40, approximately 42 miles west of Needles and nearly 100 miles east of Barstow, exit on Essex Road. Head north 9.5 miles to the junction of Essex Road and Black Canyon Road. Bear right on the latter road, which soon turns to dirt. (Well-graded Black Canyon Road is suitable for passenger cars.) After 8.5 miles of travel you'll spot the Hole-in-the-Wall information center on your left. Follow the dirt road past the visitor center to the parking area at the picnic ground.

THE HIKE Enjoy the view from the overlook west to the parking area, then start your hike at the exhibit. The path plunges into a wall of rocks. Grasp the iron rings and lower yourself into Banshee Canyon. Descend amidst the impressive pock-marked canyon walls. You can turn around at the canyon bottom or continue as your route curves north toward Wild Horse Canyon.

Iron rings make for an adventurous descent into Hole-in-the-Wall.

Hole-in-the-Wall is not the only place in this area with a colorful name. Banshee is named not for the shrieking elves of the Scottish Highlands, but for the sounds said to be heard here at night that resemble their cries. Horned owls and the sound of the wind whistling through the holes make a quiet night in the canyon unlikely.

You can extend your walk past Banshee Canyon into Wild Horse Canyon.

Follow Banshee to its opening, then turn north to follow the wash, picking your way cross-country to the indistinct trail leading northward. The trail climbs gently onto a low mesa that offers good views of Wild Horse Mesa to the left and desert varnish-covered rock formations on the right.

Continue northward through a magnificent devil's garden filled with yucca, cholla, beavertail, barrel, and prickly pear cactus. In the springtime, the cactus bloom spreads bright yellow and hot pink across the canyon.

As you near the end of the canyon, enjoy the view of the juniper-filled basin to the north, and the mountains and mesas in every direction. If you continued northward, you would reach Mid Hills, but the hike between the two camp-grounds is best done north to south.

For an enjoyable additionn to the hike, you can make a 1-mile loop around the unnamed hill behind the information center. When you exit Banshee Canyon, keep the hillside on your left, circling its base. A faint trail leads past a small group of petroglyphs and back to the information center.

■ KELSO DUNES
Kelso Dunes Trail
To top of Kelso Dunes is 3 miles round trip
with 400-foot elevation gain

In the heart of the heart of the East Mojave lie Kelso Dunes, one of the tallest dune systems in America.

And the dunes give off good vibrations, say many desert explorers. The good vibrations may be the desert's spiritual emanations—which many visitors find con-siderable—but more likely are the Kelso Dunes' rare ability to make a low rum-bling sound when sand slides down the steep slopes. This sound has been variously described as that of a kettle drum, a low-flying airplane, or a Tibetan gong.

The sand that forms Kelso Dunes blows in from the Mojave River basin. After traveling east 35 miles across a stark plain known as the Devil's Play-ground, it's deposited in hills nearly 600 feet high. The westerlies carrying the sand rush headlong into winds from other directions, which is why the sand is dropped here and why it stays here.

For further confirmation of the circular pattern of winds that formed the dunes, examine the bunches of grass on the lower slopes. You'll notice that the tips of the tall grasses have etched 360-degree circles on the sand.

Kelso Dunes

Other patterns on the sand are made by the desert's abundant but rarely seen wildlife. You might see the tracks of a coyote, kit fox, antelope ground squirrel, packrat, raven, or sidewinder. Footprints of lizards and mice can be seen tacking this way and that over the sand. The dune's surface records the lightest pressure of the smallest feet.

The Kelso Dunes may boom, but they still offer hikers plenty of opportunity for solitude and quiet times.

DIRECTIONS TO TRAILHEAD From Interstate 15 in Baker, some 60 miles northeast of Barstow, turn south on Kelbaker Road and proceed about 35 miles to the town of Kelso. Pause to admire the classic neo-Spanish-style Kelso Railroad Depot next to the Union Pacific tracks. The building has been restored as a visitor center, the preserve's premier information center.

From Kelso, continue on Kelbaker Road for another 7 miles to a signed dirt road and turn right (west). Drive slowly along this road (navigable for all but very low-slung passenger cars) 3 miles to a parking area. The trail to Kelso Dunes begins just up the dirt road from the parking area.

THE HIKE Only the first 0.25 mile or so of the walk to the dunes is on established trail. Once the trail peters out, angle toward the low saddle atop the dunes, just to the right of the highest point.

Know the old saying "One step forward, two steps back"? This will take on new meaning if you attempt to take the most direct route to the top of the dunes by walking straight up the tallest sand hill.

As you cross the lower dunes, you'll pass some mesquite and creosote bushes. During spring of a good wildflower year, the lower dunes are bedecked with yellow and white desert primrose, pink sand verbena, and yellow sunflowers.

When you reach the saddle located to the right of the high point, turn left and trek another hundred yards or so to the top. The black material crowning the top of the dunes is magnetite, an iron oxide, and one of about two dozen minerals found within the dune system.

Enjoy the view from the top: the Kelso Mountains to the north, the Bristol Mountains to the southwest, the Granite Mountains to the south, the Providence Mountains to the east. Everywhere you look there are mountain ranges, small and large.

In fact, despite evidence to the contrary—most notably the stunning dunes beneath your feet—the East Mojave is really a desert of mountains, not sand.

While atop the dunes, perhaps your footsteps will cause mini-avalanches and the dunes will sha-boom-sha-boom for you. There's speculation that the extreme dryness of the area, combined with the wind-polished, rounded nature of the individual sand grains, has something to do with their musical ability. After picking up good vibrations, descend the steep dune face (much easier on the way down!) and return to the trailhead.

■ GRANITE MOUNTAINS
Silver Peak Trail
To Silver Peak is 8.5 miles round trip
with 2,400-foot elevation gain

G eologists often call the eastern Mojave a desert of mountains. Most prominent of these many mountains is the chain that trends southwest-northeast across Mojave National Preserve—a high-profile combination formed by the Granite, Providence, Mid Hill, and New York ranges.

The Granite Mountains, southernmost in the chain, are a little-visited wilderness, the domain of desert bighorn sheep. In fact, the craggy shoulders of these 6,000-foot mountains are favored haunts of the elusive creatures. A lack of asphalt (the sheep refuse to step over paved roads) and scarce human activity in this southern corner of the preserve means a bighorn-friendly environment.

The rugged Granite Mountains—and the other granite ranges in the eastern Mojave—have been highly eroded; characteristic of this action is the buildup of loose sedimentary materials at the base of the mountains. These apron-shaped formations are called alluvial fans.

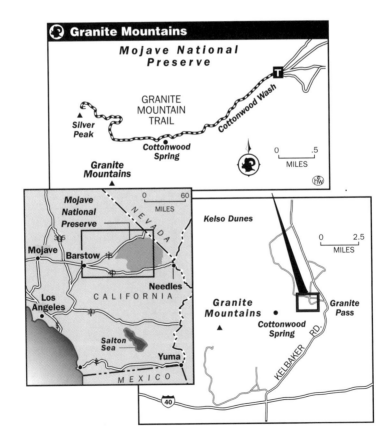

At 6,365 feet in elevation, Silver Peak is not the highest summit in the Granite Mountains (that honor belongs to Granite Mountain, the 6,762-foot signature summit located a few miles south of Silver Peak), but it does boast the only decent trail in the range. Your reward for the steep climb to Silver Peak are vistas of some of Mojave National Preserve's most famed features, including Cima Dome, the Providence Mountains, and Kelso Dunes.

Portions of these mountains are part of the University of California's Granite Mountains Natural Reserve. Such reserves represent a wide variety of the state's ecosystems, including Big Sur, the Eel River, plus a dozen more. UC reserves are dedicated to ecological research and education, and they typically serve as outdoor classrooms and field laboratories for students and faculty.

Some 9,000 acres in the Granite Mountains are in the UC reserve, of which 2,500 acres are owned by the University of California. To avoid disturbing any of the natural sciences research projects conducted in the Granite Mountains, please heed the reserve's no trespassing signs and stay on the area's main trails.

The rapid change in elevation along Silver Peak Trail is accompanied by distinct changes in vegetation. At lower elevations in Cottonwood Wash, sage and yucca are among the dominant plants. Higher elevations bring cholla-dotted slopes and then a woodland of pinyon pine and juniper.

DIRECTIONS TO TRAILHEAD From Interstate 40, about 78 miles east of Barstow and 65 miles west of Needles, exit on Kelbaker Road and head north into Mojave National Preserve.

Ten miles from I-40, look left (west) for an unsigned dirt road. (Clue: another dirt road, nearly opposite this one, heads east from the other side of Kelbaker Road.) Those traveling from northern preserve locations on Kelbaker Road will find the above-mentioned turnoff about 4.6 miles south of the turnoff for Kelso Dunes.

Drive 1.75 miles to a small rise, where there is a backcountry camping area (no facilities) and the signed boundary of the wilderness.

THE HIKE Head west into Cottonwood Wash. After 0.1 mile, the road forks. Stay right and hike up the wash.

Reminders of the area's ranching days come in the form of fencing and dirt tracks leading off to water tanks and corrals.

After about 1.25 miles, the old road narrows to a trail and begins an aggressive ascent up Silver Peak. The steep path passes amidst pinyon pine and juniper. A bit more than 3 miles out, the trail angles west for 0.5 mile, then north again.

The path ends 0.25 mile and about 300 feet in elevation short of the summit. Cairns help guide you over a very steep and rocky slope to the summit.

■ MITCHELL CAVERNS STATE RESERVE

Caverns Trail

1.5-mile guided tour of the caverns

Trail trivia question: Where in Southern California can you explore some stunning scenery, be assured that it won't rain, and know that the temperature for your walk will always be a comfortable 65°F?

Hint: One of the overlooked gems of the California state park system.

If you're in the dark, then you're on the right path—the trail through Mitchell Caverns State Reserve, which is part of Providence Mountains State Recreation Area. Ranger-led walks through the dramatic limestone caves offer a fascinating geology lesson that the whole family can enjoy.

In 1932, Jack Mitchell abandoned his Depression-shattered business in Los Angeles and moved to the desert. For a time, he prospected for silver, but his real fascination was with what he called the "Providence" or "Crystal Caves" and their potential as a tourist attraction. He constructed several stone buildings to use for lodging. (Today's park visitor center is one of these buildings.)

Mitchell Cavern's stalactites—underground desert wonders.

Mitchell and his wife, Ida, provided food, lodging, and guided tours of the caverns until 1954. By all accounts, Jack Mitchell was quite a yarn-spinner. He was known for telling visitors tall tales of ghosts, lost treasure, and bottomless pits.

DIRECTIONS TO TRAILHEAD From Interstate Highway 40, about 80 miles east of Barstow, exit on Essex Road and drive 16 miles to road's end at the Providence Mountains State Recreation Area parking lot. Sign up at the visitor center for tours.

THE HIKE Now that the caverns are part of the state park system, rangers lead the tours. They're an enthusiastic lot and quite informative. Visitors walk through the two main caves, which Mitchell named El Pakiva (the Devil's House) and Tecopa (after a Shoshonean chieftain). You'll get

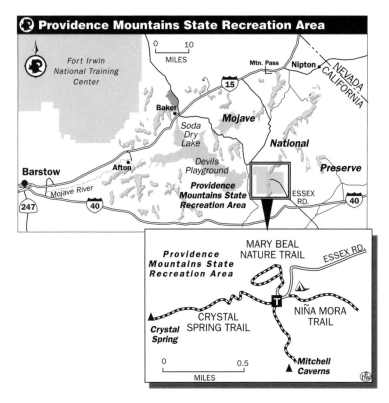

a close-up view of stalactites and stalagmites, cave ribbon, cave spaghetti, and flow stone. And you'll learn about some of the caverns' former inhabitants— the Chemehuevi Indians and a Pleistocene ground sloth that stumbled into the darkness some 15,000 years ago.

During Jack Mitchell's day, visitors had to be nimble rock climbers who waited for their tour leader to toss flares into the darkness. Nowadays, the caverns are equipped with stairs and special lighting.

Guided tours are conducted Monday through Friday at 1:30 PM On Saturday and Sunday, tours begin at 10 AM, 1:30 PM, and 3 PM. A tour takes an hour and a half to two hours depending on your group's enthusiasm and collective curiosity, and a fee is charged.

Because you can only tour the caverns with a park ranger, and because you wouldn't want me to spoil the many surprises of the cave walk with a step-by-step description, I won't further detail the Mitchell Caverns Trail. However, after exploring "the great indoors," allow some time to explore the park's outdoor pathways.

■ PROVIDENCE MOUNTAINS STATE RECREATION AREA
Mary Beal Nature Trail
0.5 mile round trip

Pick up an interpretive booklet from the park visitor center and walk the Mary Beal Nature Trail, which offers a great introduction to high-desert flora. Cliffrose and blue sage share the hillsides with cholla, catsclaw, and creosote.

The trail honors Mary Beal, a Riverside librarian who was "exiled" to the desert by her doctor for health reasons. For a half century, this remarkable woman wandered through the Providence Mountains and other remote Mojave Desert locales gathering and classifying hundreds of varieties of wildflowers and other plants. The trail was dedicated in 1952 on Beal's 75th birthday.

DIRECTIONS TO TRAILHEAD   From Interstate Highway 40, about 80 miles east of Barstow, exit on Essex Road and drive 16 miles to road's end at the Providence Mountains State Recreation Area parking lot. Walk the road north of the visitor center to the signed start of the trail.

THE HIKE The path meanders an alluvial plain. Prickly pear, cholla, and assorted yuccas spike surrounding slopes. Benches offer restful places from which to contemplate the cacti, admire the volcanic boulders, and count the speedy roadrunners often seem scurrying across the trail. Also savor views of the Providence Mountains and Clipper Valley.

■ CRYSTAL SPRING CANYON
Crystal Spring Trail
From Mitchell Caverns to Crystal Spring is 2 miles round tip with 600-foot elevation gain

Crystal Spring Trail leads into the pinyon pine- and juniper-dotted Providence Mountains by way of Crystal Canyon. Bighorn sheep often travel through this canyon.

Crystal Canyon is walled with limestone and rhyolite, a red volcanic rock. High above the canyon, castle-like formations of this rhyolite crown the Providence Mountains. The steep and rather rocky trail offers both an exploration of an inviting high-desert canyon and engaging vistas of the spires of Providence Mountains peaks and a slice of Arizona.

DIRECTIONS TO THE TRAILHEAD From Interstate Highway 40, about 80 miles east of Barstow, exit on Essex Road and drive 16 miles to road's end at the Providence Mountains State Recreation Area parking lot. Join the signed trail ascending the slope near the beginning of the Mitchell Caverns Trail.

THE HIKE In less than a 0.25-mile ascent, enter a unique desert landscape framed by bold rhyolite outcroppings. Pinyon pine join a veritable cactus garden of barrel, cholla and prickly pear cacti.

About 0.5 mile out, keen-eyed hikers may spy the pipeline Jack Mitchell built in the 1930s to supply his tourist attraction-in-the-making. The path crosses to the canyon's right side and continues a last 0.25 mile to the end of the trail, just short of willow-screened Crystal Spring. Intrepid hikers may proceed on fainter trail to the spring and to a viewpoint a short distance beyond.

See Map on Page 143

■ CAMEL HUMPS
Niña Mora Trail
0.5 mile round trip

Experience the grandeur and isolation of the Providence Mountains, as well as grand vistas, by walking the short Niña Mora Trail. The path ascends the summit of one of a pair of hills known as Camel Humps.

From atop the hump, gaze out over some 300 square miles of desert. Clear-day views include Arizona's Hualapai Mountains, located about 100 miles to the east.

The trail was named for the *niña* (child) Mora, daughter of a Mexican silver miner who toiled in the region's diggings in the early 1900s. A miner's life—as well as the lives of his family members—was often a short one. And so it was with little Mora, who died at a very early age and lies buried in a grave near the trail that bears her name.

DIRECTIONS TO TRAILHEAD From Interstate Highway 40, about 80 miles east of Barstow, exit on Essex Road and drive 16 miles to road's end at the Providence Mountains State Recreation Area parking lot. Join the signed path at the east end of the park's tiny campground.

THE HIKE From the campground, the path leads over a barrel cactus- and yucca-dotted ridge, and past the grave marker of Niña Mora.

In no time, you reach trail's end and a viewpoint that offers a good perspective on the weathered rhyolite crags of the Providence Mountains looming to the west. Below is Clipper Valley and to the east is Table Mountain.

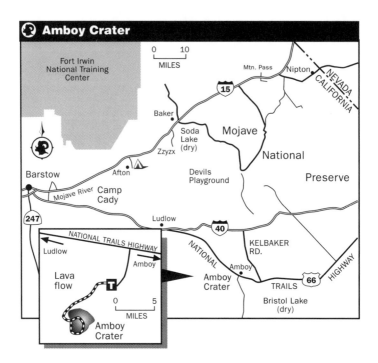

■ AMBOY CRATER
Amboy Crater Trail
3 miles round trip with 200-foot elevation gain

We're fascinated by volcanoes and, as long as they're not too hot and not active, we like to visit them. Amboy Crater, located out in the eastern Mojave Desert with the old-time diners and abandoned gas stations along historic Route 66, has long been a curiosity for generations of desert travelers. The little volcano can be reached with a short hike, an ideal leg-stretcher for motorists desiring a break from interminable Interstate 40.

Getting to the volcano's trailhead via Route 66 can be thoroughly enjoyable. The stretch of Route 66 from just outside Barstow to just west of Needles is the longest stretch of the historic route in California.

About 28 miles east of Ludlow, you'll notice extensive Hawaiian-like lava fields. Amboy Crater, the cause of this flow, lies just south of the road.

Some writers have been repelled, not attracted, by this scene. In *The Grapes of Wrath*, John Steinbeck wrote, "And 66 goes on over the terrible desert, where the distance shimmers and the black cinder mountains hang unbearably in the distance." Many of the black cinder mountains (and red ones, too) are now part of the Mojave National Preserve.

The town of Amboy, a few miles east of the crater, has never consisted of much more than a cafe or two and a motel. Built in the mid-1940s, the stop was a popular one with motorists during the Route 66 heyday. Gas is still available here.

About 2.5 miles east of town, Kelbaker Road extends north to the heart of Mojave National Preserve. The volcanically inclined visitor can count a dozen or two cones and a number of lava flows on the drive to Kelso and the heart of the preserve.

Between Amboy and Essex, you'll notice abandoned autos, closed-down diners and service stations. The buildings may still stand, but the spirit and life behind them appears to have just dried up and blown away—exactly what happened when Route 66 was bypassed by Interstate 40.

Amboy Crater and environs are covered with two kinds of lava: *aa* (pronounced ah-ah), sharp, hiking boot-assaulting hunks of basalt, and *pahoehoe* (pa-hoy-hoy), smoother, rope-like lava.

While it's difficult to get lost because Route 66 and Amboy Crater are almost always in view, it is possible to get quite frustrated if you get sidetracked in the lava field labyrinth and end up involuntarily extending your short hike to the volcano. It's only a little more than a mile from the parking area to the crater, but it can seem much longer if you do a lot of zigzagging over the lava. Forget trying to follow any one path and instead make a beeline for the base of the crater. Look back occasionally to establish landmarks to assist you on your return trip.

DIRECTIONS TO THE TRAILHEAD From Barstow, head east on Interstate 40 some 52 miles and take the Ludlow exit. Join National Trails Highway (the modern moniker for old Route 66) and drive 28 miles southeast to just short of Amboy and the intersection with Amboy Road. Turn south on an unsigned dirt road leading 0.4 mile down a short graded road. Proceed slowly along this road (littered with sharp, potentially tire-shredding lava chunks) to a dirt parking area.

THE HIKE From the parking area, follow the vehicle road, which soon ends in a spaghetti-tangle of trails. Eyeball the crater and simply start walking straight toward it. The hiker will soon figure out that the easiest traveling is over the smooth, sandy stretches between the rough lava flows.

Approaching the cinder cone, angle right toward Amboy's west ridge. A footpath climbs to a wide opening in the crater rim. Climb into this breach in the cone, then continue on this west side to the rim. Walk along the rim for panoramic vistas of the surrounding lavascape and the East Mojave desert. Continue walking clockwise around the rim, then retrace your steps back to the parking area.

Joshua tree—the namesake for the national park.

CHAPTER 4

JOSHUA TREE NATIONAL PARK

For many visitors, the Joshua trees are not only the essence but the whole of their park experience. Joshua Tree National Park, however, is much more than a tableau of twisted yucca and beckons the explorer with a diversity of desert environments, including sand dunes, native palm oases, cactus gardens, and jumbles of jumbo granite.

The Joshua tree's distribution defines the very boundaries of the Mojave Desert. Here in its namesake national park, it reaches the southernmost limit of its range.

The park area is sometimes known as the "connecting" desert because of its location between the Mojave and the Colorado Desert, and because it shares characteristics of each. The Mojave, a desert of mountains, is (relatively) cooler-wetter-higher and forms the northern and western parts of the park. Southern and eastern sections of the park are part of the hotter-drier-lower Colorado Desert, characterized by a wide variety of desert flora, including, ironwood, smoketree, and native California fan palms. Cacti, especially cholla and ocotillo, thrive in the more southerly Colorado Desert (a part of the larger Sonoran Desert).

In 1994, under provisions of the federal California Desert Protection Act, Joshua Tree was "upgraded" to national park status (from national

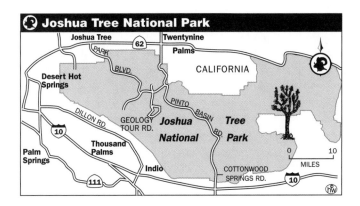

monument) and expanded by about a quarter-million acres. The park attracts campers, hikers, and especially rock-climbers. From Hidden Valley to the Wonderland of Rocks, the park has emerged as one of the world's premier rock-climbing destinations. The park offers some 3,500 climbing routes, ranging from the easiest of bouldering to some of the sport's most difficult technical climbs.

The visitor center is located alongside one of the park's four palm oases— the Oasis of Mara, also know as Twentynine Palms. For many hundreds of years native Americans lived at "the place of little springs and much grass."

Two paved roads explore the heart of the park. The first loops through the high northwest section, visiting Queen and Lost Horse Valleys, as well as the awesome boulder piles at Jumbo Rocks and Wonderland of Rocks. The second angles northwest-southeast across the park, and crosses both the Mojave Desert Joshua tree woodland and cactus gardens of the Colorado Desert.

From Oasis Visitor Center, drive south to Jumbo Rocks, which is kind of Joshua Tree National Park to the max: a vast array of rock formations, a Joshua tree forest, the yucca-dotted desert open and wide. Check out Skull Rock (one of the many rocks in the area that appear to resemble humans, dinosaurs, monsters, cathedrals, and castles) via a 1.5-mile long nature trail that provides an introduction to the park's flora, wildlife, and geology.

In Queen Valley, just west of Jumbo Rocks, is the signed beginning of Geology Tour Road, a rough dirt road (four-wheel drive recommended)

Barker Dam Loop, one of Joshua Tree's best jaunts.

extending 18 miles into the heart of the park. Motorists get close-up looks at the considerable erosive forces that shaped this land, forming the flattest of desert playas, or dry lake beds, as well as massive heaps of boulders that tower over the valley floor. Some good hikes begin off Geology Tour Road, which delivers a Joshua tree woodland, an historic spring, abandoned mines, and some fascinating native petroglyphs.

Farther west of Jumbo Rocks is Indian Cave, typical of the kind of shelter sought by the nomadic Cahuilla and Serrano Indian clans that traveled this desert land. A number of bedrock mortars found in the cave suggest its use as a work

Mid-day at the oasis.

site by its aboriginal inhabitants. A 4-mile round trip trail climbs through a lunar landscape of rocks and Joshua trees to the top of 5,470-foot Ryan Mountain. Reward for the climb is one of the park's best views.

At Cap Rock Junction, the paved park road swings north toward the Wonderland of Rocks, 12 square miles of massive jumbled granite. This curious maze of stone hides groves of Joshua trees, trackless washes, and several small pools of water.

Easiest, and certainly the safest way to explore the Wonderland is to follow the 1.25-mile Barker Dam Loop Trail. The first part of the journey is on a nature trail that interprets botanical highlights; the second part visits some native petroglyphs and a little lake created a century ago by cattle ranchers.

Cottonwood Spring, near the south end of the park is a little palm- and cottonwood-shaded oasis that attracts desert birds and bird-watchers. From Cottonwood Campground a trail leads to the old Mastodon Gold Mine,

Boulders are a distinctive feature in Joshua Tree.

then climbs behemoth-looking Mastodon Peak for a view from Mt. San Jac-into above Palm Springs to the Salton Sea.

The national park holds two more of California's loveliest palm oases. Fortynine Palms Oasis winds up and over a hot rocky crest to the dripping springs, pools, and the blessed shade of palms and cottonwoods. Lost Palms Oasis Trail visits the park's premier palm grove.

You'll see plenty of Joshua trees along the park's pathways, but there's much more for the hiker to discover. Two of my favorite footpaths are Black Rock Canyon Trail which follows a classic desert wash, then ascends to the crest of the Little San Bernardino Mountains at Warren Peak. Desert and mountain views from the peak are stunning. Lost Horse Mine Trail visits one of the area's most successful gold mines, and offers a close-up look back into a colorful era, and some fine views into the heart of the park.

■ HIGH VIEW
High View Nature Trail
1.3 mile-loop with 300-foot elevation gain

If one word could sum up the view from High View, it might be "transitions." The naturalist can contemplate two subtle transitions—that between the Mojave and Colorado deserts, and that between the desert and San Bernardino Mountains.

A far less subtle and far more abrupt transition is also obvious from High View: the desert communities of Joshua Tree, Yucca Valley and Twentynine Palms sprawling along the northern border of Joshua Tree National Park.

An interpretive brochure, keyed to two dozen numbered sites along the nature trail, explains the region's ecology and geography. Pick up a copy of the leaflet (far more lyrical and engaging than the usual nature trail guide) at the Black Rock Canyon Ranger Station.

DIRECTIONS TO TRAILHEAD From Highway 62 in Yucca Valley, drive 5 miles south on Joshua Lane toward Black Rock Campground. Just before reaching the campground entrance, turn right on the unsigned dirt access road for South Park and drive 0.75 mile to road's end at the trailhead parking lot.

THE HIKE Begin with a meander past tall yuccas then embark on a mellow ascent up and around pinyon pine-dotted slopes. Strategically placed benches offer the hiker rest and places from which to regard the surrounding desert.

The trail passes both the Joshua tree and its close cousin, the nolina, distinguished by its long, flexible leaves.

Reach the summit at the 0.5-mile mark and enjoy clear-day views of the San Gabriel and San Bernardino Mountains, including Mt. San Gorgonio, the Southland's highest peak. The path descends through a grove of manzanita to a wash as it circles back to the trailhead.

Hill View Nature Trail's yucca trees.

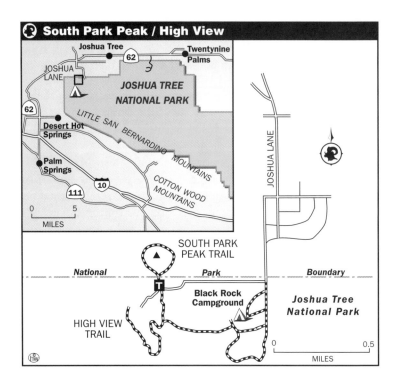

■ BLACK ROCK CANYON

Black Rock Canyon Trail

From Black Rock Campground to Warren Peak is 6 miles
round trip with 1,000-foot elevation gain

A hike through Black Rock Canyon has just about everything a desert hike should have: plenty of cactus, pinyon pine-dotted peaks, a sandy wash, dramatic rock formations, a hidden spring, grand vistas. And much more.

Tucked away in the northwest corner of the park, the Black Rock Canyon area also hosts forests of the shaggy Joshuas. *Yucca brevifolia* thrive at the higher elevations of this end of the national park.

More than 200 species of birds, including speedy roadrunners, have been observed in and around Black Rock Canyon. Hikers frequently spot mule deer and rabbits—desert cottontails and black-tailed jack rabbits. Bighorn sheep are also sighted occasionally. A bit off the tourist track, Black Rock Canyon rarely makes the "must see" list of natural attractions at the national park. Ironically though, while Black Rock is often overlooked, it is one of the easiest places to reach. The canyon is close to Yucca Valley's commercial strip, very close to a residential neighborhood.

Maybe we nature-lovers practice a curious logic: if a beautiful place is near civilization it can't be that beautiful, right? In Black Rock Canyon's case, our logic would be faulty. The canyon matches the allure of much more remote regions of the national park.

Black Rock Canyon Trail follows a classic desert wash, then ascends to the crest of the Little San Bernardino Mountains at Warren Peak. Desert and mountain views from the peak are stunning.

DIRECTIONS TO TRAILHEAD From Highway 62 (Twentynine Palms Highway) in Yucca Valley, turn south on Joshua Lane and drive 5 miles through a residential area to Black Rock Ranger Station. Park at the station. The station has some interpretive displays and sells books and maps. Ask rangers for the latest trail information.

Walk uphill through the campground to campsite #30 and the trailhead.

THE HIKE From the upper end of the campground, the trail leads to a water tank, goes left a very short distance on a park service road, then angles right. After a few hundred yards, the trail splits. The main trail descends directly into Black Rock Canyon wash. (An upper trail crests a hill before it too descends into the wash.)

A quarter mile from the trailhead, the path drops into the dry, sandy creekbed of Black Rock Canyon. You'll bear right and head up the wide canyon mouth, passing Joshua trees, desert willow, and cholla.

A mile of wash walking leads you to the remains of some so-called "tanks," or rock basins that were built by early ranchers to hold water for their cattle.

Another quarter mile up the wash is Black Rock Spring, sometimes dry, sometimes a trickle. Beyond the spring, the canyon narrows. You wend your way around beavertail cactus, pinyon pine, and juniper.

(Near the head of the canyon, the trail splits. Turning left [east] cross-country will lead along a rough ridge to Peak 5195.)

If you follow the right fork of the rough trail, you'll climb to a dramatic ridge crest of the Little San Bernardino Mountains, then angle right (west) along the crest. A steep, 0.25-mile ascent past contorted wind-blown juniper and pinyon pine brings you to the top of Warren Peak.

Oh what a grand clear-day view! North is the Mojave Desert. To the west is snowy Mt. San Gorgonio, Southern California's highest peak, as

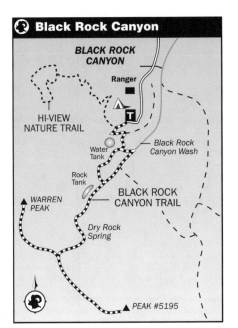

Black Rock Canyon

BLACK ROCK CANYON

Ranger

HI-VIEW NATURE TRAIL

Water Tank

Black Rock Canyon Wash

Rock Tank

WARREN PEAK

BLACK ROCK CANYON TRAIL

Dry Rock Spring

PEAK #5195

well as the San Bernardino Mountains and the deep trough of San Gorgonio Pass. Southwest lies mighty Mt. San Jacinto and to the south (this is often the murky part of the view) Palm Springs and the Coachella Valley. The peaks of the Little San Bernardino Mountains extend southeast, marching toward the Salton Sea.

■ EUREKA PEAK
California Riding and Hiking Trail, Eureka Peak Trail
From Black Rock Canyon Campground to Eureka Peak is 11 miles round trip with 1,500-foot elevation gain

M any hikers claim the panoramic view from 5,516-foot Eureka Peak is one of the best in the national park. During winter and spring, snow-capped Mt. San Jacinto towers over the Coachella Valley. Mt. San Gorgonio, highest peak in Southern California, and other 10,000-foot summits in the San Gorgonio Wilderness, are also majestic sights.

Much to the lament of hikers, motorists can drive to within a hundred yards of Eureka Peak and get the same view. Nevertheless, there is much to be recommended for using two feet instead of four wheels to climb Eureka.

From Black Rock Campground, a 2-mile length of the California Riding and Hiking Trail ascends the hills fringing the Yucca Valley, then delivers you to a

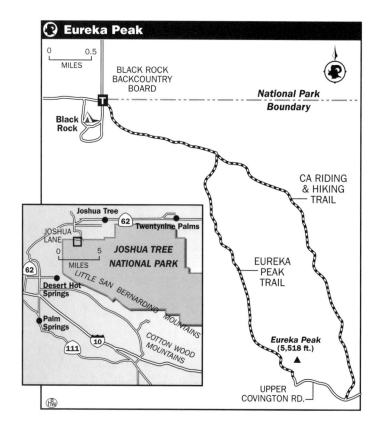

Eureka Peak

0   0.5
MILES

BLACK ROCK
BACKCOUNTRY
BOARD

National Park
Boundary

T

Black
Rock

CA RIDING
& HIKING
TRAIL

Joshua Tree

62 Twentynine Palms

JOSHUA
LANE

0   5
MILES

JOSHUA TREE
NATIONAL PARK

EUREKA
PEAK
TRAIL

62

LITTLE SAN BERNARDINO MOUNTAINS

Desert Hot
Springs

Palm
Springs

COTTON WOOD
MOUNTAINS

Eureka Peak
(5,518 ft.)

111   10

UPPER
COVINGTON RD.

series of washes and narrow canyons that you follow to the summit of Eureka Peak. Occasional signposts help you negotiate the trailless stretches of the route.

Once atop the peak, the hiker has several options: A return to Black Rock Campground via the CR&HT (my favorite option); pick up by a friend from atop the peak; continuing 2 miles by dirt road to Covington Flat and then getting a ride.

DIRECTIONS TO TRAILHEAD From Highway 62 (Twentynine Palms Highway) in Yucca Valley, turn south on Joshua Lane and drive 5 miles through a residential area to Black Rock Ranger Station. Park at the station. Signed California Riding and Hiking Trail is located on the east side of Black Rock Campground.

THE HIKE The CR&HT passes through some pretty country dotted with Joshua trees, pinyon pine, and juniper. Enjoy the view of the fast-developing Yucca Valley. After 2 miles, the path reaches a convergence of 2 washes. CR&HT heads east, but your route is the south fork to the right.

After 0.5 mile or so, the wash forks and you'll bear right, following this branch of the wash 2 miles to its end, then heading left (southeast) over a ridge. Cresting this ridge, you'll continue to angle south-southeast around to the south side of Eureka Peak. Lastly, you'll join the short summit trail (and those motorists taking the easy way to the top!) ascending from the parking area.

■ WONDERLAND AND WILLOW HOLE
Boy Scout Trail
From Keys View Backcountry Board to Indian Cove
Backcountry Board is 8 miles one way with 1,300-foot
elevation loss; optional 4-mile round trip extension
to Willow Hole

Boy Scout Trail tours a quintessential Joshua Tree National Park landscape: a vast array of rock formations, a Joshua tree forest, the yucca-dotted desert open and wide.

And, if the allure of this uncommon landscape is not sufficient motivation to take this hike, Boy Scout Trail has one more attraction—it's a nearly all-downhill walk.

Boy Scout Trail, one of the park's premier footpaths, skirts the wild western edge of the Wonderland of Rocks, 12 square miles of massive jumbled granite. The path also offers the hikers some engaging wash-walking along narrow, sandy canyons dotted with pinyon pine and juniper.

Although Boy Scout Trail can be hiked as a 16-mile out-and-back, it's more commonly enjoyed as a one-way trek aided by a car shuttle. Usually hikers prefer the downhill walk from Keys View trailhead to the Indian Cove trailhead, however, the elevation change is not that great, so hiking the reverse, uphill route is definitely doable.

DIRECTIONS TO TRAILHEAD From Highway 62 in the town of Joshua Tree, turn south on Park Boulevard and drive 5 miles to the west entrance of Joshua Tree National Park. Continue another 7 miles to Keys View Backcountry Board and the trailhead, located on the left (north) side of the road.

For a car shuttle: From Highway 62, 10 miles east of the town of Joshua Tree and the Park Boulevard turnoff, turn south on Indian Cove Road and proceed 1.5 miles to the Indian Cove Backcountry Board and trailhead on the right (west) side of the road.

THE HIKE Boy Scout Trail climbs gently past a Joshua tree forest. As it travels along the west side of the Wonderland of Rocks, views open up to the southwest of the sometimes snow-capped San Bernardino Mountains.

At a signed junction 1.25 miles from the trailhead, the path forks. The left fork is the continuation of the Boy Scout Trail; the right branch leads to Willow Hole.

(Willow Hole-bound hikers will join the sandy trail on a mellow 1.2-mile descent past granite towers to a wash, then follow the wash 0.8 mile to willow lined seasonal pools tucked in a cliff-encircled rock bowl.)

Boy Scout Trail traverses a fairly flat, Joshua tree- and yucca-dotted plateau. About 3 miles from the trailhead, the path drops into a rocky canyon, where park service markers help you stay on the trail; at 3.5 miles, the trail follows a wash and at 4 miles, this hike's halfway point, you'll encounter a cement water tank.

After another 0.25 mile of wash-walking concentrate on sticking with the

trail, which exits the wash and bends sharply to the west. The now rocky trail dips and rises, then switchbacks down to another wash at the 5-mile mark. After a mile of wash-walking, the path crosses over to a second, wider wash, and follows the latter for 0.5 mile.

The trail climbs out of the wash and crosses a broad alluvial fan spiked with cholla and yucca. A final 1.5 miles of walking across the fan leads to the Indian Cove Backcountry Board.

Boy Scout Trail; girls welcome.

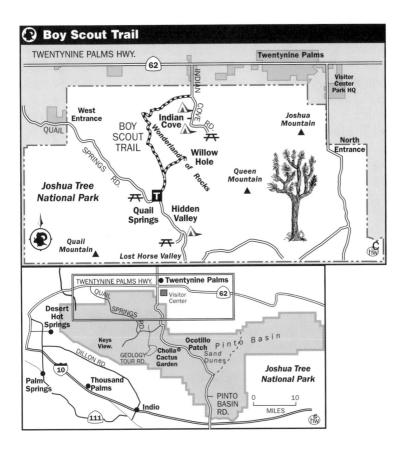

Boy Scout Trail

TWENTYNINE PALMS HWY.
62
Twentynine Palms

Visitor Center Park HQ

West Entrance

BOY SCOUT TRAIL

QUAIL

Indian Cove

INDIAN COVE RD.

Joshua Mountain

SPRINGS RD.

Wonderland of Rocks

Willow Hole

North Entrance

Joshua Tree National Park

Queen Mountain

Quail Springs

Hidden Valley

Quail Mountain

Lost Horse Valley

TWENTYNINE PALMS HWY.
Twentynine Palms

QUAIL

Visitor Center
62

SPRINGS RD.

Desert Hot Springs

Keys View.

Ocotillo Patch

Pinto Basin

GEOLOGY TOUR RD.

Cholla Cactus Garden

Sand Dunes

DILLON RD.

Joshua Tree National Park

10

Palm Springs

Thousand Palms

Indio

PINTO BASIN RD.

0   10

MILES

111

See Map on Page 160

■ INDIAN COVE

Indian Cove Nature Trail
0.6 mile round trip

Indian Cove has been a popular campground for hundreds of years. Long before park visitors pulled trailers and pitched tents in the cove, the native Chemehuevi, Cahuilla, and Serrano stopped here on their winter migrations.

Twentieth-century campers discovered *ollas* (earthenware jars) in the cove. The Indians stored seeds, nuts, and other foodstuffs in the ollas which were cached in the nooks and crannies of the cove's rock walls. Pottery shards and other evidence of village sites are scattered about the Indian Cove area.

Indian Cove appears most cove-like near sunset when dark shadows fill the sandscape floor between encircling rock formations. In the right light, one can imagine "Mojave Bay," a landlocked desert harbor.

Signs along Indian Cove Nature Trail interpret desert flora and wildlife, as well as offering some history about the earliest human inhabitants of this land.

DIRECTIONS TO TRAILHEAD From Highway 62, some 7 miles west of Twentynine Palms and 10 miles east of Joshua Tree (the town), turn south on signed Indian Cove Road and drive 3 miles south to the national park's Indian Cove Campground. From the campground, follow the signs to the parking area for the signed nature trail.

A 0.2-mile spur trail links the group campground with the northernmost segment of the Indian Cove Nature Trail.

THE HIKE The path begins in the shadow of boulders, the northern fringe of the Wonderland of Rocks. Rock overhangs and caves in the surrounding hills offered shelter to the native Serrano.

The trail descends into a wash where interpretive signs discuss the kinds of plants and wildlife that inhabit this kind of environment. Close the loop by walking past the curious paperbag bush and assorted cacti, then ascending out of the wash back to the trailhead.

■ RATTLESNAKE CANYON
Rattlesnake Canyon Cross-country Route
1 to 3 miles round trip

N orthern access point to the famed 10-square mile Wonderland of Rocks is via Indian Cove. This favorite camping spot and picnic area is the jump-off spot for an exploration of one of the Wonderland's more intriguing slot canyons—Rattlesnake Canyon.

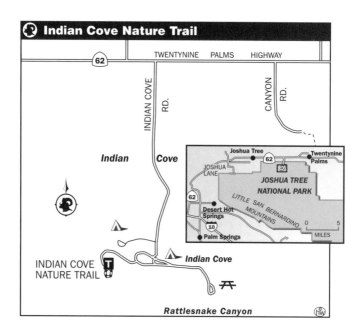

Considering this area of the park is known as one of the drier ones, it's surprising to discover a (seasonal) little creek tumbling over the boulder-strewn Rattlesnake Canyon. A half-mile from the mouth of the canyon is a small waterfall, where the creek tumbles over the polished rocks. Tiny cascades and some lovely pools complete the attractive scene.

Not only is Rattlesnake Canyon easy on the eye, it's pleasing to the ear when water is flowing. The reverberation of the running water in the narrow canyon overwhelms all sounds of nearby civilization. At night, the soprano peeping of the resident tree frogs echoes through the canyon.

Beyond the waterfall area, Rattlesnake Canyon is difficult to traverse and recommended only for experienced hikers with boulder scrambling experience.

DIRECTIONS TO TRAILHEAD From Yucca Valley, drive east on Highway 62 for 14 miles to Indian Cove Road. Turn south (right), proceed a mile to the ranger station, then 3.3 more miles to the picnic area at road's end.

THE HIKE From the picnic area, march east into what is usually the dry creekbed of Rattlesnake Canyon. Head south (up-canyon) dodging creosote bush and yucca and working your way around the canyon's many boulders to the base of the falls.

Experienced hikers will climb around and above the falls and continue up-canyon. After much scrambling, you'll eventually reach a sandy wash and a more open part of the canyon.

■ FORTYNINE PALMS
Fortynine Palms Trail
To Fortynine Palms Oasis is 3 miles round trip with 400-foot elevation gain

Fortynine Palms Oasis has retained a wonderful air of remoteness. From the parking area, an old Indian trail climbs a steep ridge and offers expansive views of the Sheephole and Bullion mountain ranges.

On the exposed ridge, barrel cacti, creosote, yucca, and brittlebush brave the heat. As the trail winds up and over a rocky crest, the restful green of the oasis comes into view.

At the oasis, nature's personality abruptly changes and the dry, sunbaked ridges give way to dripping springs, pools, and the blessed shade of palms and cottonwoods.

Unlike some oases, which are strung out for miles along a stream, Fortynine Palms is a close-knit palm family centered around a generous supply of surface water. Seeps and springs fill numerous basins set among the rocks at different levels. Other basins are supplied by "rain" drip-drip-dripping from the upper levels. Mesquite and willow thrive alongside the palms. Singing house finches and croaking frogs provide a musical interlude.

Perched on a steep canyon wall, Fortynine Palms Oasis overlooks the town of Twentynine Palms, but its untouched beauty makes it seem a lot farther removed from civilization.

DIRECTIONS TO TRAILHEAD From Interstate 10, a few miles east of the Highway 111 turnoff going to Palm Springs, bear north on Highway 62. After passing the town of Yucca Valley, but before reaching the outskirts of Twentynine Palms, turn right on Canyon Road. (Hint: Look for an animal hospital at the corner of Highway 62 and Canyon Road) Follow Canyon Road 1.75 miles to its end at a National Park Service parking area and the trailhead.

THE HIKE The trail rises through a Spartan rockscape dotted with cacti and jojoba. After a brisk climb, catch your breath atop a ridgetop and enjoy the view of Twentynine Palms and the surrounding desert.

You may notice colorful patches of lichen adhering to the rocks. Lichen, which conducts the business of life as a limited partnership of algae and fungi, is very sensitive to air pollution; the health of this tiny plant is considered by some botanists to be related to air quality. Contemplate the abstract impressionist patterns of the lichen, inhale great drafts of fresh air, then follow the trail as it descends from the ridgetop.

Palms with their feet in the water and their heads in the sun.

The trail leads down slopes dotted with barrel cactus and mesquite. Soon the oasis comes into view. Lucky hikers may get a fleeting glimpse of bighorn sheep drinking from oasis pools or gamboling over nearby steep slopes.

As the path leads you to the palms, you'll notice many fire-blackened tree trunks. The grove has burned several times during the last 100 years. Fortunately, palms are among the most fire-proof trees in existence, and fire—whether caused by man or lightning—seldom kills them. Fire may actually be beneficial for the palms because it serves to temporarily eliminate the competition of such trees as mesquite and cottonwood and bushes like arrowweed, all of them thirsty fellows and able to push their roots much deeper in search of water than

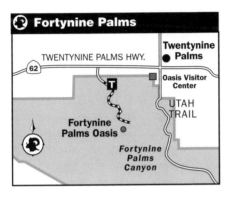

palms. Burning also opens the oasis floor to sunlight, which seedling palms need.

Fortynine Palms Oasis celebrates life. Our native California fan palm clusters near handsome boulder-lined pools. Fuzzy cattails, ferns, and grasses sway in the breeze. An oasis like this one gives the hiker a chance to view the desert in terms that are the exact opposite of its stereotypical dry hostility.

■ CONTACT MINE
Contact Mine Trail
From Park Route 12 to Contact Mine is
3.4 miles round trip with 700-foot elevation gain

Explore an early 1900s silver and gold mine site on a trail leading into the rugged terrain close to the park's north entry station. The Contact Mine's considerable remains include several mine shafts, ore car tracks, and a cable winch.

The mine's layout, equipment, and the road leading to it all suggest some excellent early twentieth-century engineering was carefully applied to the endeavor. The access road with its supporting rock foundations and the way it contours over rocky slopes is a particularly good expression of the road builder's art.

Two words of advice about the old road, now a hiking trail. The first stretch of trail is sketchy and you don't actually join the mine road until the 0.75-mile mark. Also, a century of erosion has made the road a rocky one.

DIRECTIONS TO TRAILHEAD
From Highway 62 in Twentynine Palms, drive 4 miles south on Utah Trail to an entry kiosk on the national park's north boundary. Continue another 0.5 mile south to a pullout; parking and an information board are on the right (west) side of the road.

THE HIKE From the information board, follow the very faint road southwest across flat, sandy, cholla-dotted terrain. After 0.1 mile the trail

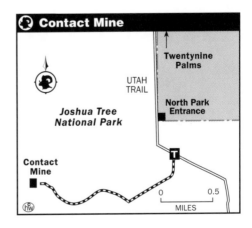

crosses a low dirt dike and soon reaches a second dike that traces a wash. Follow the wash to the right as it curves toward the mountains.

At 0.4 mile, the wash forks and you bear right, heading toward those rocky mountains. Concentrate on the trail but do look up to admire vistas of the Pinto Mountains and the surrounding parkland.

About 0.75 mile of travel from the trailhead brings you to not-very-obvious junction with another wash. Watch for rock cairns, bear right, climb out of the wash, and join the old mining road. The quite rocky road ascends rapidly for a mile. Not long after you spot the first mining equipment, the old road delivers you to the ruins of the Contact Mine. Be careful around the shafts and mine site debris.

■ HIDDEN VALLEY
Hidden Valley Trail
1 mile round trip

Hidden Valley certainly isn't hidden; the trail leading to it begins just off Park Boulevard. In the 1880s, however, the valley was sufficiently isolated for lawbreakers to hide from view.

As the story goes, cattle rustlers stashed bovines stolen from the Arizona Territory in Hidden Valley. Quite possibly, the climate was a bit wetter in those days, thus providing sufficient vegetation for the hidden cows. After re-branding the cattle, the rustlers then sold them to customers on terms that no doubt included no questions asked, no returns, and cash-only. Local "ranchers" who made good use of Hidden Valley included brothers Bill and John McHaney, who made a profitable career change to mining in later years. Their Desert Queen Mine yielded a small fortune in gold.

With its Joshua trees and rock formations, this nature trail has always been a popular one with my family. The nature trail is a good learning experience; the interpretive signs are insightful, not intrusive.

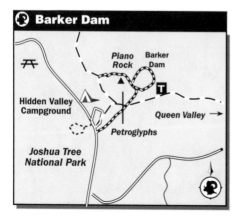

DIRECTIONS TO TRAILHEAD From Highway 62 in Joshua Tree, proceed 14 miles south on Park Boulevard to the signed turnoff for Hidden Valley Picnic Area and Nature Trail. Turn right and proceed 0.25 to parking and the signed trailhead.

THE HIKE Join the path, paved at first, as it ascends between big boulders and soon forks. Head to the left on the sandy trail and hike past the varied vegetation that keeps company

Rock out on this excellent nature trail.

with the Joshuas: turbinella oak, juniper, and pinyon pine, as well as cholla and beavertail cactus.

The trail loops around the edges of the rock-surrounded valley as it closes the loop and returns you to the trailhead.

■ WONDERLAND OF ROCKS
Barker Dam Loop Trail
From Parking Area to Barker Dam is 1.25 miles round trip

One of the many wonders of Joshua Tree National Park is the Wonderland of Rocks, 12 square miles of massive jumbled granite. This curious maze of stone hides groves of Joshua trees, trackless washes, and several small pools of water.

Perhaps the easiest, and certainly the safest way to explore the Wonderland is to follow the Barker Dam Loop Trail. The first part of the journey is on a nature trail that interprets the botanical highlights of the area. The last part of the loop trail visits some Indian petroglyphs.

This hike's main destination is the small lake created by Barker Dam. A century ago, cowboys took advantage of the water catchment of this natural basin and brought their cattle to this corner of the Wonderland of Rocks. Barker and Shay Cattle Co. constructed the dam, which was later raised to its present height by Bill Keys and his family in the 1950s. Family members inscribed their names atop the dam's south wall and renamed it Bighorn Dam, however, Barker was the name that stuck.

The trail to Barker Dam, while interesting, is not likely to occupy much of a day for the intrepid walker. One way to explore a little more of the Wonderland of Rocks is to pick up the Wonderland Wash Ranch Trail to the Astrodomes. Departing from the next spur road and parking area past the Barker Dam trailhead, this path leads to the ruins of a pink house known as the Worth Bagley House. From the back corner of the house, you'll pick up a wash and follow an intermittent trail through boulder clusters. The trail is popular with rock climbers, who use this trail to reach the Astrodomes— steep, 300-foot-tall rocks that tower above the wash.

A myriad of narrow canyons and washes lead into the Wonderland, but route-finding is extremely complex and recommended only for the very experienced with map and compass skills.

By park service regulation, the area is open only from 8 AM to 6 PM; this restriction is designed to allow the shy bighorn sheep a chance to reach water without human interference.

DIRECTIONS TO TRAILHEAD From I-10, a little east past the Highway 111 turnoff to Palm Springs, take Highway 62 northeast to the town of Joshua Tree. Continue 4 miles south to the park entrance, then another 10 miles to Hidden Valley Campground. A dirt road leads 2 miles from Hidden Valley Campground to Barker Dam parking area.

THE HIKE From the north end of the parking area, join the signed trail that immediately penetrates the Wonderland of Rocks. You'll pass a special kind of oak, the turbinella, which has adjusted to the harsh conditions of desert life. The oaks are habitat for a multitude of birds and ground squirrels.

For the first 0.5 mile, interpretive signs point out the unique botany of this desert land. The path then squeezes through a narrow rock passageway and leads directly to the edge of the lake. Bird-watching is excellent here because many migratory species not normally associated with the desert are attracted to the lake. The morning and late afternoon hours are particularly tranquil times to visit the lake and to contemplate the ever-changing reflections of the Wonderland of Rocks on the water.

The trail is a bit indistinct near Barker Dam, but resumes again in fine form near a strange-looking circular water trough, a holdover from the area's cattle ranching days. A toilet-like float mechanism controlled the flow of water to the thirsty livestock.

The path turns southerly and soon passes a huge boulder known as Piano Rock. When this land was in private ownership, a piano was hauled atop this rock and played for the amusement of visitors and locals.

Beyond Piano Rock the trail enters a rock-rimmed valley. A brief leftward detour at a junction brings you to the Movie Petroglyphs, so named because in less enlightened times, the native rock art was painted over by a film crew in order to make it more visible to the camera's eye.

Back on the main trail, you'll parallel some cliffs, perhaps get a glimpse of some Indian bedrock mortars, and loop back to the parking area.

See Map
on Page
168

■ DESERT QUEEN MINE
Desert Queen Mine Trail
1.2 miles round trip

Perched atop cliffs north of Jumbo Rocks Campground are the considerable ruins of the Desert Queen Mine, one of the more profitable gold mines dug in the desert we now call Joshua Tree National Park. Shafts, stone building foundations, and rusting machinery are scattered about the slopes above Desert Queen Wash.

If murder and intrigue are what fascinate us about desert mines, then the Desert Queen is quite a story. The tale begins in 1894 when a prospector named Frank James discovered some rich gold ore in the hills north of Jumbo Rocks. Word of his discovery reached cattle rustler Jim McHaney who, as the story goes, ordered his men to follow James to his claim and talk things over. One of McHaney's thugs, Charles Martin, shot him dead (though an inquest jury decided Martin acted in self-defense and did not need to stand trial). Jim McHaney and his more respectable brother, Bill, owned the Desert Queen for 2 years; however, the 30–40,000 dollars yielded from a good-sized pocket of ore was squandered by high-living Jim (later to be convicted of counterfitting) and the bank reclaimed the mine.

Hard-rock miner William Keys took control of the mine in 1915, Altadena jeweler Frederick Morton in 1931. Morton was convinced by a dubious "mining engineer" to acquire and to invest heavily in the Desert Queen. Against all

There's gold in them thar hills north of Jumbo Rocks.

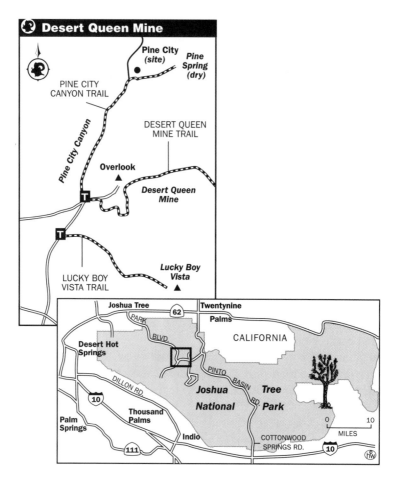

odds, the miners under the supervision of "Mr. Hapwell" actually struck pay dirt. Hapwell set up a secret stamp mill nearby to process the ore and, of course, pocketed the profits. Meanwhile the fast-going-broke Morton sold stock in the Desert Queen without incorporating—a violation of securities law that soon got him convicted of fraud. The mysterious, and by some accounts wealthy, Mr. Hapwell, dropped out of sight.

You can visit the ruins of the Desert Queen from a northern trailhead shared with the path to Pine City or from a southern trailhead at Split Rock Picnic Area.

DIRECTIONS TO TRAILHEAD From the park highway, opposite the Geology Tour Road, turn right (north) for 1.25 miles to a parking area for the mine.

THE HIKE The path, an old mine road, heads east, past some building foundations. The trail forks. The right fork goes 2 miles south, past the site of the Eagle Cliff Mine to Split Rock Picnic Area.

Adventurous hikers can take the left fork and climb a bit through pinyon pine- and juniper-dotted Desert Queen Wash, passing a mining area called John's Camp and traveling 3 miles to the park road.

■ PINE CITY
Pine City Trail
To Pine City is 3 miles round trip with
100-foot elevation gain

The name Pine City is a half-truth. It's not a city, or even a town or hamlet, just a long-abandoned mining camp. Not even a single building stands at the site of this early twentieth-century enterprise.

But pines it has aplenty. This bold, boulder-piled country, watered very occasionally by rains and runoff, is prime habitat for scores of pinyon pine. Turbinella oak and juniper join the pines and weave dark green designs onto the earthtone-colored background of this desert tapestry.

DIRECTIONS TO TRAILHEAD From Highway 62 in Joshua Tree (the town), drive 16 miles south on Park Boulevard to Cap Rock Junction. Go left and proceed 6 miles to the signed Geology Tour Road. However, don't turn right on it; instead, turn north (left) on the dirt road opposite it and travel 1.3 miles to a parking area and the trailhead.

(The parking area is also the trailhead for the Desert Queen Mine hike.)

THE HIKE March along the old mining road across Joshua tree-dotted terrain. Your route crosses several washes.

About a mile out, the trail begins a very modest ascent as it approaches great jumbles of boulders. Substantial stands of pinyon pine around the rocks herald your arrival at Pine City.

After exploring the many unusual rock formations and recesses, and a couple of fenced mine shafts, return the way you came.

See Map on Page 168

■ LUCKY BOY VISTA
Lucky Boy Vista Trail
To Elton Mine and Vista is 2.5 miles
round trip with 100-foot elevation gain

Lucky is the hiker who enjoys a clear-day view from Lucky Boy Vista. The mini-panorama includes Split Rock and nature's stonework surrounding it, as well as the hills and valleys of the great high desert beyond.

The national park boasts many viewpoints and summits that deliver more far-reaching views, but there is something about the vista from Lucky Boy that's more intimate, and very special. For the solitary hiker, such an overlook seems to inspire contemplation and when viewed with fellow hikers, seems to nudge conversation into philosophical directions.

Only a fenced-off mine shaft remains of the Elton Mine, an early twentieth-century endeavor. This hike's goal is the vista point and the fine desert saunter leading to it.

DIRECTIONS TO TRAILHEAD From Highway 62 in Joshua Tree (the town), drive 16 miles south on Park Boulevard to Cap Rock Junction. Go left and proceed 6 miles to the signed Geology Tour Road; however, don't turn right on it. Instead, turn left (north) on the dirt road opposite it and travel 0.9 mile to a parking area and the trailhead.

THE HIKE The old dirt road ascends very gradually. Joining the ubiquitous yuccas and Joshua trees dotting the desertscape are pinyon pines. Pine "City" (see Pine City Hike) is nearby.

Pause to admire the snow-capped summits of Mt. San Jacinto and Mt. San Gorgonio. Stay on the main road to the farthest edge of the plateau to reach the overlook.

■ RYAN MOUNTAIN
Ryan Mountain Trail
From Sheep Pass to Ryan Mountain is 4 miles round trip with 700-foot elevation gain

This hike tours some Joshua trees, visits Indian Cave, and ascends Ryan Mountain for a nice view of the rocky wonderland in this part of Joshua Tree National Park. Ryan Mountain is named for the Ryan brothers, Thomas and Jep, who had a homestead at the base of the mountain.

The view from atop Ryan Mountain is to be savored, and is one of the finest in the National Park.

DIRECTIONS TO TRAILHEAD From the Joshua Tree National Park Visitor Center at Twentynine Palms, drive 3 miles south on Utah Trail Road (the main park road), keeping right at "Pinto Wye" junction and continuing another 8 miles to Sheep Pass Campground on your left. Park in the Ryan Mountain parking area. You may also begin this hike from the Indian Cave Turnout just up the road. Be sure to visit Indian Cave; a number of bedrock mortars found in the cave suggests its use as a work site by its aboriginal inhabitants.

THE HIKE From Sheep Pass Campground, the trail skirts the base of Ryan Mountain and passes through a lunar landscape of rocks and Joshua trees.

Soon you intersect a well-worn side trail coming up from your right. If you like, follow this brief trail down to Indian Cave, typical of the kind of shelter sought by the nomadic Cahuilla and Serrano clans that traveled this desert land.

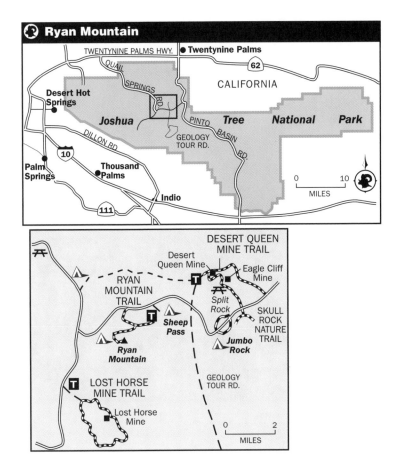

Continuing past the junction, Ryan Mountain Trail ascends moderately-to-steeply toward the peak. En route, you'll pass some very old rocks which make up the core off this mountain and the nearby Little San Bernardino range. For eons, these rocks have, since their creation, been metamorphosed by heat and pressure into completely new types, primarily gneiss and schist. No one knows their exact age, but geologists believe they're several hundred million years old.

Atop Ryan Mountain (5,470 feet) you can sign the summit register, located in a tin can stuck in a pile of rocks that marks the top of the mountain. From the peak, you're treated to a panoramic view of Lost Horse, Queen, Hidden, and Pleasant valleys. There's a lot of geologic history in the rocks shimmering on the ocean of sand below. Not all the rocks you see are as ancient as the ones on Ryan Mountain. Middle-aged rocks, predominately quartz monzonite, are found at Hidden Valley, Jumbo Rocks and White Tank. Younger rocks made of basaltic lava are mere infants at less than a million years old; they are found in Pleasant Valley.

Sunsets are spectacular on Ryan Mountain.

■ LOST HORSE MINE
Lost Horse Mine Trail
To Lost Horse Mine is 3.5 miles round trip
with 400-foot elevation gain

Lost Horse Mine was the most successful gold mining operation in this part of the Mojave. More than 9,000 ounces of gold were processed from ore dug here in the late 1890s. The mine's 10-stamp mill still stands, along with a couple of large cyanide settling tanks and a huge winch used on the main shaft. The trail to the mine offers a close-up look back into a colorful era and some fine views into the heart of the national park.

Many are the legends that swirl like the desert winds around the Lost Horse Mine. As the story goes, Johnny Lang in 1893 was camping in Pleasant Valley when his horse got loose. He tracked it out to the ranch belonging to Jim McHaney, who told Lang his horse was "no longer lost" and threatened Lang's health and future.

Lang wandered over to the camp of fellow prospector Dutch Diebold, who told him that he, too, had been threatened by McHaney and his cowboys. A pity too, because he, Diebold had discovered a promising gold prospect, but had been unable to mark his claim's boundaries. After sneaking in to inspect the claim, Johnny Lang and his father, George, purchased all rights from Diebold for $1,000.

At first it looked like a bad investment, because the Langs were prevented by McHaney's thugs from reaching their claim. Partners came and went, and by 1895, Johnny Lang owned the mine with the Ryan brothers, Thomas and Jep. Peak production years for the mine were 1896 through 1899. Gold ingots were hidden in a freight wagon and transported to Indio. The ruse fooled any would-be highwaymen.

But thievery of another sort plagued the Lost Horse Mine. The theft was of amalgam, lumps of quicksilver from which gold could later be separated. Seems in this matter of amalgam, the mill's day shift, supervised by Jep Ryan, far out-produced the night shift, supervised by Lang. One of Ryan's men espied Lang stealing the amalgam. When Ryan gave Lang a choice—sell his share of the mine for $12,000 or go to the penitentiary—Lang sold out.

Alas, Johnny Lang came to a sad end. Apparently, his stolen and buried amalgams supported him for quite some time, but by the end of 1924, he was old, weak, and living in an isolated cabin. And hungry. He had shot and eaten his four burros and was forced to walk into town for food. He never made it. His partially mummified body wrapped in a canvas sleeping bag was found by prospector/rancher Bill Keys alongside present-day Keys View Road. He was buried where he fell.

DIRECTIONS TO TRAILHEAD From the central part of Joshua Tree National Park, turn south from Caprock Junction on Keys Road and drive 2.5 miles. Turn left on a short dirt road. Here you'll find a Park Service interpretive display about Johnny Lang's checkered career. (You can also visit Lang's grave, located a hundred feet north of the Lost Horse Mine turnoff on Keys Road.) The trail, a continuation of Lost Horse Mine Road, begins at a road barrier.

THE HIKE The trail, the old mine road, climbs above the left side of a wash.

An alternative route, for the first (or last) mile, is to walk from the parking area directly up the wash. Pinyon pine and the nolina (often mistaken for a yucca) dot the wash. Nolina leaves are more flexible than those of yucca, and its flowers smaller. The wash widens in about 0.75 mile and forks; bear left and a short ascent will take you to the mine road. Turn right on the road and follow it to the mine.

A few open shafts remain near the Lost Horse, so be careful when you explore the mine ruins. Note the stone foundations opposite the mill site. A little village for the mine workers was built here in the late 1890s. Scramble up to the top of the hill above the mine for a panoramic view of Queen Valley, Pleasant Valley, and the desert ranges beyond.

■ CAP ROCK
Cap Rock Nature Trail
0.4-mile loop

Perched atop a monolithic dome is a visor-shaped boulder resembling the bill on a baseball cap. Signs along the nature trail interpret Mojave Desert geology and plant life.

The path loops among boulder formations and affords good views of Cap Rock and the many climbers who scale it.

DIRECTIONS TO TRAILHEAD   From Highway 62 in Joshua Tree (the town) drive 5 miles south on Park Blvd to the national park's west entrance. Continue 15 more miles to a junction and turn right on Keys View Road. The signed parking area for Cap Rock is located just 0.1 mile down the road from the intersection on the left (east) side of Keys View Road.

THE HIKE   Signs along the level, paved, wheelchair-accessible path interpret what author Mary Austin called a "land of little rain." Bone-dry this land may be but it's certainly not lifeless. Mormon tea, Mojave yucca, peachthorn, and more grow alongside cholla and beavertail cactus.

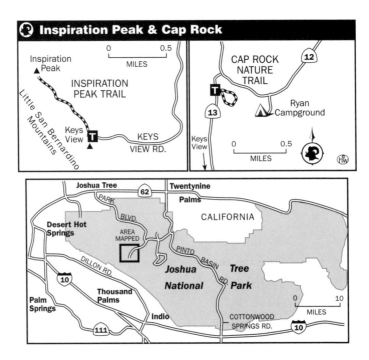

Some see a baseball cap atop this dome—hence the name, Cap Rock.

■ KEYS VIEW
Inspiration Peak Trail
From Keys View to Inspiration Peak
is 1.5 miles round trip with 400-foot elevation gain

Hikers know that the very best views are not often found by following short paved trails to official, guardrail-lined park overlooks. Keys View is a case in point. This viewpoint, arguably the best in the national park, offers magnificent vistas by any standard; however, the vistas are even better from adjacent Inspiration Peak.

At 5,558 feet in elevation, Inspiration Peak is a bit higher than such well-known park summits as Warren Peak, Eureka Peak, and Ryan Mountain and the view offered unequaled. A short but steep climb to the point rewards the hiker with all the vistas available from Keys View plus additional panoramas of the national park and a glimpse of the mountains in Mexico.

Keys View and Inspiration Peak are perched on the crest of the Little San Bernardino Mountains, a rather mellow-looking range when viewed from the north side. From the crest, however, the mountains appear anything but gentle as the south side plunges precipitously thousands of feet toward the Coachella Valley far below.

Clear-day views encompass the Coachella Valley with the Salton Sea shimmering mirage-like at the valley's south end. The Santa Rosa and San Jacinto

Mountains (crowned by 10,894-foot Mt. San Jacinto) form the valley's far wall. Mighty Mt. San Gorgonio (11,499 feet), the Southland's highest peak, is visible to the northwest.

It's often quite breezy atop Keys View and Inspiration Peak and on days when smog obscures Palm Springs and its desert suburbs, I'm overtaken with the urge to send some fresh air down below where its so obviously needed. Park service interpretive displays explain the effects of air pollution on the valley, the park, and the Keys View view.

DIRECTIONS TO TRAILHEAD From Highway 62 in Joshua Tree (the town), head south on Park Boulevard 15 miles to Cap Rock Junction at the turnoff for Keys View. Continue south 6.2 miles to road's end and parking.

THE HIKE First join the paved path to Keys View and partake of the fine vistas. Retrace your steps and locate Inspiration Peak Trail, signed by a hiker symbol, on the north side of the parking lot.

As you ascend steeply above Keys View, ever more expansive vistas unfold. Continue past Inspiration Peak's first summit to a second higher one, crowned by piles of dark boulders.

On a clear day, you can see forever—or at least to the Salton Sea.

■ JUMBO ROCKS
Skull Rock Interpretive Trail
1.7-mile loop from Jumbo Rocks Campground

The terrain crossed by Skull Rock Interpretive Trail is Joshua Tree National Park to the max: a vast array of rock formations, a Joshua tree forest, the yucca-dotted desert open and wide. While the scenery is superb, the path per se is not. (I hold a distinctly minority viewpoint; the trail is one of the park's most popular.)

Skull Rock, the highlight of the hike, is one of the many rocks in the area that appear to resemble humans, dinosaurs, monsters, cathedrals, and castles.

Half the hike is via a nature trail that provides an introduction to the park's flora, wildlife, and geology. The diversity of flora en route includes the pint-sized turbinella oak and the teddy bear cholla. The other half winds among rock monoliths on the opposite side of the park road from Jumbo Rocks Campground.

A certain dogged determination is required to make this hike a loop. The trail north of the road is tricky to follow in places—though you won't get lost because it's not far from the road. For a loop route, you have to walk on paved road through Jumbo Rocks Campground.

DIRECTIONS TO TRAILHEAD Begin in the Jumbo Rocks Campground, located 4 miles west of Pinto Wye on the park's main road. Look for trailhead parking and the signed trail opposite the campground entrance on the north side of the road. A second signed trailhead, where this walk begins, is inside Jumbo Rocks Campground at the camp's Loop E entrance.

THE HIKE Descend the camp road to the signed nature trail. Signs pointing out plants from catsclaw acacia to creosote complement your traverse of this handsome high desert environment. After 0.5 mile of educational adventure, the path reaches the base of Skull Rock.

The return loop crosses the park road and meanders through a wash and among boulders and across rock outcroppings. Rock cairns mark the way as you head back to the trailhead opposite the entrance of Jumbo Rocks Campground.

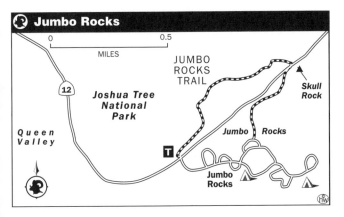

■ LIVE OAK AND IVANPAH TANKS
Ivanpah Tank Trail
1-mile loop

Ivanpah is one of the many tanks—rock- and cement-lined water catchment basins—built by early twentieth-century cattle ranchers (see the Wonderland of Rocks hike). This hike visits Ivanpah Tank and Live Oak Tank, both of which hold much more sand than water these days, via a handsome little desert wash.

Live Oak, which names a tank, a road, and a picnic area, refers to an unusual oak that botanists believe is a hybrid between the valley oak, found between the Santa Monica Mountains near Los Angeles and the San Joaquin Valley, and the small-sized turbinella oak, which thrives in the park's uplands.

Ivanpah Tank Trail follows a wash past the famed oak to Live Oak and Ivanpah tanks, then loops back to the picnic area.

DIRECTIONS TO TRAILHEAD The path begins at the west end of Live Oak Picnic Area.

THE HIKE From the picnic area, head south toward the big old oak located at the base of the rock cluster known as the Pope's Hat. Down-canyon a short ways from the "Live Oak" is a low stone wall—what remains of Live Oak Tank.

The sandy wash angles east below rocky, juiper-dotted canyon walls, soon opening up a bit and reaching sand-filled Ivanpah Tank.

Energetic hikers may continue following the wash down-canyon a mile or so. Otherwise, ascend the left wall of the wash and return by a dirt road that once provided access to Ivanpah Tank. The old road leads back to the east side of the picnic area, whereupon you follow the picnic ground road back to the trailhead.

■ PINYON WELL
AND PUSHAWALLA PLATEAU
Pinyon Well Trail
From parking area to Pinyon Well site is 1.5 miles round trip;
to Pushawalla Plateau is 6.5 miles round trip with 1,500-foot
elevation gain

Water, especially in the desert where there is so little of it, is the very essence of life. Pinyon Well was one such life-giving source, a critical water supply for teamsters, miners and their families.

During the 1890s, prospectors constructed a crude arrasta, then a more elaborate stamp mill at Pinyon Well in order to extract gold from ore dug from the Lost Horse, the Desert Queen, and other nearby mines. Teamsters guided their wagons through Pushawalla Canyon to Pinyon Well.

At the dawn of the twentieth century, Pinyon Well was a little mining hamlet, a community that included women and children—an unusual state of affairs. In later years, Pinyon Well's valuable water was piped to the Piute Basin, serving mining operations until the early 1930s.

Pinyon Well put a gleam in the eye of one 1920s developer, who envisioned a resort community rising from the the wide open spaces. Pinyon Well, however, could not provide sufficient water to become another Palm Springs.

This hike follows traces of the old road and visits Pinyon Well, where water still seeps and attracts birds and wildlife. Past the well, the trail ascends Pushawalla Plateau for excellent views of the Coachella Valley and Palm Springs.

DIRECTIONS TO TRAILHEAD Follow the Geology Tour Road 9.5 miles until it reaches the signed Pinyon Well turnoff.

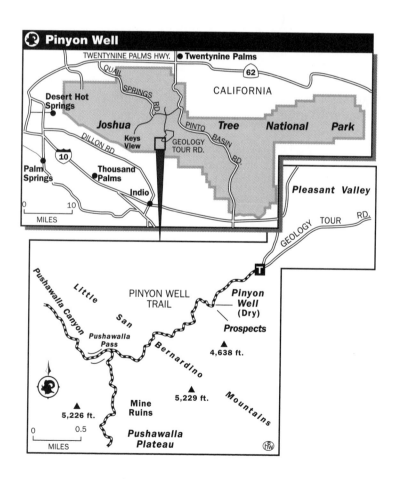

THE HIKE Proceed up-canyon 0.75 mile to Pinyon Well. Some cement tanks, rusty pipes, and foundations of old cabins mark the site of Pinyon Wells. It seems a bit forlorn, desolate even, and it's easier to imagine teamsters swearing at their mules than happy families living here.

The path continues with the canyon another 0.75 mile and forks left. In another 0.25 mile the canyon turns south, but you stay to the right with the somewhat faint road. A little farther along, the road becomes steeper and rockier as it climbs to Pushawalla Plateau. Atop the broad, pinyon pine- and Joshua tree-covered plateau is a view of Mt. San Jacinto and some of the northern valleys and ranges of the park.

A trail continues some 8 more miles over the plateau and the crest of the Little San Bernardino Mountains all the way out to Dillon Road in Desert Hot Springs.

■ ARCH ROCK
Arch Rock Nature Trail
0.3 mile round trip

Arch Rock crowns one of the many granite monoliths located near White Tank Campground. The natural arch, 135 million years in the making, looks like it might be a scaled-down version of the great sandstone arches of the American Southwest, but actually is a special variety of igneous rock known as White Tank granite.

The complex forces required to create the arch and the area's unique geology are detailed by trailside signs and displays. These en route explanations go well beyond the usual once-over-lightly geology lessons of a typical nature path. While some of the textbook-style interpretation might be difficult to understand, everyone will appreciate the visual aids provided by this outdoor classroom—the splendid boulder formations.

DIRECTIONS TO TRAILHEAD From Highway 62 in Twentynine Palms, drive 9 miles south on Utah Trail to the park's Y junction. Head left and continue 3 more miles to the turnoff (left) for White Tank Campground. Drive into the campground and look for the signed Arch Rock Nature Trail near campsite 9.

THE HIKE The trail curves through intriguing stone formations to the base of the arch. Arch Rock extends some 15 feet skyward and spans about 30 feet.

Before joining the return leg of the loop, take a short trip to White Tank, the old cattle tank that gave the campground as well as a variety of granite its name. To reach the tank from the front of Arch Rock, you'll scramble northeast among boulders about a hundred yards.

Cattle ranchers made the tank in the early 1900s by constructing a rock and cement dam across the width of a narrow wash. Rainwater and hillside run-off

Guess how Arch Rock got its name.

pooled behind the dam and provided water to slake the considerable thirst of the desert-grazing cows. White Tank fell into disuse and filled with sand long ago; however, the still-moist environment attracts birds and wildlife.

■ CHOLLA CACTUS GARDEN
Cholla Cactus Garden Nature Trail
0.25-mile loop

Highlight of this easy path is a dense concentration of Bigelow cholla, often called "teddy bear" cactus because of the (deceptively) soft, even fluffy appearance of its sharp spines. A closer look reveals a cholla that's not really fuzzy-wuzzy like a teddy bear, but more like the acupuncturist from hell armed with thousands of fine needles.

While prickly cacti of all kinds have plagued desert travelers from time immemorial, the Bigelow has long been regarded as a particularly irksome menace. Merely brushing against this cholla results in its spines jabbing and affixing to clothing and bare skin. Botanists tell us that Bigelows have microscopic barbs on the ends of their bristles.

The extensive cholla patch lies on the southernmost edge of the transitional region between the Mojave and Colorado deserts. If you drive to the garden from the northern part of the park, you might notice the shift in flora: Goodbye Joshua tree (strict in its loyalty to the Mojave Desert) and hello creosote, characteristic of the Colorado Desert.

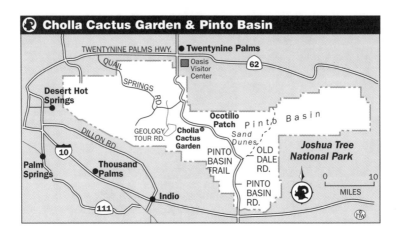

While an interpretive pamphlet (never available when I've walked this nature trail) might be helpful, it's not really necessary to enjoy Cholla Cactus Garden. The beauty of this path is in the abundant Bigelows and views out to the Pinto Mountains to the north and the Hexie Mountains to the southwest.

DIRECTIONS TO TRAILHEAD From Highway 62 in Twentynine Palms, drive 9 miles south to Pinto Wye. Bear left and continue 6.2 miles south to signed Cholla Cactus Garden on the right side of the road.

THE HIKE This easy interpretive path is best hiked early or late in the day when the cholla are backlit and particularly photogenic. The cactus with its dark brown bases, rust-colored torso, and green top is a wonder to behold—and photograph.

■ PINTO BASIN DUNES
Pinto Basin Trail
To sand dunes is 2 miles or so round trip

As a habitat for humans, Pinto Basin is, to say the least, forbidding: a barren lowland surrounded by austere mountains, and punctuated by sand dunes.

Nevertheless, some two to four thousand years ago, native people lived here. Environmental conditions were friendlier then—creeks flowed across the center of the basin and a forest cloaked the mountainsides.

Still, even in these better times, the people who lived had to make adaptations to desert living and forge some specialized tools; so unique were these ancients, anthropologists describe them as "Pinto Man." A gifted amateur archeologist from Twentynine Palms, Elizabeth Campbell began recovering artifacts from the Pinto Basin in the 1930s. Since then, evidence of "Pinto Man

Culture" has been found in other widely scattered parts of the California Desert.

While today's visitor has a difficult time imagining how even the most primitive of people could have survived in the harsh environs of the Pinto Basin, real estate developers of the 1920s were not at all discouraged by the forbidding land and began selling parcels for homes and ranches. The Lake County Development Syndicate promised would-be buyers that an investment in Pinto Basin real estate would soon pay off big time—as soon as a water source was developed. The water never came, of course, and the Depression of the 1930s ended the developer's scheme.

The hike to Pinto Basin's sand dunes begins at Turkey Flat, the site of an unsuccessful poultry farm in the 1920s. For experienced, well-conditioned hikers, Turkey Flat is the departure point for the climb of 3,983-foot Pinto Mountain, which lords over the north side of the basin. Three routes, 9 to 13 miles round trip, ascend washes, then tackle the shoulders of the peak.

DIRECTIONS TO TRAILHEAD This hike begins from the Turkey Flat Trailhead off Pinto Basin Road, 5 miles east of Ocotillo Patch and some 12 miles west of the junction with Old Dale Road.

THE HIKE The mellow ramble to the dunes, bedecked by lilies and other spring wildflowers, is one for the whole family. From the parking area, head northeast to the low sandy ridge. Frolic in the sand until tired and return the same way.

■ COTTONWOOD SPRING OASIS
Cottonwood Spring Nature Trail
1 mile round trip

An interpreted nature trail travels through rolling hills on its way to Cottonwood Spring Oasis, haven for birds and desert wildlife. Nearby are some Native American bedrock mortars.

Largely human-made Cottonwood Spring Oasis was a popular rest and overnight stop for freight-haulers and prospectors journeying from Banning to the Dale Goldfield east of Twentynine Palms. For a time, the spring's abundant waters (some 3,000 gallons a day during the early 1900s) were pumped up to the Iron Chief Mine in the Eagle Mountains.

The spring's output declined over the decades, dwindling to just a few gallons per day. Seismic activity related to the 1971 San Fernando Earthquake prompted an increased flow of water, geologists believe.

One of the park's best interpretive paths, Cottonwood Spring Nature Trail extends between Cottonwood Spring Campground and Cottonwood Spring Oasis, and can be hiked from either direction. Those hikers adhering to the save-the-best-for-last theory will start from the camp and hike to the oasis.

DIRECTIONS TO TRAILHEAD From Highway 62 in Twentynine Palms, travel 9 miles south on Utah Trail to the Pinto Wye junction, bear left, and travel 32 miles to Cottonwood Spring Campground. The trailhead is located at the end of camp, near site 13.

From Interstate 10, some 25 miles east of Indio, exit on Cottonwood Canyon Road head north 8 miles to Cottonwood Spring Visitor Center.

THE HIKE Signs en route interpret plants and animals of the Colorado Desert, which predominates in the southeastern portion of the national park. Particularly intriguing are explanations of how the native Cahuilla used a wide variety of plants for food and medicine.

The path meanders through rolling hills to Cottonwood Spring, where the cottonwoods and palms planted long ago by miners and desert travelers now shade a lovely oasis.

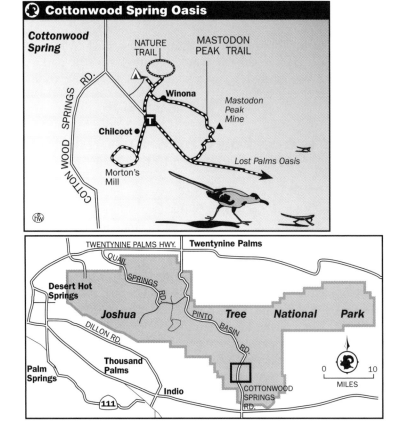

MOORTEN'S MILL
Moorten's Mill Trail
1 mile round trip

During the 1930s, "Cactus" Slim Moorten operated a stamp mill that processed ore from mines in the Cottonwood Springs area. After his mining days, Moorten turned desert landscaper and developed a reputation for locating and transplanting exotic cactus species during the worldwide cactus craze in the early 1950s. Moorten, and his wife, Patricia, eventually founded Moorten's Botanical Garden in Palm Springs.

Except for some building foundations and rusted tanks, not much remains of the mill site; however, another historic attraction nearby invites a visit.

In the early 1900s, teamsters drove their teams over a stretch of nasty road near Cottonwood Spring known as "Little Chilcoot Pass," a comparison to the infamous divide that faced Yukon prospectors on the way to the Klondike gold fields in 1898.

The pass—a bypass, really—was built to get over a low cliff in a wash. Even by 1906 accounts it was clear this so-called shortcut wasn't; heavily laden ore wagons and their teams found passage extremely difficult. Misuse of public funds and moronic engineering were two common complaints about the pass while the reaction of teamsters to this road cannot be printed here.

DIRECTIONS TO TRAILHEAD From the Cottonwood Spring Visitor Center, drive 1.2 mile east to Cottonwood Spring.

THE HIKE From Cottonwood Spring, follow the wash downstream. You'll travel past smoke trees and mesquite and other wash-typical flora.

Cottonwood Canyon soon narrows and you pass below high, cactus-dotted rock walls. Next is the Little Chilcoot Pass; digging it with hand tools must have been quite an ordeal. Beyond the pass are the rusty ruins of Moorten's Mill.

See Map on Page 184

■ MASTODON PEAK
Mastodon Peak Trail
3-mile loop with 400-foot elevation gain

Mastodon Peak Trail packs a lot of sightseeing into a 3-mile hike: a cottonwood-shaded oasis, gold mine, and grand desert view.

Mastodon Peak, named by early prospectors for its behemoth-like profile, was the site of the Mastodon Mine, a gold mine worked intermittently from 1919 to 1932. The ore was of high quality; however, the main ore body was cut off by a fault.

A mile down the trail from the mine is Winona, where some concrete foundations remain to mark the former mill and little town. Winona was home to workers at the Mastodon Mine, as well as workers at the mill, which processed ore from a number of nearby mines.

Views from elephantine-shaped Mastodon Peak include the Cottonwood Springs area and the Eagle Mountains. Clear-day panoramas extend from Mt. San Jacinto above Palm Springs to the Salton Sea.

DIRECTIONS TO TRAILHEAD Entering the national park from the south (via Interstate 10), travel 8 miles north of the park boundary to Cottonwood Spring Campground. Park at the Cottonwood Spring day-use area.

THE HIKE From the parking area, the path proceeds immediately to Cottonwood Spring, a collection of cottonwoods, California fan palms and cattails crowded around a trickling spring.

The path continues 0.5 mile, following a wash to a junction. Lost Palms Trail heads right, but you take the left fork to ascend Mastodon Peak. A short spur trail leads to the summit. Enjoy the views from Cottonwood Campground just below to the Coachella Valley beyond.

The main trail descends to the shafts and ruins of Mastodon Mine. Another mile of travel brings you to Winona. Some shady trees—including eucalyptus planted by miners—offer a pleasant rest stop. A last 0.25 mile brings you to a fork in the road. The right fork leads to the campground; the left fork returns to Cottonwood Spring parking lot.

See Map on Page 184

■ LOST PALMS OASIS
Lost Palms Oasis Trail
From Cottonwood Springs Campground to Lost Palms Oasis is 8 miles round trip with 300-foot elevation gain

Lost Palms Oasis Trail passes through a cactus garden, crosses a number of desert washes, and takes you to the two southern oases in the National Park: Cottonwood and Lost Palms.

Largely human-made, Cottonwood Spring Oasis was once a popular overnight stop for freight-haulers and prospectors during the mining years of 1870 to 1910. Travelers and teamsters journeying from Banning to the Dale Goldfield east of Twentynine Palms rested at the oasis.

Lost Palms Oasis is a hidden gem. Nearly 100 palms are found in the deep canyon where steep igneous walls sparkle in the desert sun.

DIRECTIONS TO TRAILHEAD From the south end of Joshua Tree National Park, follow the park road 8 miles to Cottonwood Spring Campground. Park your car at the campground. The trailhead is at the end of the campground.

THE HIKE Leaving Cottonwood Spring Campground, the trail ambles through a low desert environment of green-trunked palo verde, ironwood and cottonwood trees, spindly ocotillo plants, and cholla cactus. Park Service identification plaques describe the area's flora and fauna.

The trail, a bit difficult to follow through the sandy wash, brings you to Cottonwood Spring Oasis in 0.5 mile. Cottonwood Spring is home to a wide variety of birds and a large number of bees.

From Cottonwood Spring, the trail marches over sandy hills, past heaps of huge rocks and along sandy draws and washes. A number of Park Service signs point the way at possibly confusing junctions. Finally, you rise above the washes and climb to a rocky outcropping overlooking the canyon harboring Lost Palms Oasis. From the overlook, descend the steep path around the boulders to the palms.

Little surface water is present at Lost Palms Oasis, but enough is underground for the palms to remain healthy. Lost Palms remained relatively untouched throughout the mining years, though some of its water was pumped to settlements 8 miles to the south at Chiriaco Summit. Adjacent to Lost Palms Canyon is a handsome upper canyon called Dike Springs.

Shy and reclusive desert bighorn sheep are often seen around this oasis—particularly in hot weather when they need water more often.

The palm oasis: A world apart from the world-class resort—a spectacular natural attraction.

CHAPTER 5

PALM SPRINGS
AND THE COACHELLA VALLEY

I n the early years of the twentieth century, it was called a "Desert Eden," "Our Araby" and "A Garden in the Sun." Now it's called a "Desert Hollywood," "Fairway Living" and "Rodeo Drive East."

Palm Springs today means different things to different people, but one thing is for certain—the golf courses, condos and country clubs of the resort are a far cry from what the first residents of Agua Caliente intended.

What most Palm Springs pioneers intended was to leave this desert land more or less alone. Early twentieth-century health-seekers and nature lovers recognized their discovery for what it was—a true oasis. Here was a palm-dotted retreat where an ancient hot springs gushed forth. Here was nature, simple and unadorned.

Some residents championed the creation of Palm Canyon National Monument, in order to preserve the canyons on the outskirts of Palm Springs known collectively as the Indian Canyons—Palm, Murray, and Andreas. The national monument was approved by Congress in 1922 but no funds were ever allocated and the palm canyons never did win National Park Service protection.

Finally, in 1990, a sizable portion of the palm canyons, as well as the surrounding mountains came under federal protection with the establishment of the Santa Rosa Mountains National Scenic Area, administered by the U.S. Bureau of Land Management. More recently the name was changed to Santa Rosa and San Jacinto Mountains National Monument, a better reflection of the monument's boundaries and mission. National forest, state parks, and BLM land is included within the monument.

What makes Palm Springs and the Coachella Valley so compelling to the hiker is the backdrop of majestic mountains. The mountains beckon the sojourner afoot with world renowned scenic beauty, unique cultural and historical sites, an exceptional biodiversity, and a wide-ranging and substantial collection of parklands.

When high and steep mountains thrust skyward from a low-elevation desert floor, the result is multiple habitats in close proximity and an unusual array of plant species and wildlife. An extraordinary biodiversity occurs in the life zones where the Santa Rosa and San Jacinto ranges rise from the Coachella Valley. Majestic palm oases and some 500 species of plants are part of that remarkable diversity found in the region.

The mountains are critical habitat for the Peninsular Ranges bighorn sheep. Shrinking habitat and other factors may be contributing to the bighorn's serious population decline. One of the national monument's most important missions is to ensure the survival of the sheep.

The Santa Rosa Mountains have been the home of the native Cahuilla for at least 3,000 years and continue to have a strong heritage value to the contemporary Cahuilla. This chapter highlights hiking in many locales that were important to the Cahuilla, including San Andreas Canyon, Tahquitz Canyon, and Pinyon Flat.

The Palm Springs area offers hiking for all levels of ability and degrees of enthusiasm. Experienced hikers can roam nearly 100,000 acres preserved in four wilderness areas in the Santa Rosa and San Jacinto Mountains National Monument. Those looking for gentler journeys on the edge of Palm Springs can hike what the BLM calls the Bogart Trail Complex, a network of canyon and foothill pathways.

During the 1980s, 1990s, and now in the twenty-first century, the Coachella Valley has undergone, and continues to undergo, tremendous residential and resort development. Thus, the surrounding parkland is becoming an even more valuable resource and natural attraction to residents, as well as to visitors from around the world.

"Essentially, the desert is Nature in her simplest expression," wrote nature writer and Palm Springs resident Joseph Smeaton Chase. The Living Desert Preserve, Palm Canyon, Santa Rosa and San Jacinto Mountains National Monument, Big Morongo Canyon, and the Coachella Valley Preserve are places for the hiker to commune with this simple nature.

■ BIG MORONGO CANYON
Big Morongo Canyon Trail
To waterfall is 2.5 miles round trip; to canyon mouth is 12 miles round trip with 1,900-foot elevation loss

For many centuries native peoples used Big Morongo Canyon as a passageway between the high and low deserts. The last of these nomads to inhabit the canyon were Serrano people known as the Morongo, for whom the canyon is named. When settlers entered the area in the mid-nineteenth century, the Morongos were forced onto a reservation and the canyon became the property of ranchers. Today, Big Morongo Canyon is managed and protected by the Nature Conservancy and the U.S. Bureau of Land Management.

The relative abundance of water is the key to both Big Morongo's long human history and its botanical uniqueness. Several springs bubble up in the reserve and

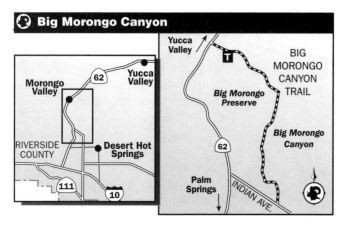

Big Morongo Canyon

one of the California desert's very few year-round creeks flows through the canyon. Dense thickets of cottonwood and willow, as well as numerous water-loving shrubs line Big Morongo Creek. This lush, crowded riparian vegetation sharply contrasts with the well-spaced creosote community typical of the high and dry slopes of the reserve and of the open desert beyond.

The oasis at Big Morongo is a crucial water supply for the fox, bobcat, raccoon, coyote and bighorn sheep. Gopher snakes, rosy boas, chuckawallas and California tree frogs are among the amphibians and reptiles in residence. The permanent water supply also makes it possible for the showy western tiger swallowtail and other butterflies to thrive, along with several species of dragon flies and water bugs.

Big Morongo Canyon is best known for its wide variety of birds, which are numerous because the canyon is not only at the intersection of two deserts, but also at the merging of two climate zones—arid and coastal. These climates, coupled with the wet world of the oasis, means the preserve is an attractive stopover for birds on their spring and fall migrations.

More than two hundred bird species have been sighted, including the rare vermilion flycatcher and the least Bell's vireo. Commonly seen all-year residents include starlings, house finches and varieties of quail and hummingbirds.

The preserve offers several short loop trails ranging from a quarter to one mile long. Some of the wetter canyon bottom sections of trail are crossed by wooden boardwalks, which keep hikers dry and fragile creekside flora from being trampled. Desert Wash, Cottonwood, Willow, Yucca Ridge, and Mesquite Trails explore the environments suggested by their names.

A longer path, Canyon Trail, travels the 6-mile length of Big Morongo Canyon. You could make this a one-way, all downhill journey by arranging a car shuttle or by having someone pick you up on Indian Avenue. Families with small children or those desiring a shorter jaunt will enjoy a 2.5-mile round trip canyon walk to a small waterfall.

DIRECTIONS TO TRAILHEAD From Interstate 10, 15 miles east of Banning and a bit past the Highway 111 turnoff to Palm Springs, exit on Highway 62. Drive 10 miles north to the signed turnoff on your right for Big Morongo

One glimpse of desert bighorn sheep will last a lifetime.

Wildlife Preserve. Turn east and after 0.1 mile you'll see the preserve's service road leading to a parking area.

To reach the end of the trail at the mouth of Big Morongo Canyon, you'll exit on Highway 62 on Indian Avenue and drive exactly a mile to a dirt road on your left. A dip sign precedes the turnoff and a pump enclosed by a chain link fence suggests your parking space.

THE HIKE From the parking lot, you may pick up the trail by the Preserve's interpretive displays or join the dirt road that leads past the caretaker's residence.

Off to the right of the old ranch road, you'll see a pasture lined with cottonwood and a barn built in the 1880s. Often the road is muddy, so detour with the signed and aptly named Mesquite Trail which utilizes a wooden boardwalk to get over the wet spots. As you stand on the boardwalk in the midst of Big Morongo Creek, take a moment to listen to the sound of running water, the many chirping birds, and croaking frogs.

Canyon Trail meanders with the creek for a gentle mile or so and arrives at a corrugated metal check dam that has created a small waterfall. For the less energetic, this is a good turnaround point. The trail continues descending through the canyon with Big Morongo Creek until a bit over 3 miles from the trailhead, the creek suddenly disappears. Actually, the water continues flowing underground through layers of sand.

The canyon widens and so does the trail. About 5 miles from the trailhead is the south gate of the preserve. Compensating for Big Morongo's somewhat inglorious end is a stirring view of snow-capped Mt. San Jacinto, which lies straight ahead. Stick to your right at every opportunity as you exit the canyon and a dirt road will soon deliver you to Indian Avenue.

■ COACHELLA VALLEY PRESERVE
McCallum, Smoke Tree Ranch, Indian Palms Trails
1- to 5-mile loop

I f it looks like a movie set, don't be surprised. Thousand Palms Oasis was the setting for Cecil B. DeMille's 1924 silent film epic, *King of Kings*, and the 1969 movie, *Tell Them Willie Boy is Here*, starring Robert Redford and Katherine Ross. The oasis is something special, and deserving of protection, but that's not why Coachella Valley Preserve was established. The reserve's raison d'être is habitat for the threatened Coachella Valley fringe-toed lizard.

For the most part, *Uma inornata* goes about the business of being a lizard beneath the surface of sand dunes, but scientists have been able to discover some of the peculiar habits of this creature, which manages to survive in places where a summer's day surface temperature may reach 160°F.

The 8-inch reptile is also known as the "sand swimmer" for its ability to dive through sand dunes. Its entrenching tool-shaped skull rams through the sand, while round scales on its skin reduce friction as it "swims." Fringes (large scales) on its toes give the lizard traction —as well as its name.

Alas, all is not fun in the sun for the fringe-toed lizard. The creature must avoid becoming dinner for such predators as roadrunners, snakes, and loggerhead shrikes. But the biggest threat to the lizards continues to be real estate development and consequent loss of habitat.

Fortunately for the fringe-toed lizard, real estate developers, the U.S. Bureau of Land Management, Congress, the California Department of Fish and Game, the U.S. Wildlife Service, and the Nature Conservancy were able to find a common ground and establish a 13,000-acre preserve in 1986. Some conservationists believe the 25-million-dollar price tag accounts for one of the most expensive single species preservation effort of all time.

Still, the reserve would be something special even without its namesake lizard. It protects flora and fauna once common in the Coachella Valley before it grew grapefruit, golf courses, and subdivisions.

Thousand Palms Oasis is California's second-largest collection of native California fan palms. Thousand Palms, along with

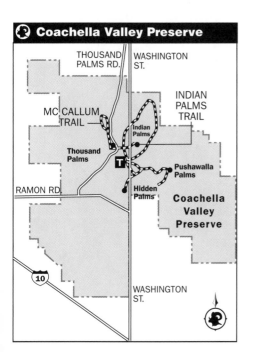

Coachella Valley Preserve hosts the threatened fringe-toed lizard—and plenty of fan palms, too.

Indian Palms, Horseshoe Palms, and a couple of other oases in the reserve came into existence as the result of earthquake faults which brought water to the surface.

Before the reserve was set aside, the Thousand Palms area was purchased in the early 1900s by rancher Louis Wilhelm and his family. The Wilhelms built "Palm House" (now the reserve's visitor center) and by the 1930s were using it as a commissary for campers, scientists, scout troops, and others who wanted to enjoy a weekend in one of their palm-shaded cottages.

DIRECTIONS TO TRAILHEAD From Interstate 10, about 10 miles east of where Highway 111 leads off to Palm Springs, exit on Washington Street/ Ramon Road. Head north on Washington Street, which bends west and continues as Ramon Road. Soon after the bend, turn right (north again) onto Thousand Palms Canyon Road. Continue to the entrance to Coachella Valley Preserve and park in the dirt lot.

THE HIKE Hikers can explore Coachella Valley Preserve on a half-dozen trails. Three of these trails depart from Thousand Palms Oasis. Shortest (a 15-minute walk) is Smoke Tree Ranch Trail, which encircles the palm oasis. Good birdwatching is possible in the mesquite thickets and among the smoke trees. Watch for the smoke tree's bright blue-purple flowers in May or June.

Don't miss McCallum Trail, a 1.5-mile round trip nature trail. It meanders by a jungle of willows, palms, cottonwoods, and mesquite. At the trailhead, pick up an interpretive pamphlet that's keyed to numbered posts along the path.

Indian Palms Trail leads 0.5 mile to small Indian Palm Oasis.

More ambitious hikers will head for Wash Trail which, true to its name, winds through washes in the northern portion of the reserve. You can also visit Bee Rock Mesa, where Malpais Indians camped 5,000 years ago, hike into adjoining Indio Hills County Park, and visit more oases—Horseshoe Palms and Pushawalla Palms.

■ PALM SPRINGS DESERT MUSEUM
Lykken Trail
From Palm Springs Desert Museum to Desert Riders Overlook is 2 miles round trip with 800-foot elevation gain; to Ramon Drive is 4 miles round trip with 800-foot gain

Museum and Lykken Trails offer a good overview of the resort. This hike begins at Palm Springs Desert Museum, where natural science exhibits recreate the unique ecology of Palm Springs and the surrounding Colorado Desert.

Steep Museum Trail ascends the western base of Mt. San Jacinto and junctions with Lykken Trail, which winds through the Palm Springs hills north to Tramway Road and south to Ramon Road. Lykken Trail honors Carl Lykken,

Palms Springs pioneer and the town's first post-master. Lykken, who arrived in 1913, owned a general merchandise store, and later a depart-ment/hardware store.

DIRECTIONS TO TRAILHEAD From Highway 111 (Palm Canyon Drive) in the middle of down-town Palm Springs, turn west on Tahquitz Drive, then a right on Museum Drive. Park in Palm Springs Desert Museum's north lot.

The trail begins back of the museum, between the museum and an administration building, by a plaque honoring Carl Lykken. The trail is closed during the summer months for health reasons (yours).

THE HIKE The trail ascends the rocky slope above the museum. Soon you'll intersect a private road, jog left, then resume trail walking up the mountainside. As you rapidly gain elevation, the view widens from the Desert Fashion Plaza to the outskirts of Palm Springs to the wide-open spaces of the Coachella Valley.

A mile's ascent brings you to a picnic area, built by the Desert Riders, local equestrians whose membership included Carl Lykken. One Desert Rider, for-mer Palm Springs Mayor Frank Bogart, has been a real trail enthusiast whose efforts contributed much to the state's trail system. Bear left (south) on Lykken Trail, which travels the hills above town before descending to Ramon Road near the mouth of Tahquitz Canyon.

■ TAHQUITZ CANYON
Tahquitz Canyon Trail
2 miles round trip with 350-foot elevation gain

After a 30-year closure, the lovely canyon named after the Cahuilla shaman Tahquitz was reopened to hikers in 2001. Storied Tahquitz Canyon, locat-ed just 2 miles as the phainopepla flies from downtown Palm Springs, was acces-sible by tribal ranger-led guided tours until 2005, and is now open for both escorted and independent hiking.

Hike highlights include ancient rock art, diverse desert flora, an early irriga-tion system, and a 60-foot waterfall featured in Frank Capra's classic 1937 film, *Lost Horizon*, starring Ronald Coleman and Jane Wyatt.

As legend has it, Tahquitz, the Cahuilla's first shaman, at first practiced his art to good effect, but soon became increasingly mischievous, then downright dangerous. Such is his power that he can appear to people in downtown Palm Springs or manifest himself as an earthquake or as a fireball in the sky.

The Cahuilla closed the canyon to the public in 1969 when a rowdy crowd left a rock concert and descended into Tahquitz Canyon for several days of partying. In later years, NO TRESPASSING signs, locked gates, and fences slowed but did not stop visitors. Most of the hikers and skinny-dippers enjoyed the picturesque falls and were respectful to the serene scene, but a number of vandals dumped garbage on the canyon floor and spray-painted graffiti on the rocks and boulders. Hippies, hermits, hobos, and homeless folks took up residence in the canyon's caves.

With proceeds from the tribe's Spa Resort & Casino, the Agua Caliente band of the Cahuilla embarked on a 3-year clean-up effort and built a visitor center with educational and cultural exhibits. Visitors can view "The Legend of Tahquitz Canyon" video in a special screening room.

I recommend getting an early start (Tahquitz Canyon Visitor Center opens at 7:30 AM) and arriving in time to watch the rising sun probe the dark recesses of the high walls of Tahquitz Canyon. If you take the first (8 AM) tour of the day or choose to hit the trail early on your own, you'll beat the crowds, beat the heat, and have the best chance of spotting wildlife.

The interpreted hike proceeds at a very slow pace, and is unlikely to appeal to younger children, who will probably not appreciate the tribal ranger's narrative about the Cahuilla's uses of native plants, and may become a distraction to their parents and other hikers. Contact the visitor center for the schedule of guided hiking tours.

Taking a hike in Tahquitz Canyon will cost you considerably more than the usual park entry fee. At this writing, admission for adults is $12.50, children $6. There is no additional cost for the 2.5-hour guided hikes.

DIRECTIONS TO TRAILHEAD From Highway 111 in Palm Springs, head south on Palm Spring Drive through downtown to Mesquite Avenue. Turn right (west) and proceed 0.5 mile to the parking area below the Tahquitz Canyon Visitor Center.

THE HIKE At just 2 miles long, the hike through Tahquitz Canyon is a family-friendly one. The canyon is chock-full of native plants including brittle bush, creosote, cholla, hedgehog cactus, Mormon tea, and desert lavender.

The hiker's view down-canyon over the sometimes smog-obscured Coachella Valley sprawl can be a bit discouraging; up-canyon vistas, however, are glorious. From Tahquitz Peak, a subsidiary summit of Mt. San Jacinto, a lively creek tumbles through an impressive gash in the towering rock walls.

The hike highlight is, of course, the waterfall—"Shangri-La" indeed.

■ MURRAY AND ANDREAS CANYONS
Murray Canyon Trail
From Andreas Canyon to Murray Canyon is 2 miles round trip
with 200-foot elevation gain

I n the foothills above Palm Springs are two lovely palm-lined canyons—
Andreas and Murray. Both have hundreds of palms, crystalline streams, and
dramatic rock walls. Andreas, with about 700 native California fan palms and
Murray with about 1,000 palms, are among the most populous palm groves in
the state. The two canyons are tributaries of nearby Palm Canyon, undisputed
king of California's palm oases.

Both canyons honor Palm Springs pioneers. Andreas is named after a Cahuilla Indian chieftain of the late 1800s, while Murray honors irascible Scotsman
and dedicated botanist Dr. Welwood Murray, who built a hotel/health resort in
the very early days of Palm Springs. Many of those making their way to the
Murray Hotel came for the curative climate and the rejuvenation of their health,
but a number of literary figures also visited and these scribes soon spread the
word that Palm Springs was a very special place indeed.

Andreas Canyon was once a summer retreat for the Agua Caliente band of
the Cahuilla. The Indians spent the winter months in the warm Coachella Valley then sought the relative coolness of Andreas and other palm canyons during
the warmer months.

Unlike most palm oases, which are fed by underground springs or sluggish
seeps, Andreas is watered by a running stream. Fortunately for the palms and
other canyon life, settlers were legally prevented from diverting this stream to
the emerging village of Palm Springs. Ranchers and townspeople had to turn
to the larger, but notoriously unde-pendable Whitewater River.

Meandering through the tall palms, hikers can travel a ways upstream
through Andreas Canyon. Adding to the lush scene are alders and willows,
cottonwoods and sycamores.

The trail between Andreas Canyon and Murray Canyon is only a mile long,
but you can travel a few more miles up the canyons themselves.

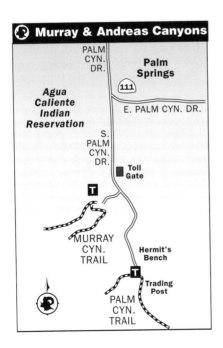

DIRECTIONS TO TRAILHEAD
From the junction of State Highway
111 and South Palm Canyon Drive in

Palm Springs, proceed south on the latter road for 1.5 miles, bearing right at a signed fork. After another mile you'll reach the Agua Caliente Indians Reservation tollgate.

Just after the tollgate, bear right at a signed fork and travel 0.75 mile to Andreas Canyon picnic ground. The trail begins at the east end of the splendid picnic area.

THE HIKE Notice the soaring, reddish-brown rocks near the trailhead. At the base of these rocks are grinding holes once used by the Cahuilla.

The trail extends south along the base of the mountains. A dramatic backdrop to the path is the desert-facing side of the San Jacinto Mountains.

It's an easy walk, occasionally following a dry streambed. Here, away from water, you encounter more typical desert flora: cholla, hedgehog cacti, burrobush.

When you reach Murray Canyon, you can follow the palms and stream quite a ways up-canyon. Joining the palms are willows, cottonwoods, mesquite, arrowweed, and desert lavender. Mistletoe is sometimes draped atop the mesquite and attracts lots of birds.

As you take the trail back to Andreas Canyon you can't help noticing the luxury housing and resort life reaching toward the palm canyons. And you can't help being thankful that these tranquil palm oases are still ours to enjoy.

■ PALM CANYON
Palm Canyon Trail
From Hermit's Bench to turnaround is 4 miles round trip with 200-foot elevation gain

The hills and canyons bordering Palm Springs have the greatest concentration of palm trees in the United States, and in number of trees, Palm Canyon is the uncrowned king of America's desert oases. A meandering stream and lush undergrowth complement over 3.000 palms, creating a jungle-like atmosphere in some places.

Palm fans will enjoy viewing the largest concentration of California fan palms while visiting the Agua Caliente Indian Reservation.

DIRECTIONS TO TRAILHEAD From Interstate 10, exit on Highway 111 (Palm Canyon Drive) and proceed to downtown Palm Springs. Continue through town on Palm Canyon Drive. At a fork, Highway 111 veers east and becomes known as East Palm Canyon Drive. You head straight ahead, on South Palm Canyon Drive, following the signs to "Indian Canyons." You reach the Agua Caliente Indians tollgate, where you must pay a fee to enter tribal lands. The reservation is open daily from 8:30 AM to 5 PM Parking is a short distance beyond the tollgate at the head of Palm Canyon at Hermit's Bench, where there is a trading post and a good view north into Palm Springs. Many signs remind visitors that they must be off the reservation before closing time.

THE HIKE From the trading post, the trail descends into the canyon. Some of the palms stand 60 feet tall, with 3-foot trunk diameters. The trail follows the canyon for 2 miles to a tiny grotto that seems an ideal place to turn around.

Hearty adventurers will relish the challenge of proceeding up Palm Canyon 7 more miles, gaining 3,000 feet in elevation, before reaching a junction with Highway 74, the Palms-to-Pines Highway. Note: This extremely strenuous hike is best done by beginning at the Highway 74 trailhead, hiking down Palm Canyon, and convincing a friend to pick you up at Hermit's Bench. Contact the BLM in Palm Springs for the latest trail advice.

■ SANTA ROSA AND SAN JACINTO MOUNTAINS NATIONAL MONUMENT
Fern Canyon, Vandeventer, Palm Canyon Trails
8 miles round trip with 600-foot elevation gain

Gentle sandscapes, rugged mountains, and hidden palm oases are some of the highlights of the Santa Rosa and San Jacinto Mountains National Monument. The area includes significant portions of these mountain ranges, which form that postcard-perfect background for Palm Springs and the Coachella Valley.

Land-use planners evaluated the Santa Rosa Mountains under the government's Visual Resources Management Program and gave the range a "scenic quality rating of 'A', or excellent." Any hiker who looks out over the blooming ocotillo as the sun sets over the western escarpment of the Santa Rosas will likely agree with this rating. Adding to the area's scenic qualities is a variety of plant life—miles of creosote and salt bush, chaparral, pinyon-juniper woodland, palm oases, and high conifer forests.

Besides their visual appeal, the Santa Rosa Mountains were declared a scenic area because they serve as habitat for America's largest remaining population of peninsular bighorn sheep. The bighorn need lots of room to roam.

Other wildlife in the scenic area includes golden eagles, red-tailed hawks, coyotes, bobcats, and mule deer.

One of my favorite hikes in the scenic area, which offers an alternative to the well-traveled Palm Canyon, is the jaunt to Fern Canyon where the hikers will find ferns growing in this arid land—a sight as surprising as the palm oases!

DIRECTIONS TO TRAILHEAD From Interstate 10, exit on Highway 111 (Palm Canyon Drive) and proceed to downtown Palm Springs. Continue through town on Palm Canyon Drive. At a fork, Highway 111 veers east and becomes known as East Palm Canyon Drive. You head straight ahead on South Palm Canyon Drive, following the signs to "Indian Canyons." You reach the Aqua Caliente Indians tollgate, where you must pay a fee to enter tribal lands. The reservation is open daily from 8:30 AM to 5 PM. Parking is a short distance beyond the tollgate at the head of Palm Canyon at Hermit's Bench, where there is a trading post and a good view north into Palm Springs. Many signs remind visitors that they must be off the reservation before closing time.

Fern Canyon Trail begins just below the trading post.

THE HIKE The trail climbs steeply to meet a palm oasis at the base of a huge rock, where ferns now thrive. Ascend away from Palm Canyon, then trek through the thick vegetation and push past the palm fronds in the bottom of Wentworth Canyon. Expect some boulder-hopping along the way.

Eventually the trail ascends out of the canyon and joins much-easier-to-follow, sandy, Vandeventer Trail and circles back to Palm Canyon at the south end of the Victor Trail just above the intersection to the Palm Canyon Trail.

■ THE LIVING DESERT
Jaeger Nature Trail
2-mile loop through Living Desert Reserve; return via Eisenhower Trail and Eisenhower Mountain is 5 miles round trip with 500-foot elevation gain

A superb introduction to desert plant life and wildlife, The Living Desert is a combination zoo, botanic garden, and hiking area. The 1,200-acre, nonprofit facility is dedicated to conservation, education, and research.

Gardens represent major desert regions including California's Mojave, Arizona's Sonoran, and Mexico's Chihuahuan. Wildlife-watchers will enjoy observing coyotes in their burrows and bighorn sheep atop their mountain peak. The reserve also has a walk-through aviary and a pond inhabited by the rare desert pupfish.

Nature and hiking trails provide an opportunity to form an even closer acquaintance with an uncrowded, undeveloped sandscape. Easy trails lead past the Arabian oryx and bighorn sheep, past desert flora with name tags and ecosystems with interpretive displays, and over to areas that resemble the open desert of yesteryear.

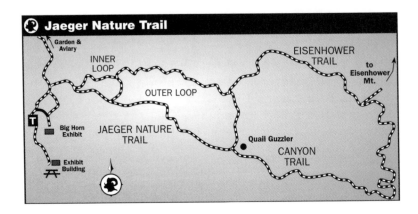

Presidents Eisenhower, Nixon, Ford, and Reagan relaxed in Palm Springs. Eisenhower spent many winters at the El Dorado Country Club at the base of the mountain that now bears his name. Palm Desert boosters petitioned the Federal Board of Geographic Names to name the 1,952 (coincidentally, 1952 was the year of his election)-foot peak for part-time Palm Springs resident Dwight D. Eisenhower.

The first part of the walk through The Living Desert uses a nature trail named after the great naturalist Edmund Jaeger. It's keyed to a booklet available from the entrance station. An inner loop of two-thirds of a mile and an outer loop of 1.5 miles lead past a wide array of desert flora and 60 interpretive stops. A longer loop can be made using Canyon Trail and Eisenhower Trail. The hike to Ike's peak ascends about halfway up the bald mountain and offers great views of the Coachella Valley.

DIRECTIONS TO TRAILHEAD From Highway 111 in Palm Desert, turn south on Portola Avenue and drive 1.5 miles south to the park. Closed mid-June to the end of August.

THE HIKE The trail begins at the exhibit buildings. Follow either the numbered nature trail, beginning at number one, or make a short rightward detour to the bighorn sheep enclosure.

The trail junctions once more and you begin heading up the alluvial plain of Deep Canyon. Walking up the wash, you'll observe the many moisture-loving plants that thrive in such environments, including smoke trees, desert willows, and palo verde.

Stay right at the next junction and begin the outer loop of the Jaeger Nature Trail. You'll pass plenty of that common desert dweller, the creosote bush, and wind along the base of some sand dunes.

The trail climbs out of the wash and into a kind of plain that true desert rats call a bajada. Here you'll find a quail guzzler which stores rainwater to aid California's state bird in the hot summer months. And here you'll find a junction with Canyon Trail (the south loop of the Eisenhower Trail).

Canyon Trail heads up the bajada. After climbing through a little canyon, the trail winds up the south slope of Eisenhower Mountain to a picnic area and a plaque describing the region's date industry.

From the picnic area, you'll descend Eisenhower Mountain, getting good views of the mountains and the Coachella Valley. After passing the signed Eisenhower trailhead, you'll reach the north loop of the Nature Trail and begin heading west down the brittlebush-dotted floodplain back to the exhibit buildings and the central part of the preserve.

■ DESERT VIEW
Desert View Trail
From Mountain Station to Desert View is 2 miles round trip; to Round Valley is 6 miles round trip

Starting in Chino Canyon near Palm Springs, Palm Springs Aerial Tramway takes passengers from 2,643-foot Lower Tramway Terminal (Valley Station) to 8,516-foot Upper Tramway Terminal (Mountain Station) at the edge of the Wilderness.

The Swiss-made gondola rapidly leaves terra firma behind. Too rapidly, you might think. It carries you over one of the most abrupt mountain faces in the world, over cliffs only a bighorn sheep can scale, over several life zones, from palms to pines. Nature-lovers enjoy witnessing flora and fauna changes equivalent to those viewed on a motor trip from the Mojave Desert to the Arctic Circle in just minutes.

For an introduction to the alpine environment of Mount San Jacinto State Park, take the short nature that begins at Mountain Station, then join Desert View Trail for a superb panorama of Palm Springs. After enjoying the view of

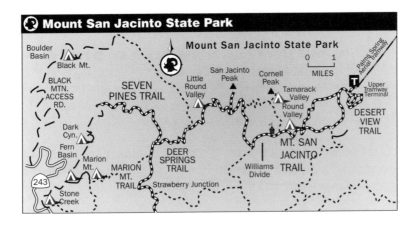

the arid lands below, you can extend your hike by looping through lush Round Valley.

DIRECTIONS TO TRAILHEAD From Interstate 10, exit on California 111 (the road to Palm Springs). Proceed 9 miles to Tramway Road, turn right, and follow the road 2.5 miles to its end at Mountain Station. Contact the Tramway office for information about prices and schedules.

THE HIKE From Mountain Station, walk down the paved pathway to the signed beginning of the trail to Desert View. Join the Nature Trail for a short distance, and soon get the first of a couple great desert views. The view takes in Palm Springs, Tahquitz, and other palm-lined canyons of the Agua Caliente Indian Reservation, along with the basin and hills of the Coachella Valley.

Continue on Desert View Trail, which makes a full circle and junctions with the path back up to Mountain Station. For a longer hike, walk through the Long Valley Picnic Area to the state park ranger station. Obtain a wilderness permit here.

Continue west on the trail, following the signs to Round Valley. The trail parallels Long Valley Creek through a mixed forest of pine and white fir, then climbs into lodgepole pine country. Lupine, monkeyflower, scarlet bugler, and Indian paintbrush are some of the wildflowers that add seasonal splashes of color.

After passing a junction with a trail leading toward Willow Creek, another 0.3 mile brings you to Round Valley. There's a trail camp and a backcountry ranger station in the valley, and splendid places to picnic in the meadow or among the lodgepole pines. The truly intrepid hiker will head for the summit of Mount San Jacinto, a 3.5 mile ascent from Round Valley.

An alternative to returning the same way is to retrace your steps 0.3 mile back to the junction with Willow Creek Trail, take this trail a mile through the pines to another signed junction, and follow the signed trail north back to Long Valley Ranger Station. This alternative adds only about 0.25 mile to your walk and allows you to make a loop.

See Map
on Page
203

■ MOUNT SAN JACINTO STATE PARK
San Jacinto Peak Trail
From Mountain Station to Round Valley is 4 miles round trip with 600-foot elevation gain; to San Jacinto Peak is 11 miles round trip with 2,300-foot elevation gain

The San Jacinto Mountain range is one of those magical places that lures visitors back year after year. Hikers enjoy the contrasts this range offers—the feeling of hiking in Switzerland while gazing down at the Sahara.

Palm Springs Aerial Tramway makes it easy to enter Mount San Jacinto State Wilderness. The day hiker accustomed to remote trailheads may find it a bit bizarre to enter Valley Station and find excited tourists sipping drinks and shopping for souvenirs. When you disembark at Mountain Station, your ears will pop and you'll have quite a head start up Mount San Jacinto.

The wild areas in the San Jacinto Mountains are administered by both state park and national forest rangers. The middle of the region, including San Jacinto Peak, is part of the state park; most of it is managed as a wilderness area. On both sides of the peak, north and south, the wilderness is part of the San Bernardino National Forest.

The meadows and High Sierra-like scenery can be glimpsed on a moderate hike to Round Valley; the ascent through the lodgepole pine forest to the top of Mt. San Jacinto is absolutely splendid, as are the views from the peak.

DIRECTIONS TO TRAILHEAD From Interstate 10, exit on California 111 (the road to Palm Springs). Proceed nine miles to Tramway Road, turn right, and follow the road 2.5 miles to its end at Mountain Station. Contact the Tramway office for information about prices and schedules.

THE HIKE From Mountain Station, walk down the cement walkway through the Long Valley Picnic Area. Soon you will arrive at the state park ranger station. Obtain a wilderness permit here.

Continue west on the trail, following the signs to Round Valley. The trail parallels Long Valley Creek through a mixed forest of pine and white fir, then climbs into lodgepole pine country. Lupine, monkeyflower, scarlet bugler, and Indian paintbrush are some of the wildflowers that add seasonal splashes of color.

After passing a junction with a trail leading toward Willow Creek, another 0.3 mile of hiking brings you to Round Valley. There's a trail camp and a backcountry ranger station in the valley, and splendid places to picnic in the meadow or among the lodgepole pines.

An alternative to returning the same way is to retrace your steps 0.3 mile back to the junction with the Willow Creek Trail, take this trail a mile through the pines to another signed trail north back to Long Valley Ranger Station. This alternative route adds only about a 0.25 mile to your day hike, and allows you to make a loop.

To Mount San Jacinto Peak: From Round Valley, peak-bound hikers follow the sign for Wellman Divide Junction. From the Divide, a trail leads down to Humber Park. At the divide, you'll be treated to spectacular views of Tahquitz Peak and Red Tahquitz, as well as the more-distant Toro Peak and Santa Rosa Mountain. You continue toward the peak on some vigorous switchbacks. The lodgepole pines grow sparse among the crumbly granite. At another junction, a half mile from the top, the trail continues to Little Round Valley but you take the summit trail to the peak. Soon you arrive at a stone shelter—an example of

Civilian Conservation Corps handiwork during the 1930s—built for mountaineers who have the misfortune to be caught in winter storms. From the stone hut, you boulder-hop to the top of the peak.

The view from the summit—San Gorgonio Pass, the shimmering Pacific, the Colorado Desert, distant Mexico—has struck some visitors speechless, while others have been unable to control their superlatives. Helen Hunt Jackson's heroine Ramona found "a remoteness from earth which comes only on mountain heights," and John Muir found the view "the most sublime spectacle to be found anywhere on this earth!"

■ SANTA ROSA WILDERNESS
Cactus Spring Trail
From Pinyon Flat to Horsethief Creek is 5 miles round trip with a 900-foot loss; to Cactus Spring is 9 miles round trip with a 300-foot gain

The Santa Rosas are primarily a desert range and a unique blend of high and low desert environments. Desert-facing slopes of these mountains are treeless—scorched and sparse as the desert itself. Throughout the foothills and canyons, lower Sonoran vegetation—chamise, barrel cactus, ocotillo and waxy creosote—predominate. In some of the canyons with water on or near the surface, oases of native California fan palms form verdant islands on the sand. With an increase in elevation, the wrinkled canyons and dry arroyos give way to mountain crests bristling with pine and juniper.

The Santa Rosa Wilderness, set aside in 1984, lies within the boundaries of the San Bernardino National Forest. Trails are few in the Santa Rosas; most are

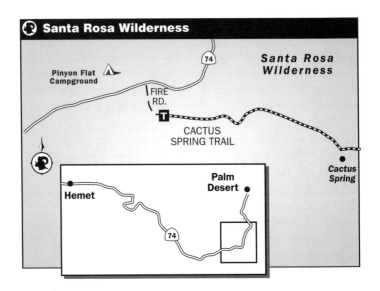

faint traces of Cahuilla pathways. The ancients climbed the mountains to hunt deer, gather pinyon pine nuts, and escape the desert heat. When the snows began, they descended from the high country to the gentle, wintering areas below.

Cactus Spring Trail, an old Indian path overhauled by the Forest Service, gives the hiker a wonderful introduction to the delights of the Santa Rosas.

The trail first takes you to Horsethief Creek, a perennial waterway that traverses high desert country. A hundred years ago, horse thieves pastured their stolen animals in this region before driving them to San Bernardino to sell. The cottonwood-shaded creek invites a picnic. Continuing on the Cactus Spring Trail, you'll arrive at Cactus Spring. Along the trail is some wild country, as undisturbed as it was in 1774 when early Spanish trailblazer Juan Bautista de Anza first saw it.

DIRECTIONS TO TRAILHEAD From Highway 111 in Palm Desert, drive 16 miles up Highway 74 to the Pinyon Flat Campground. (From Hemet, it's a 40-mile drive along Highway 74 to Pinyon Flat Campground.) Opposite the campground is Pinyon Flat Transfer Station Road, also signed "Elks Mountain Retreat." You'll follow this road about 0.75 mile. Just before reaching the (trash) Transfer Station, a rough dirt road veers to the left. Follow this road 200 yards to road's end.

THE HIKE Follow the dirt road east a short distance to Fire Road 7S01, then head south for 0.25 mile. You'll then take the first road on your left. A sign reassures you that you are indeed on the way to Cactus Spring, and you'll soon pass the abandoned Dolomite Mine, where limestone was once quarried. Approximately 0.25 mile past the mine site, the dirt road peters out and the trail begins. Here you'll find a sign and a trail register.

The trail bears east to the east and dips in and out of several (usually) dry gullies. A half mile past the sign-in register, a sign welcomes you to the Santa Rosa Wilderness. Cactus Spring Trail does not contour over the hills, but zigs and zags, apparently without rhyme or reason. The bewitching, but easy-to-follow trail finally drops down to Horsethief Creek. At the creek crossing, Horsethief Camp welcomes the weary with flowing water and shade.

Return the same way, explore up and down the handsome canyon cut by Horsethief Creek, or continue to Cactus Spring.

To reach Cactus Spring, cross the creek, then climb east out of the canyon on a rough and steep trail past sentinel yuccas guarding the dry slopes. The trail stays with a wash for a spell (the route through the wash is unmarked except for occasional rock ducks), then gently ascends over pinyon pine-covered slopes. It's rolling wild country, a good place to hide out. Alas, Cactus Spring, located a few hundred yards north of the trail, is almost always dry.

■ TORO PEAK
Santa Rosa Mountain Trail
To Toro Peak summit is 3 miles round trip
with 800-foot elevation gain

They're rugged, young, and restless. They're the Santa Rosa Mountains which, by all appearances, are a youthful range: precipitous slopes, minimal flora, steep canyons. Geologists say the range arose only 3 to 4 million years ago (quite recently in geologic time) and is still rising—due to its location near the center of the San Jacinto Fault, one of the region's most active.

The mountains are severely eroded, Rain falls on steep, nearly bare earth slopes, and washes loose soil and rock all the way down to the desert floor. Water scours canyons, carrying great loads of sand and boulders below and spreading it about the canyon mouths in deposits called alluvial fans.

Toro Peak (elevation 8,716 feet) is the high point of the range and towers over all other desert topography including nearby range namesake Santa Rosa Mountain (8,046 feet). The trail to the summit is really Santa Rosa Mountain Road, the last length of which is closed to vehicles.

The peak, crowned by communications facilities, offers memorable desert views of Anza-Borrego Desert State Park. Toro Peak's view is an intriguing contrast to the one offered at Santa Rosa Overlook: a vista from the desert floor up at Toro Peak.

DIRECTIONS TO TRAILHEAD The trail to the summit is really Santa Rosa Mountain Road, the last length of which is closed to vehicles.

Depending on your level of affection for driving on rugged dirt roads, getting there may—or may not—be half the fun. "Tortuous" might be the most polite way to describe Santa Rosa Road in a family-oriented book.

The drive to the Toro Peak trailhead is both the best of times and the worst of times—in that order. Palms to Palms Highway (74) offers numerous viewpoints of the Santa Rosa National Scenic Area as it ascends some 23 miles from Palm Desert to Santa Rosa Summit. As the highway gains elevation, you'll motor past contrasting environments from palms and ocotillo to pinyon pine and juniper.

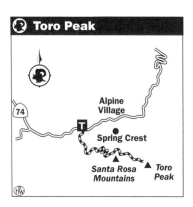

At about 7,000 feet in elevation, those with sturdy, high-clearance vehicles (four-wheel drive is best) turn left (south) on signed Santa Rosa Mountain Road. The (sometimes) graded road, which can have major potholes, wash-outs, and eroded stretches, leads about 11.5 miles to a locked gate.

A handsome mixed forest of sugar pine, Jeffrey pine, and fir cloaks the upper face of the mountain. Roadslide pull-outs offer woodsy car-camping opportunities.

Before tackling this road, the prudent motorist will contact the San Jacinto and Santa Rosa Mountains National Scenic Area office for the latest road and weather conditions. Snowfall prompts authorities to closure (from about December through March, somtimes later) the uppermost 5 miles of the road. Rather than be disappointed by this road closure, hikers looking for a special adventure will enjoy trampling the snow-dusted road through the lovely, quiet forest.

THE HIKE Not much to this summit climb, except a steep ascent up the road for 1.25 mile to a fork. Bear right to the summit, which hosts a microwave relay station.

Behold the entirety of the Santa Rosa Mountains, the San Jacinto Mountains, the Salton Sea, and Coachella Valley.

■ DESERT DIVIDE
Spitler Peak, Pacific Crest Trails
From Apple Canyon to Desert Divide is 10 miles
round trip with 2,000-foot gain; to Apache Peak
is 12 miles round trip with 2,600-foot gain;
to Antsell Rock is 14 miles round trip with 2,600-foot gain

Riding the Palm Springs Aerial Tramway or driving the Palms to Pines Highway are two ways to view the astonishing change in vegetation that occurs with a change in elevation in the San Jacinto Mountains. A third way to observe the startling contrast between desert and alpine environments is to hike up the back side of the San Jacinto Mountains to aptly named Desert Divide. The imposing granite divide, which reminds some mountaineers of the High Sierra, offers far-reaching views of the canyons on the fringes of Palm Springs and of the Coachella Valley.

Most visitors to the San Jacinto Mountains begin their explorations in Idyllwild or from the top of the tramway. Few hike—or even think about—Desert Divide. Too bad, because this land of pine forest, wide meadows, and soaring granite peaks has much to offer.

The trail begins in Garner Valley, a long meadowland bordered by tall pine. Meandering across the valley floor is the South Fork of the San Jacinto River, whose waters are impounded at the lower end of the valley by Lake Hemet. Splashing spring color across the meadow are purple penstemon, golden yarrow, owl's clover and tidy tips. Autumn brings a showy "river" of rust-colored buckwheat winding through the valley.

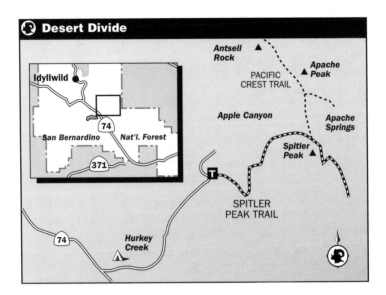

Spitler Peak Trail offers a moderate-to-strenuous route up to Desert Divide. You can enjoy the great views from the divide and call it a day right there, or join Pacific Crest Trail and continue to the top of Apache Peak or Antsell Rock.

DIRECTIONS TO TRAILHEAD The hamlet of Mountain Center is some 20 miles up Highway 74 from Hemet and a few miles up Highway 243 from Idyllwild. From the intersection of Highway 243 (Banning-Idyllwild Highway) and Highway 74 in Mountain Center, proceed southeast on the latter highway. After 3 miles, turn left at the signed junction for Hurkey Creek County Park. Instead of turning into the park, you'll continue 1.75 mile on Apple Canyon Road to signed Spitler Peak Trail on the right. Park in the turnout just south of the trailhead.

THE HIKE Spitler Peak Trail begins among oak woodland and chaparral. The mellow, well-graded path contours quite some distance to the east before beginning a more earnest northerly ascent. Enjoy over-the-shoulder views of Lake Hemet and of Garner Valley. Actually, geologists say Garner Valley is not a valley at all but a graben, a long narrow area that dropped between two bordering faults.

Garner Graben?

Nope, just doesn't have the right ring to it.

The trail climbs steadily into juniper/Jeffrey pine/Coulter pine forest. Most of the time your path is under conifers or the occasional oak. There always seem to be quite a number of deadfalls to climb over, climb under, or walk around along this stretch of trail.

About a mile from the divide the going gets steeper and you rapidly gain elevation. Finally you gain the windblown divide just northwest of Spitler Peak and intersect signed Pacific Crest Trail. Enjoy the vistas of forest and desert. Picnic atop one of the divide's many rock outcroppings.

PCT, sometimes known as Desert Divide Trail in these parts, offers the energetic a range of options. PCT heads north and soon passes through a section of recovering forest—charred by the 1980 Palm Canyon Fire that roared up these slopes from Palm Springs. After a half mile you'll pass a side trail that descends steeply another 0.5-mile to Apache Springs. Another 0.5-mile along the PCT brings you to a side trail leading up to bare 7,567-foot Apache Peak.

Another mile brings you to a point just below 7,720-foot Antsell Rock. Unless you're a very good rock climber, stay off the unstable slopes and avoid the urge to ascend to the very top of the rock.

■ PAINTED CANYON
Ladder Canyon Loop
5 miles round trip with 500-foot elevation gain

Distinctly colored canyons, palm oases, narrows, slot canyons and ridgetops with far-reaching vistas are reasons for a hiking pilgrimage to the Mecca Hills located in the Coachella Valley near the Salton Sea.

The Mecca Hills offer geology textbook displays of the power of earthquakes and faulting to shape strata. Ancient rock (some 600 million years old) has been pushed up, turned, and overturned. Geologists think the last big push took place about a million years ago when the Mecca Hills were thrust upward between the Painted Canyon and San Andreas faults.

Painted Canyon, in the heart of the hills, exhibits a multitude of colorful mineral deposits. Pink, rose, red, purple, and green hues tint the moonscape. Keen-eyed wildflower lovers will stalk the rare Mecca aster, a lilac-tinted bloom that resembles a daisy.

One highlight is Ladder Canyon, so called because of the ladder that aids ascent into a slot canyon.

DIRECTIONS TO TRAILHEAD From Palm Springs, Palm Desert, or any of the other Coachella Valley cities, follow California 111 east to Mecca. Turn east at 66th Avenue. The street takes the name Box Canyon Road, and after 4.5 miles it bends northeast. A quarter of a mile after crossing the Coachella Canal, you'll spot a sign for Painted Canyon Road on the left. Turn left onto this road and proceed 4 miles to parking and the Painted Canyon Trail.

THE HIKE Head east (right) up the wide canyon 0.25 mile to the entrance for Ladder Canyon. The route skirts a rockslide and soon brings you to the first ladder. Climb the ladder to a long slot canyon, continue the ascent 0.3 mile or so, then join a switchbacking trail to a ridge.

Inexperienced hikers will want to turn around here and retrace their steps to the trailhead.

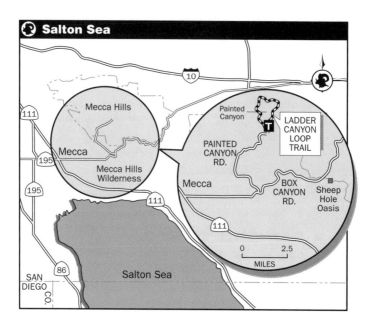

Experienced desert hikers with a good sense of direction can follow the path north along the ridge as it serves up view of the Mecca Hills, the Salton Sea to the south, and Mt. San Jacinto to the west. After following the ridge for slightly more than a mile, the trail descends into Painted Canyon. Bear south, down the canyon.

Continue to a narrow spot where another ladder helps you reach the canyon bottom. The trailhead is slightly less than a mile farther.

■ SHEEP HOLE PALMS OASIS
Sheep Hole Oasis Trail
To Sheep Hole Oasis is 3.5 miles round trip;
to Hidden Spring Oasis is 6 miles round trip

The end of the Mecca Hills features complex canyons, intricate passageways in sandstone in a variety of shapes and colors. A National Park Service study once described the hills as having the most diverse geology, concentrated in one place, of any area in the Mojave Desert.

The trail begins in long, serpentine patterned Box Canyon, which provides a border of sorts between the Mecca Hills and the foothills of the Orocopia Mountains. Ancient Cahuilla pathways plus hiker/horse-compacted use trails are part of the sketchy trail system.

The hike also offers eye-popping vistas of the Salton Sea and the lower Coachella Valley. In spring, purple blossoms adorn the desert ironwood and smoke trees growing in the washes.

You'll be hiking in the vicinity of the Bradshaw Stageline route. Between the 1860s and the early years of the twentieth century, the former Native American trade route turned desert road was promoted by its namesake booster soldier-mountain man William D. Bradshaw.

Stout Washingtonia palms cluster in Sheep Hole Oasis, a waterhole occasionally visited by bighorn sheep. Hikers can extend their tour with a visit to Hidden Spring (no exaggeration) Oasis, which offered water to earlier generations of desert travelers.

Experienced desert explorers with good navigation skills will find their way to The Grottoes, cave-like passageways in the mud hills.

A rare sighting of a coyote in the California desert.

DIRECTION TO TRAILHEAD From Highway 111 in Mecca, located a few miles north of the north shore of the Salton Sea, turn east on Highway 195. After 4.5 miles, the road bends northeast and, 0.25 mile after crossing the Coachella Canal, you'll spot signed Painted Canyon Road on the left.

Continue another 5 miles (that's about 10 miles from Highway 111) and look for the trailhead parking on the north (right) side of the road.

THE HIKE From road's end at the mouth of a small tributary canyon, hike 150 feet or so up the ravine and join the unsigned trail as it ascends the ravine's right slope. Follow this reworked Cahuilla path for a mile to Sheep Hole Oasis.

Continue 0.25 mile past the oasis and look leftward for a path ascending out of the wash. Join this path as it surmounts a minor ridge and drops into Hidden Springs Canyon. Walk up the bottom of the canyon, which, after 0.75 mile, narrows as it turns right. Just beyond this bend look to the left for a narrow (only 7 feet wide) arroyo. Head up this gray-and red-rocked framed passage a few hundred feet to Hidden Spring Oasis.

The brilliant red of an ocotillo in bloom is a spectacular springtime attraction in Anza-Borrego.

CHAPTER 6

ANZA-BORREGO DESERT STATE PARK

When Butterfield Overland stagecoaches sped from St. Louis through the Colorado Desert toward Pueblo de Los Angeles in the 1850s, the serpentine canyons and jagged mountains that are now part of Anza-Borrego Desert State Park stood as the last obstacle to the trip across the continent. Stagecoach passengers were only too happy to leave behind this vast desolate wilderness. Since the 1930s however, when a half-million acres of palm oases, cactus flats, and fantastic badlands were preserved in a state park, this very vastness and desolation have attracted visitors.

East-west Highway 78 crosses the state park and reveals a land as intriguing as its names: Earthquake Valley, Grapevine Hills, Nude Wash. And Angelina Spring, Narrows Earth Trail, and Ocotillo Wells. At Yaqui Well grow the spiny ironwood trees, and at Alma Wash grow those botanical oddities, the puffy-looking elephant trees. At Split Mountain the road separates two mountain ranges and offers an inside-out look at hundreds of sedimentary layers of ancient sea bottoms and fossil shell reefs.

Another long desert highway, S-22, the Borrego-Salton Seaway, also crosses the park from east to west. In 1929 Alfred "Doc" Beatty led a mule-drawn Fresno scraper through the Borrego Badlands to the Truckhaven Cafe on old Highway 99. Truckhaven Trail became a popular jeep road after World War II. When Highway S-22 was built in 1968 it followed Doc's road closely for much of its length. S-22 offers access to lonely Seventeen Palms Canyon, where a desert seep enables a group of fan palms to survive, and to the twisted sandstone formations of Calcite Canyon, where calcite, useful for making gun sights, was mined during World War II.

S-22, like a good many desert roads, has evolved from trail to jeep road to highway. But if Colorado Desert roads have changed a great deal over the past half century, desert vistas have not. One of my favorite views is off S-22 at Font's Point, where an overlook offers a breathtakingly beautiful panorama of Baja California, the Salton Sea, Borrego Valley, and the sculptured maze of the Borrego Badlands. This view has remained exactly the same as it was in the 1930s when *Los Angeles Times* outdoors writer Lynn J. Rogers stepped out of his Chevrolet and observed: "A myriad of furrowed canyons drop down into a wild confusion of tumbled gorges and pinnacles. Beyond is spread the great bowl of the Borrego Valley with scattered clearings and patches of brown mesquite stretched out in the aching clearness of the desert morning light."

Anza-Borrego Desert State Park includes virtually all the features visitors associate with a desert: washes, badlands, mesas, palm oases, and much more. This diverse desert park boasts more than 20 palm groves and year-round creeks, great stands of cholla and elephant trees, slot canyons, and badland formations.

Anza-Borrego is diverse, and it is huge; more than 3 times the size of Zion National Park. The 650,000-acre park stretches almost the whole length of San Diego County's eastern border between Riverside County and Mexico. Its elevation ranges from 100 feet below sea level near the Salton Sea to 6,000 feet above sea level atop San Ysidro Mountain.

California's largest state park preserves a 60-mile long, 30-mile wide stretch of Colorado Desert from the Santa Rosa Mountains to the Mexican border. Lower in elevation than the Mojave Desert, the Colorado Desert is also hotter and drier. (The Colorado Desert in the extreme southeastern portion of California is only a small part of the larger Sonoran Desert, which covers about 120,000 acres of the American Southwest.)

The park, set aside in 1933, is named for the Mexican explorer (Juan Bautista de Anza) and the Spanish word for bighorn sheep, *borrego*. Anza traveled through the area in 1774, and the bighorn sheep still roam this land.

Travelers are welcomed to Anza-Borrego by what is probably the best visitor center in the state park system. Numerous self-guided nature trails and automobile tours allow visitors to set their own pace. An active natural history association and foundation sponsors many regularly scheduled ranger- and naturalist-led activities.

While the park is oriented to exploration by vehicle, a number of fine hikes await the desert trekker. A note to the uninitiated: Hiking in this section of the Colorado Desert is guaranteed to make a desert rat out of anyone.

Among the sights are Calcite Canyon, where nature's cutting tools, wind and water, have shaped the ageless sandstone into steep, bizarre formations. The elephant tree grove is another strange sight. Its surreal color scheme, parchment-like bark and stout elephant-like trunk is something to behold.

■ BORREGO PALM CANYON
Borrego Palm Canyon Trail
To Falls is 3 miles round trip with 600-foot elevation gain; to South Fork is 6.5 miles round trip with 1,400-foot gain

Borrego Palm Canyon was the first site sought for a desert state park back in the 1920s. It's a beautiful, well-watered oasis, tucked away in a rocky V-shaped gorge. The canyon's many charms, along with its easy access from the park visitor center, combine to make it the most popular sight to see in the park by far—at least for those willing to take a short hike.

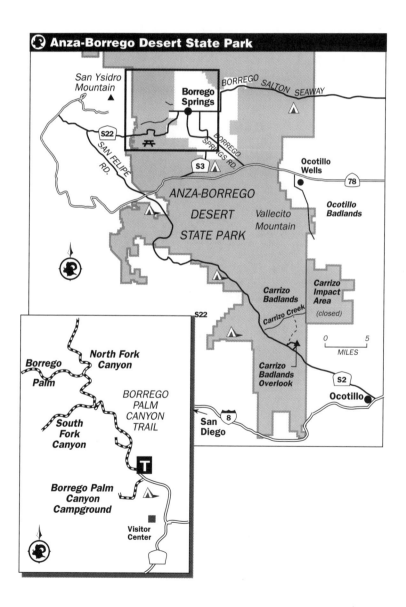

With more than a thousand palms, the oasis once ranked number three among the state's native fan palm gatherings. However, the palm population was decimated by a flash flood in September 2004. A 10-foot-high wall of water washed away some 70 percent of the Borrego's palms.

The oasis-bound hiker will find many a toppled palm lying in or near the boulder-strewn riverbed. Fortunately, there are sufficient survivors to perpetuate the species.

The still-enjoyable trail makes its way to a much-reduced palm grove and seasonal waterfall A longer option takes you exploring up-canyon.

In winter, the trail to the falls is mighty popular; get an early start to beat the crowd and for a better chance of sighting the bighorn sheep that frequently visit the canyon. In the summer, you'll probably have the oasis all to yourself.

DIRECTIONS TO TRAILHEAD The trail begins at Borrego Palm Canyon Campground, located 1 mile north of park headquarters. Trailhead parking is available at the west end of the campground near the campfire circle.

Little hiker with a heart! Spot rocks of all shapes and sizes in the riverbed.

THE HIKE Beginning at the pupfish pond, you walk up-canyon past many desert plants used by the Indians for food and shelter. Willow was used for home-building and bow-making; brittle bush and creosote were used for their healing qualities; honey, along with mesquite and beavertail cactus, was a food staple. You might also notice shallow grinding holes in the granite.

The broad alluvial fan at the mouth of the canyon narrows and the sheer rock walls of the canyon soon enclose you as the trail continues along the healthy, but seasonal stream. Already surprised to learn how an apparently lifeless canyon could provide all the Native Americans' necessary survival ingredients, you're surprised once more when Borrego

Palm Oasis comes into view. Just beyond the first group of palms is a damp grotto, where a waterfall cascades over huge boulders. The grotto is a popular picnic area and rest stop.

From the falls, you may take an alternate trail back to the campground. This trail takes you along the south side of the creek, past some magnificent ocotillos, and gives you a different perspective on this unique desert environment. By following the optional route, you can continue hiking up the canyon. Hiking is more difficult up-canyon after the falls, with lots of dense undergrowth and boulders to navigate around.

To South Fork: From the "tourist turnaround" continue up the canyon. The creek is a fairly dependable water supply and is usually running late in the fall. The canyon is wet, so watch your footing on the slippery, fallen palm fronds. The canyon narrows even further and the trail dwindles to nothing. Parallel the streambed and boulder-hop back and forth across the water. The canyon zigs and zags quite a bit, so you can never see much more than a few hundred yards ahead. The walk is well-worth the effort though, because most of the 800 or so palms in the canyon are found in its upper reaches. Sometimes you'll spot rock-climbers practicing their holds on the steep red-rock cliffs above you.

The canyon splits 1.75 miles from the falls. Straight ahead, to the southwest, is South Fork. The rocky gorge of South Fork, smothered with bamboo, is in possession of all the canyon's water. It's quite difficult to negotiate. South Fork ascends to the upper slopes of San Ysidro Mountain (6,417 feet). The Middle Fork (the way you came) of Borrego Pam Canyon is dry and more passable. It's possible to hike quite a distance first up Middle Fork, then North Fork of Borrego Palm Canyon, but check with park rangers first. It's extremely rugged terrain.

■ SAN YSIDRO MOUNTAIN
Panorama Overlook Trail
From Borrego Palm Canyon Campground is 1 mile round trip;
from visitor center is 2 miles round trip

Panorama Overlook Trail delivers what it promises: vistas of the Borrego Valley and Borrego Badlands, the Vallecito Mountains, and the Santa Rosa Mountains.

Take this walk at dawn and you'll enjoy watching the rising sun chase shadows from the many mountains and canyons below the overlook. Bring along a park map to identify the considerable geography at your feet.

A state park trail second in popularity only to Borrego Palm Canyon Nature Trail, the path is a good one to take to get the lay of the land before embarking on more strenuous and far-reaching Anza-Borrego explorations.

One such (extremely) strenuous exploration begins where Panorama Overlook Trail ends. Experienced desert hikers in top form may continue up the trailless shoulder of San Ysidro Mountain past giant boulders, cactus, shrubs, and juniper to the mile-high top of the mountain. It's only a 7-mile round trip, but a brutal 4,400-foot gain, and an all-day hike to the mile-high summit. The panoramic views from the peak are magnificent.

DIRECTIONS TO TRAILHEAD Anza-Borrego Desert State Park Visitor Center is located on Palm Canyon Drive just west of Highway S-22 in Borrego Springs. You can park in the visitor center lot (sometimes crowded on the weekends), but rangers ask that you help ease congestion by continuing up the road into the campground (day-use fee required). Ignore the many signs pointing toward Borrego Palm Canyon Nature Trail and proceed to the trailhead parking area near campsite 71.

THE HIKE Before hitting the trail, check out the nature and history exhibits at the park visitor center. You can start walking from the visitor center on the signed, 0.5-mile-long Campground Trail or from a trailhead in the Borrego Palm Canyon Campground.

■ HELLHOLE CANYON
Hellhole Canyon Trail
From S-22 to Maidenhair Falls is 5 miles round trip with 900-foot elevation gain

Add Hellhole Canyon to the list of great geographical misnomers. Just as Greenland is anything but green, Hellhole Canyon is far from, well . . . hellish. Cottonwood, California fan palms, ferns, and mosses thrive in the canyon, which hosts a blissful waterfall.

Certainly this hike's destination—Maidenhair Falls—is no misnomer. Maidenhair ferns enshroud the 30-foot-high falls. The presence of a lush, fern-filled grotto in the midst of one of the West's most parched landscapes is a small miracle, an example of nature's mysterious ways. Not only is Hellhole Canyon attractive, it's convenient—just a few miles as the cactus wren flies from the Anza-Borrego Desert State Park Visitor Center.

An intermittent trail travels through the long and deep canyon. Caution: while the canyon's riparian growth is easy on the eye, it's difficult to penetrate; expect slow-going through the thick vegetation.

Begin your trek to Hellhole Canyon from the park visitor center or from a trailhead located just off S-22. I recommend the latter trailhead, which shaves a mile from the walk and avoids the sometimes congested visitor center parking lot.

DIRECTIONS TO TRAILHEAD From its intersection with Palm Canyon Drive, proceed 0.7 mile southwest on Montezuma Valley Road to the parking area on the right (west) side of the road. A bulletin board features trail and nature information.

THE HIKE Follow signed California Riding and Hiking Trail some 200 yards to a junction; the CR&HT splits left, while you bear right, heading southwest over the broad alluvial fan. The well defined, sandy trail crosses a desert garden of cholla, creosote bush, desert lavender, and ocotillo.

A bit more than a mile out, the path angles toward the mouth of Hellhole Canyon, distinguished by riparian trees and palms (and altogether different-looking than that smaller, drier tributary canyon to its right (north). The trail stays to the left of the fan, as should the hiker until entering the mouth of the canyon.

Once in the canyon, you might find yourself walking next to a wet or dry (depending on the season) watercourse. Try to steer clear of the very bottom of the canyon, an obstacle course of brush, boulders, and fallen trees. The thickest

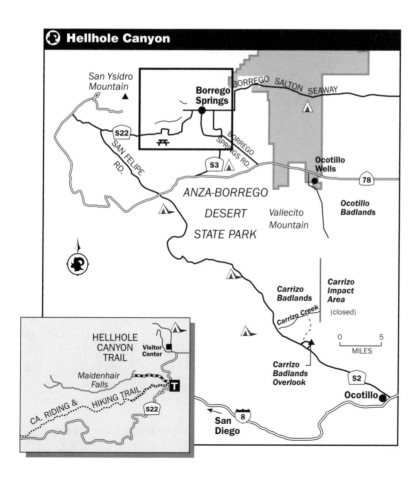

of the canyon's scattered palm groves, and the narrowing of the canyon's walls signal that you're nearing Maidenhair Falls.

Ultra-ambitious hikers can continue bushwhacking up Hellhole Canyon, but most travelers will be content to enjoy the soft light and tranquillity around the falls and return to the trailhead.

■ CALCITE CANYON

Calcite Canyon Trail

From County Road S-22 to Calcite Mine is 4 miles round trip with 500-foot elevation gain

Nature's cutting tools, wind and water, have shaped the ageless sandstone in Calcite Canyon into steep, bizarre formations. The cutting and polishing of the uplifted rock mass has exposed calcite crystals. Calcite is a common enough carbonate and found in many rocks, but only in a few places are the crystals so pure.

It was the existence of these crystals, with their unique refractive properties that brought prospectors to this part of the desert. The jeep trail was built in the mid-1930s for miners to gain access to Calcite Canyon, as it came to be called. Because of their excellent double refraction properties, calcite crystals were useful in the making of gun sights. Mining activity increased during World War II.

The calcite was taken from the canyon in long trenches, which look as if they were made yesterday. The desert takes a long time to heal.

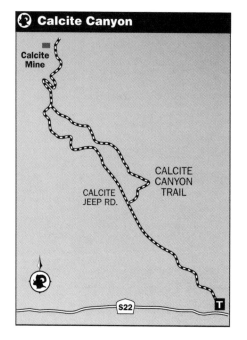

This walk takes the jeep road to its dead end at the mine. You'll see the Calcite Mine Area up-close and get a good overlook of the many washes snaking toward the Salton Sea. A return trip through Palm Wash and its tributaries lets you squeeze between perpendicular walls and gives a unique perspective on the forces that shape the desert sands. The awesome effects of flash flooding are easily discerned by the hiker and suggest a narrow wash is the last place in the world you want to be in a rainstorm.

DIRECTIONS TO TRAILHEAD

Follow County Road S-22 west from Highway 86, or 20 miles from the

Christmas Circle to Calcite Jeep Road. The jeep road is just west of a microwave tower. Don't drive down the jeep road into Calcite Canyon; this road is very eroded and dangerous even for experienced four-wheelers. Park your car up and start hiking.

THE HIKE Follow the jeep road, which first drops into the south fork of Palm Wash, then begins to climb northwest. Along the road you'll see long, human-made slots cut into the hillsides for the removal of calcite. Calcite Jeep Road dips a final time, then climbs a last 0.5 mile toward the mine. Two miles from the trailhead, the road ends at the mining area.

Calcite crystal fragments embedded in the canyon walls and scattered on the desert floor glitter in the sun. Behind the mining area, to the northeast, is a gargan-

All that glitters may be calcite crystals.

tuan hunk of white sandstone dubbed "Locomotive Rock." The imaginative can picture a great locomotive chugging up a steep grade. If you look carefully, you'll be able to see Seventeen Palms and some of the palms tucked away in Palm Wash in a bird's-eye view of the east side of the state park.

You can return the same way or descend through tributaries of the middle fork of Palm Wash. Take a last look at the steep ravines and washes to get your bearings. Middle Fork is but a hop, skip, and a jump from the mine, but the jump's a killer—a 50-foot plunge to a deep intersecting wash. To get into the wash, you need to descend 0.5-mile down Calcite Road to a small tributary wash. Descend this wash, which is fairly steep at first. The sandstone walls close in on you. One place, "Fat Man's Misery," allows only one fat man (or two skinny day hikers) to squeeze through at a time. When you reach the middle fork, a prominent canyon, follow it 0.25 mile to the brief jeep trail connecting the wash to Calcite Road. Walk back up Calcite Road 0.1 mile to the parking area.

■ YAQUI PASS
Kenyon Overlook Trail
1.25 mile loop with 100-foot elevation gain

At the V-shaped highway junction where S-3 swings north toward Borrego Valley from Highway 78, are a tumble of low ridges and canyons, a campground, and a trio of nature trails. Kenyon Overlook Trail honors William C. Kenyon, state parks superintendent and conservationist. This path begins atop Yaqui Pass; the other two begin opposite inviting Tamarisk Grove Campground, a pleasant place to overnight or to picnic.

This view is in contrast to the one enjoyed by the motorist descending north from Yaqui Pass back toward Borrego Valley—a panorama of the heart of the park, including Borrego Palm Canyon, the park visitor center and the town of Borrego Springs.

The trail continues to a second overlook, then weaves 0.75 mile through a low desert flora of creosote bush, cacti and jojoba to undeveloped Yaqui Pass Campground and trail's end. Walk two hundred yards along S-3 back to the trailhead.

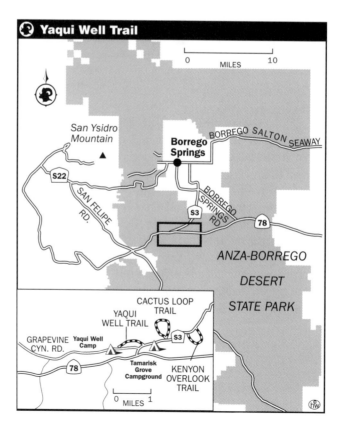

DIRECTIONS TO TRAILHEAD Bill Kenyon Trail begins at a signed trailhead atop Yaqui Pass on S-3, some 12.5 miles from the park visitor center. Drive 1.5 miles over the pass on S-3 to reach Tamarisk Grove Campground and the signed trailheads for Cactus Loop Trail and Yaqui Well Trail.

THE HIKE From Yaqui Pass, Kenyon Overlook Trail leads 0.25 mile to a viewpoint. Below sprawls the Mescal Bajada, one of the largest bajadas (delta-like fans of gravel and silt) in the state park. Mescal, or desert agave, is the dominant plant in the bajada. Also visible are the Pinyon Mountains and on clear days, the Salton Sea.

■ CACTUS LOOP
Cactus Loop Trail
1 mile round trip with 200-foot elevation gain

This nature trail (with some plant identification signs) ascends a rocky slope past a diversity of cacti—beavertail, barrel, fishhook, and cholla. Most spectacular are the large (six-foot high) teddy bear cholla.

Of all desert flora, the cholla has the most sinister reputation; its evils have been repeatedly chronicled by Western writers. Joseph Smeaton Chase, in his 1919 classic *California Desert Trails*, writes: "First, it certainly is in villainous traits and in the ill-regard of every desert traveler. It is an ugly object three or four feet high, with stubby arms standing out like amputated stumps. The older parts are usually black with decay, the rest of a sickly greenish white, and the whole thing is covered with horrible barbed spines, uncountable in quantity and detestable in every regard."

Just to make sure the reader fully understands his loathing for cholla, Chase adds in final fulmination: "if the plant bears any helpful or even innocent part in the scheme of things on this planet, I should be glad to hear of it."

DIRECTIONS TO TRAILHEAD Bill Kenyon Trail begins at a signed trailhead atop Yaqui Pass on S-3, some 12.5 miles from the park visitor center. Drive 1.5 miles over the pass on S-3 to reach Tamarisk Grove Campground and the signed trailheads for Cactus Loop Trail and Yaqui Well Trail.

THE HIKE After ascending a wash to the crest of a low ridge, the trail returns to Highway S-3.

Look, but don't touch! Pretty, back-lit teddy bear cholla.

See Map
on Page
224

■ YAQUI WELL
Yaqui Well Trail
2 miles round trip

Yaqui Well Trail leads to a waterhole that attracts birds and bird-watchers. Along the way, the cacti, as well as such characteristic desert flora as ocotillo, mesquite, and jojoba are identified and described.

DIRECTIONS TO TRAILHEAD Bill Kenyon Trail begins at a signed trailhead atop Yaqui Pass on S-3, some 12.5 miles from the park visitor center. Drive 1.5 miles over the pass on S-3 to reach Tamarisk Grove Campground and the signed trailheads for Cactus Loop Trail and Yaqui Well Trail.

THE HIKE After surmounting a few low hills, the trail leads to Yaqui Well, surrounded by thriving ironwood, willow, and mesquite. The waterhole attracts abundant wildlife. From nearby Yaqui Well Primitive Camp, you can join dirt Grapevine Canyon Road, which follows ironwood- and mesquite-lined San Felipe Creek. The road meets Highway S-3 just short of the trailhead.

■ THE NARROWS, SAN FELIPE WASH
Narrows Earth Trail
0.3 mile loop

From erosion to earthquakes, the forces that formed the land we now call Anza-Borrego have been both subtle and cataclysmic. The area's complex geologic history is the subject of an interpretive trail at "The Narrows," a narrow gap where Pinyon Ridge extends toward the Vallecitos Mountains.

The nature trail is a ramble past rocks estimated to be nearly a half-billion years old. Check out the salt and pepper granite. (The "salt" is feldspar, the "pepper" is mica.)

Common flora include ocotillo, jojoba, and assorted cacti. Keep an eye out for the chuparosa (so-called "hummingbird plant" because it attracts hummingbirds), a shrub that produces bright red flowers in early spring.

DIRECTIONS TO TRAILHEAD: From Christmas Circle, drive south on Borrego Springs Road (S-3) 13 miles to meet Highway 78. Turn left (east) on the highway and proceed 4.7 miles to the Narrow Earth Trail parking area on the right. Be careful when entering and exiting the parking area because Highway 78 is a heavily trafficked truck route.

The trail begins east of the parking area. Look carefully for Stop #1, where interpretive brochures are (usually) available.

THE HIKE When you get to the top of the seven-stop nature trail loop, you can extend your walk a bit by tramping up the wash.

■ PINYON RIDGE
Wilson Trail
To Wilson Peak is 8.5 miles round trip
with 1,400-foot elevation gain

Pinyon Ridge is just that—a large block of boulders and pinyon pine that stands just high enough above the desert floor to offer a 360-degree view. Its lower slopes are cloaked in cactus and creosote bush, its upper elevations dotted with yucca, chamise, and the pinyon pine promised by its name.

Pinyon Ridge and some of the surrounding environs are included in a state-designated wilderness area. Dirt roads abound in the area, but the one climbing the ridge, an old jeep road, is closed to all but foot traffic.

Wilson Trail and Wilson Peak take their name from Borrego Valley cattle rancher Alfred Wilson who grazed his cattle in these parts in the late nineteenth century. The trail gives out a bit before the summit, but a short, cross-country scramble will take you to the top. Rewarding your peak-climbing efforts are excellent views from Borrego Valley to the Salton Sea.

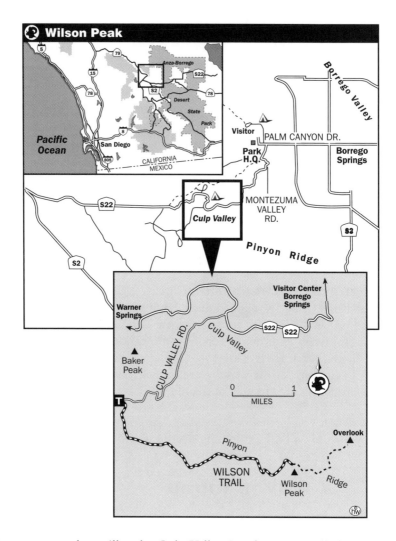

Your route to the trailhead—Culp Valley Road—can usually be traveled with two-wheel drive vehicles; however, brush does crowd the road in places. Watch out you don't scratch your paint job! If the road has deteriorated, or is too overgrown by brush for your taste, numerous turnouts along the way allow you to leave your vehicle short of the trailhead. It's a nice 2-mile road walk from Cottonwood Spring to the Wilson trailhead.

DIRECTIONS TO TRAILHEAD From Highway S-22 (Montezuma Highway) at mileage marker 10.4, turn west onto signed, dirt Culp Valley Road. At 0.4 mile, a spur road leading left (south) leads 0.2 mile to Culp Valley Picnic Area, a couple of tables beneath some shade trees offering a great view of Culp Valley's grassland floor.

At 0.6 mile, a right-branching spur road leads to a dead-end parking area for Culp Valley visitors. A mile from the highway, after passing two more left-forking roads, you'll spot three large cottonwood trees standing near Cottonwood Spring, a pipe-fed concrete water basin; the overflow nurtures a patch of lush greenery.

After 2 more miles of travel on Culp Valley Road, you'll reach a small turnaround and the signed Wilson trailhead.

THE HIKE Wilson Trail heads southeast over hard-packed sand. The climb is through an intriguing mix of both desert and mountain flora: cholla, yucca, and bearvertail cactus as well as manzanita, pinyon pine, and juniper.

The path winds south and east, passing boulders stacked upon boulders like a child's blocks.

Four miles along, the old road/trail ends, leaving you just north of Wilson Peak. Make your way between the boulders and weather-worn pinyon pine to the benchmark at the top of the peak.

The panoramic view includes the Laguna and Cuyamaca Mountains to the southwest and the Santa Rosa Mountains to the northeast.

■ HARPER CANYON
Harper Canyon Trail
9 miles round trip with 1,500-foot elevation gain

Cattle ranchers Julius and Amby Harper left their names on the land—Harper Canyon—but a name more evocative of the geography might be "Cactus Canyon" or "Ironwood Canyon."

The first mile of the hike passes a profusion of cacti known as the Cactus Garden. A half-dozen Colorado Desert cacti, especially barrel cactus, thrive here, along with ocotillo, smoke tree, desert lavender, and ironwood. Ironwood and the sweet-smelling, purple-blossoming desert lavender are abundant in the midst of Harper Canyon.

Harper Flat was heavily used by the native people, who left behind many bedrock *morteros* and hand tools in the area. In more modern times, the Flat was used by off-highway vehicles, but is now protected, along with much of the Pinyon Mountains, within a state park wilderness area.

Two-wheel drive vehicles with high clearance can proceed as far as Kane Springs. Expect lots of ruts and some soft sand along the way. The route beyond Kane Springs Road is four-wheel drive only.

The mileage and walk description assume you don't have four-wheel drive and are hiking the first leg.

DIRECTIONS TO TRAILHEAD From Highway 78, at the 87.2 marker, turn south onto a signed dirt road and proceed 1.5 miles to a T-intersection with

Kane Springs Road. Turn right (west) and proceed down a bumpy road 0.2 mile to a jeep trail on your left. (From here it is four-wheel drive only. It's a 1.5 mile journey (driving or walking) to road's end at the trailhead for Harper Canyon.

THE HIKE Your first mile of trail takes you past the Cactus Garden. Most noticeable are some basketball-sized barrel cactus.

About a mile out, be careful to stay on the road rather than straying up the wide tributary canyon to your right. (Such a detour—a scramble up the flanks of Sunset Peak for a 360-degree view can be rewarding, however.)

After reaching road's end, you'll head south up a sandy wash, the main branch of Harper Canyon. The route is a mixture of sand byways and some boulder-hopping. Stick to the center of the wash and avoid tributary canyons branching both east and west.

A mile from Harper Flat, the canyon narrows; a half mile away, the canyon opens up and levels out into a wide, willow-line wash.

Climb a large mound of juniper-spiked boulders for a great view of Harper Flat and the mountains beyond.

■ PICTOGRAPHS
Pictograph Trail
2.5 miles round trip with 500-foot elevation gain

Before settlers came this way, the native Kumeyaay camped in Blair Valley. They left behind *morteros* (grinding rocks) and pictographs (rock art), reminders of the early inhabitants who found sustenance which today can be reached via short hikes.

DIRECTIONS TO TRAILHEAD Leave Highway S-2 at mile-marker 22.9 and turn east into Blair Valley. The dirt road passes many campsites as it travels 2.8 miles to a signed junction. Stay left and drive to the road's end at the signed trail.

THE HIKE Pictograph Trail ascends a pinyon pine- and juniper-dotted ridge, then descends and follows a sandy wash named Smuggler Canyon. About 0.75 mile from the trailhead, look for the red- and yellow-hued pictographs on the face of a large boulder on the right side of the canyon.

From the pictographs, the path continues another half mile through the canyon, which narrows, then abruptly ends at a 200-foot drop-off. From the lip of a dry waterfall, carefully enjoy the good views.

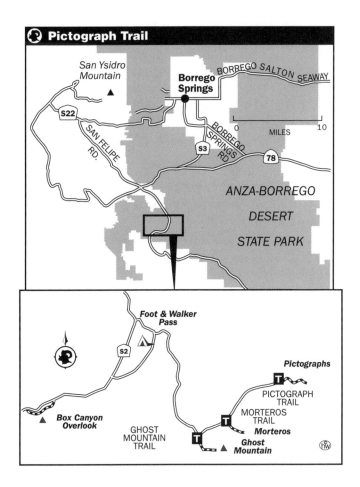

■ THE MORTEROS
Morteros Trail
0.5 mile round trip

Morteros Trail leads to an ancient village site on a rocky hillside. The highlights are dozens of grinding holes in the boulders where Kumeyaay women pulverized seeds and pods such as chia and mesquite beans.

DIRECTIONS TO TRAILHEAD Leave Highway S-2 at mile-marker 22.9 and turn east into Blair Valley. The dirt road passes many campsites as it travels 2.8 miles to a signed junction for Ghost Mountain, then continues 1.2 miles to the parking pullout for the Morteros.

THE HIKE The wide, sandy track climbs only slightly but delivers fairly impressive views of Little Blair Valley as it climbs to the mortar stones, used for more than a thousand years, some anthropologists believe.

■ GHOST MOUNTAIN
Ghost Mountain Trail
To Marshal South Cabin is 2 miles
round trip with 400-foot elevation gain

Tucked between the high desert and low desert, between Whale Peak and Granite Mountain, is Blair Valley, an inviting locale for camping and hiking. Bouldered hills fringing the valley hide secluded campsites and dirt roads and footpaths lead to cultural sites that offer a glimpse into the lives of the native Kumeyaay and the settlers who followed.

Getting to—and around—Blair Valley via Highway S-2 and two-wheel drive passable dirt roads is fairly easy these days. Not so in the stagecoach era when the Butterfield Overland Mail wagons struggled across Blair Valley and over the high desert passes. At the northern edge of the valley was a rocky incline known as Foot and Walker Pass; it was so steep that stage passengers were often forced to disembark and walk—even help push the stage—over the pass. Atop the pass is a monument commemorating the pioneers who came this way and an excellent vista of Blair Valley.

In the 1930s Marshal South, his poet wife Tanya and their three children went native in a big way. They built an adobe house called Yaquitepec, collected rainwater in cisterns, cooked on their adobe stove, and tried to live a very basic and natural life.

DIRECTIONS TO TRAILHEAD To reach the trailhead for the Marshal South Cabin, leave Highway S-2 at mile-marker 22.9 and turn east into Blair Valley. The dirt road passes many campsites as it travels 2.8 miles to a signed junction. Bear right to "Ghost Mountain Trail" and drive 0.4 mile to road's end at the signed trail.

THE HIKE The ruins of Marshal South Cabin, as it's known, can be reached by trail. Ghost Mountain Trail climbs steep, but well-graded switchbacks to the ruins of the cabin. Not much remains of the dwelling except for some walls and foundations, but the panoramic view is well worth the climb.

■ ELEPHANT TREES
Elephant Trees Discovery Trail
1.5 miles round trip with 100-foot elevation gain

A rarity in California deserts, the odd elephant tree is much admired by the visitors to Anza-Borrego Desert State Park. Its surreal color scheme (was this tree designed by committee?) of green foliage, red-tan twigs, yellow-green peeling parchment-like bark, white flowers, and blue berries, is something to behold. The stout trunk and the way the branches taper, vaguely suggests an elephant, but lots of imagination is required.

Enjoy this hike by following the 1.5 mile nature trail and/or by trekking along an alluvial fan to some elephant trees. A herd estimated at 500 elephant trees grow at this end of the state park. *Birsera microphylla* is more common in Baja California and in the Gila Range of Arizona. The park has three populations of elephant trees, but the one off Split Mountain Road is the most significant one.

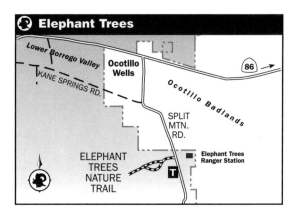

Elephant Trees Discovery Trail (brochure available), interprets various desert flora and geological features of this part of the Colorado Desert.

DIRECTIONS TO TRAILHEAD From Ocotillo Wells (located about 40 miles west of Brawley and 78 miles east of Escondido on Highway 78), turn south on Split Mountain Road and proceed 6 miles to the signed turnoff for the Elephant Trees Area. Follow a dirt road 1 mile to the trailhead.

THE HIKE Follow the nature trail until signpost #10, where you'll see the first elephant tree on the walk.

(Those experienced hikers who wish to see more elephant trees will leave the trail here and hike west up the broad alluvial fan. You'll encounter bits of trail, but really the route is cross-country. Keep the mountains on the western horizon in your sight. A mile's walk brings you to some elephant trees.)

Return the way you came back to the nature trail, which follows the numbered posts through a dry streambed and loops back to the trailhead.

■ AGUA CALIENTE SPRINGS
Squaw Pond, Moonlight Canyon Trails
1.5 to 2.5 miles round trip

Nothing like a good soak after a good hike. At Agua Caliente Springs in the middle of Anza-Borrego Desert State Park, you can have both—an inspiring walk and a soothing mineral bath. A hot spring, along with a good-sized campground, a store and the natural beauty of the Tierra Blanca Mountains, combine to make Agua Caliente County Park a popular weekend retreat.

Seismic activity (an offshoot of the Elsinore Fault) that long ago shaped the surrounding mountains also boosted water to the surface to form the mineral springs. The natural springs in the area give life to mesquite, willows, and palms and also attract many animals and birds.

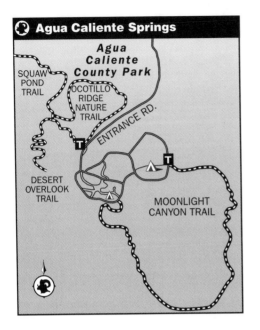

Today's visitors can soak away their cares in a large shallow outdoor pool, geothermally heated to 96°F and in an indoor pool, boosted to more than 100°F and equipped with Jacuzzi jets.

DIRECTIONS TO TRAILHEAD
Agua Caliente County Park is located on Highway S-2, some 22 miles southeast of Highway 78. Parking for Squaw Pond Trail is right next to the park entry station (day-use fee) in a picnic area. Moonlight Canyon Trail begins at Campsite 140 next to the shuffleboard courts.

THE HIKE Two trails explore the county park and visit undeveloped tiny springs (seeps) in the surrounding hills. Squaw Pond Trail visits mesquite-filled Squaw Canyon; Moonlight Canyon Trail fulfills the promise of its name.

Squaw Pond Trail ascends a mesquite-dotted slope above the park's campfire circle and soon comes to a junction. Desert Overlook Trail branches left and climbs a steep 0.25 mile to a panorama of the surrounding mountains. Ocotillo Ridge Trail, an abandoned nature trail, weaves through abundant desert flora and returns to the park entry road.

Continue on signed Squaw Pond Trail which descends a teddy bear cholla-lined draw and soon arrives at Squaw Pond, a boggy, willow-lined area nurturing a single palm tree.

From the campground, Moonlight Canyon Trail ascends briefly—but steeply—to a rocky saddle, curves east, then descends into a narrow wash. After passing a willow-lined seep in the midst of the canyon, the trail circles back to the park campground.

■ MOUNTAIN PALM SPRINGS
Six Oases Trail
2.5 miles round trip

At Mountain Palm Springs, half a dozen palm groves welcome the hiker. These groves of California fan palms in the Tierra Blanca Mountains are less secretive than most others in the Colorado Desert; some are visible from the highway, all can be visited on a mellow hike.

Palm groves abound at Mountain Palm Springs.

The palms are clustered in closely bunched communities within several narrow canyons. Abundant teddy bear cholla and the occasional elephant tree grow on the canyon walls above the palms.

The palms all lie within a square-mile of terrain so the hiker gets a lot of palms per mile with a 2.5-mile tour of Mountain Palm Springs.

DIRECTIONS TO TRAILHEAD From Highway S-2 at mile marker 47, some 54 miles from the park visitor center, turn west at the signed turnoff for Mountain Palm Springs. Follow the dirt road into the primitive campground and park at the trailhead.

THE HIKE From the parking area, two trails lead into the canyon. Begin on the main trail heading west and you'll soon reach some smallish palms in a rocky setting known as Pygmy Grove. Three-quarters of a mile from the trailhead is Southwest Grove. (A side trail leads to Torote Bowl, where elephant trees grow.)

From Southwest Grove, one of the park's largest groves, look carefully for the northbound trail that leads over a rocky ridge to Surprise Canyon and its small palm grove. It's well worth the walk to travel up-canyon to lush Palm Bowl. The path down Surprise Canyon brings you within sight of North Grove and returns you to the trailhead.

■ BOW WILLOW CANYON
Rockhouse Canyon Trail
Bow Willow Campground to Rockhouse
is 7 miles round trip with a 700-foot gain

This enjoyable day hike, for more experienced hikers, explores two intriguing canyons—Bow Willow and Rockhouse.

This looping day hike takes you climbing through a single palm canyon, visits a rock house (cattleman's line shack) and its canyon and returns via the wash on the bottom of Bow Willow Canyon. Spring scatters color in the wash. Monkeyflowers, desert stars, and a host of wildflowers brighten the sands and gravel bars. Even ocotillo changes its fit-only-for-firewood appearance and displays its new green leaves and flaming red flowers.

DIRECTIONS TO TRAILHEAD From Interstate 8 in Ocotillo, take County Road S-2 for 16 miles to the turnoff for Bow Willow Canyon and Campground. Follow the good hardpack sand road 1.5 miles to the campground. Park in the campground, but don't take a campsite someone could use.

THE HIKE Hike up Bow Willow Canyon on the signed jeep trail. Before you get much past the campground, make a 90-degree left turn (south) across a few hundred yards of wash to pick up the foot trail. A quarter mile up the trail is a beleaguered palm tree. You begin climbing steadily through a desert garden of

Head into Rockhouse Canyon for a memorable desert hike.

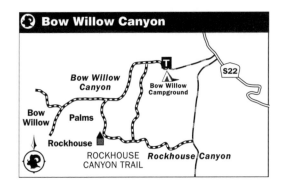

granite boulders, agave, and cholla cactus.

As you near Rockhouse Canyon, the trail descends briefly and intersects Rockhouse Canyon Jeep Trail. Follow the Jeep Trail west for 1 mile to Swartz's abandoned rock house.

From the rock house, you follow a tentative foot trail that drops down into Bow Willow Canyon. Before long you'll come to a barrier across the wash preventing off-road vehicles from ascending into the upper reaches of the canyon. Past the barrier, the canyon widens and it's an easy 2 miles over soft sand back to Bow Willow Campground.

■ CARRIZO BADLANDS
Canyon Sin Nombre Trail
4 miles round trip from mouth of canyon; 5.5 miles round trip from Highway S-2

From the Carrizo Badlands Overlook, you can peer down at 10 miles of folded and twisted terrain. Although the badlands look impenetrable, there's a way into the maze of cliffs, caves, and winding washes. One such way into the badlands is via Canyon Sin Nombre, located below the overlook.

"Canyon Without a Name" is not the dark and scary place its name might suggest. Its rocky walls, sculpted into a variety of shapes and patterns are a mosaic of blacks, browns, and grays.

The colorful canyon is a great walk; it provides a close-up look at badlands and various geological ages. Layer upon layer of deposits from ancient lakes and seas have been tilted this way and that.

The sediments comprising the badlands have been shaped and sculpted gradually over many years by wind and the scant rain that falls and also, more profoundly, by rare flash floods. Only relatively recently in geologic time—within the last 20,000 years—has this land become a desert, say scientists.

Canyon Sin Nombre is open to four-wheel drive travel, as are most of the larger washes and ravines in the Carrizo Badlands. The canyon is a major route of travel—it is the southern entrance to the park's Vallecito/Carrizo Creek area; yet on weekdays expect to meet more two-legged than four-wheeled visitors.

DIRECTIONS TO TRAILHEAD Reach the Carrizo Badlands in the southern end of Anza-Borrego Desert State Park by exiting Interstate 8 onto Highway

S-2. Drive 12 miles north to the Carrizo Badlands Overlook. Just north of the overlook at mile marker 51.3 on the east side of the road is the signed turnoff for Canyon Sin Nombre. Park in the turnout just off the highway. High-clearance vehicles can proceed 0.75 mile down the dirt road and park alongside of the road about 200 yards from the entrance to the canyon. It's sandy, narrow and rugged inside the canyon—strictly for four-wheel drive or walking.

THE HIKE Walk past some big barrel cactus into the mouth of the canyon. At the canyon entrance are brown and gray sedimentary layers estimated to be 1 to 3 million years old. In some places, once-horizontal sedimentary rocks are not vertical. Some canyon walls show S-shaped layers; the rock has been twisted downward, upward, and downward again.

The first 2 miles of Canyon Sin Nombre are the most interesting. Look for natural bridges and arches, rock formations that resemble castle walls, nests of ravens hidden on high. The jeep road eventually emerges at Carrizo Creek and links with other four-wheel drive roads.

The rugged world of Anza-Borrego includes the Carrizo Badlands.

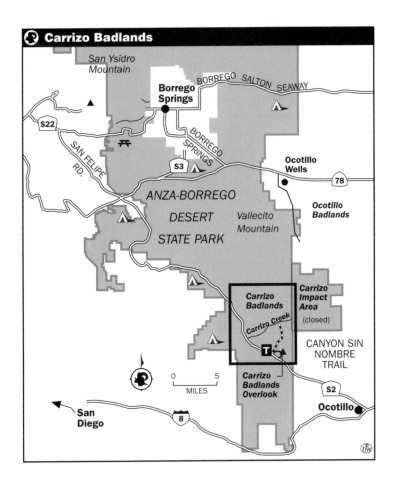

Carrizo Badlands

San Ysidro Mountain

BORREGO SALTON SEAWAY

Borrego Springs

S22

BORREGO SPRINGS

SAN FELIPE RD.

S3

Ocotillo Wells

78

ANZA-BORREGO DESERT STATE PARK

Vallecito Mountain

Ocotillo Badlands

Carrizo Badlands

Carrizo Impact Area

(closed)

Carrizo Creek

CANYON SIN NOMBRE TRAIL

0   5
MILES

Carrizo Badlands Overlook

S2

San Diego

8

Ocotillo

Anglers enjoy trying their luck in the waters of the Salton Sea.

CHAPTER 7

IMPERIAL VALLEY AND THE COLORADO RIVER

Adiversity of landscapes from sprawling farmland to a huge saltwater sea, from moonscape-looking mountains near the Mexican border to mammoth sand dunes near the Arizona border make up the Imperial Valley. Agriculture is king (some of the most productive farm land in the world is in the valley), dominating the southeastern portion of the Colorado Desert, but the area nevertheless has much to offer the hiker who knows when and where to step away from Highway 111.

Past the town of Coachella, Highway 111 becomes known as the North Shore Road and dips below sea level for much of its run to Brawley. The road is most interesting on an early winter morning when sunrise colors the Orocopia Mountains to the east and the Salton Sea to the west. Highlighting the scene are smoke trees, whose slate-gray branches from a distance resemble the plume made by a campfire.

Highway 111 edges closer to the Salton Sea, one of the world's largest inland bodies of saltwater, often referred to in the 1930s as "Coachella Valley's Sea of Galilee."

It was formed a thousand years ago when an immense lake filled the desert basin. Then over a period of hundreds of years the desert heat reduced the sea to a vast expanse of gleaming white salt flats that remained until 1905, when the Colorado River overflowed its banks, flooded the Imperial Valley, and poured into the Salton Sink. When the flood was finally checked 2 years later, a lake had been formed. Evaporation reduced the sea to its present size (35 miles by 15 miles) where it has nearly stabilized because of drainage from Imperial Valley irrigation.

Large campgrounds line the Salton Sea, the winter home of many a "snowbird"—long-term campers who've escaped colder climes for a season in the California desert. Bird-watching is simply spectacular at the Salton Sea National Wildlife Refuge. Snowbirds—and hikers—also enjoy the Algodones Dunes, handsome sand hills that reach 300 feet in height.

■ SALTON SEA STATE RECREATION AREA
Ironwood Nature Trail
From the Visitor Center to Mecca Beach is 2 miles round trip;
to Corvina Beach is 4.5 miles round trip

Between the desert and the sea is an intriguing, sun-baked shoreline, quite unlike any other locale in the California desert.

Some 18 miles of Salton Sea shoreline within the Salton Sea State Recreation Area invite the camper, angler, swimmer, and sunbather. Hikers will enjoy Ironwood Nature Trail which explores the shoreline between the visitor center and Mecca Beach.

The 15-mile-wide, 35-mile-long Salton Sea was formed in 1905 when Colorado River floodwaters overwhelmed an Imperial Valley dike during construction of the All-American Canal. For 2 years water poured into the Salton Sink, an ancient sea bed.

Surrounding rivers, washes, and canals continue to refill the lake with a combination of rainwater and agricultural runoff. Fertilizers and other minerals contribute to the high salinity (more than 10 percent "saltier" than the Pacific Ocean) of the Salton Sea.

You can learn more about the origins, present dilemmas, and possible ecological fate of the Salton Sea at the visitor center located near the park's harbor. Obtain a nature trail brochure and walk to the trailhead from here, or drive to Campsite 32 in the headquarters campground known as Los Frijoles Camp.

Plan to catch some rays or take a swim at trail's end. Sandy Mecca Beach is a popular swimming area. Showers are available to wash off the film of salt and plankton that coats the swimmer.

DIRECTIONS TO TRAILHEAD Salton Sea State Recreation Area is located some 25 miles southeast of Indio via Highway 111.

THE HIKE From the campground, enjoy the 30-stop nature trail that explores everything from salt to salt cedars to smoke trees. When you reach Mecca Beach, you can either return via the nature trail or by picking your own route closer to shore.

If you want to extend your hike, continue hiking along the shoreline to undeveloped Corvina Beach Campground or as far as you choose.

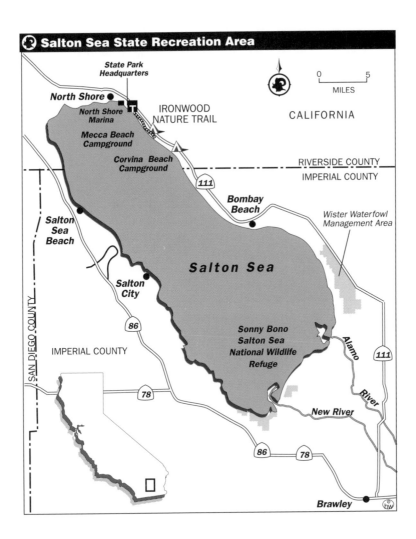

Salton Sea State Recreation Area

State Park Headquarters

North Shore ●

North Shore Marina

IRONWOOD NATURE TRAIL

CALIFORNIA

0 _____ 5
MILES

Mecca Beach Campground

Corvina Beach Campground

RIVERSIDE COUNTY
IMPERIAL COUNTY

111

Salton Sea Beach

Bombay Beach ●

Wister Waterfowl Management Area

Salton Sea

Salton City

86

IMPERIAL COUNTY

78

Sonny Bono Salton Sea National Wildlife Refuge

Alamo

111

River

New River

86   78

Brawley ●

■ SALTON SEA NATIONAL WILDLIFE REFUGE
Rock Hill Trail
2 miles round trip

The motto of the Salton Sea National Wildlife Refuge could be, "Binoculars. Don't leave home without them." In fact, few visitors who traipse the shores of the salty sea are found without their field glasses.

"We're in all the bird books," a ranger offers as explanation as to why thousands of bird-watchers a year flock to this remote wildlife sanctuary.

Sonny Bono Salton Sea National Wildlife Refuge, as it was officially renamed after the death of 1960s pop star/Palm Springs mayor/U.S. Congressman Sonny Bono, offers a superb wintering environment and migratory stopover area for birds. More than 375 bird species have been sighted at the refuge, where the avian-friendly habitat includes more than 35,000 acres of salt marsh and 2,000 acres of pasture and freshwater marsh.

Most noticeable of the feathered visitors and residents are the geese, particularly the loud-honking Canada geese who fly here in their distinct V-shaped formation. Also easy to spot are the large snow geese and the Ross geese, white geese that are similar to, but smaller than the snow geese. During some winters, the combined geese count totals 30,000 birds.

In addition to the geese, bird-watchers spot several different kinds of waterfowl—ducks, mergansers, wigeons and teals. Endangered species include the Yuma clapper rail, the California brown pelican, the southern bald eagle and the peregrine falcon. Other winged things at the refuge include bats and butterflies.

The refuge serves as a laboratory for fish and wildlife study. Scientists are studying contaminants arising from various sources in order to improve he health of birds, fish, and the unique Salton Sea ecosystem.

Rock Hill Wildlife Trail explores a kind of habitat that even the most experienced hikers may have never encountered: a coverstrip—trees and shrubs found along dikes that separate farm fields. Mesquite and palo verde in such coverstrips provide food and protection for wildlife. Characteristic coverstrip birds include Gambel's quail, mourning dove and loggerhead shrike.

The refuge, which is open all year, is especially attractive in winter when the migratory birds are in residence. A new visitor center with bird displays, a bookstore, an observation platform, and a shaded picnic area welcome bird-watchers.

I've got you, bird... more than 375 species have been spotted at this refuge.

DIRECTIONS FROM TRAILHEAD From Highway 111, 3.5 miles north of Calipatria, turn west on Sinclair Road and proceed six miles to the headquarters/visitor center of Salton Sea National Wildlife Refuge.

THE HIKE From the refuge's observation platform, the path heads west along a dike for 0.5 mile. To the south is a geothermal energy plant which captures steam from deep within the earth to drive turbines and generate electricity.

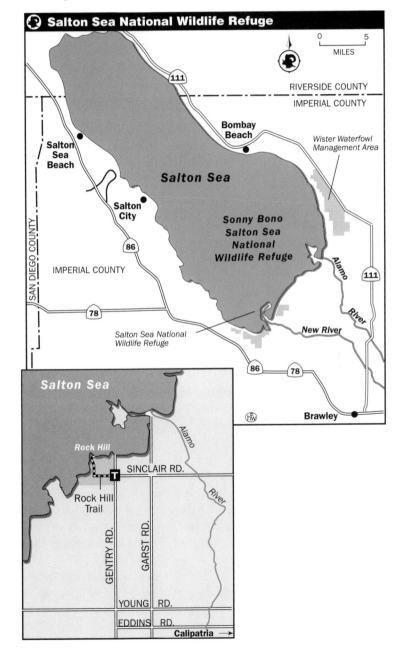

The trail turns north as it reaches the Salton Sea shoreline, lined with birds and bird-watchers. A brief ascent brings the hiker to the top of Rock Hill, a small volcanic butte. Enjoy the bird's-eye view of the Salton Sea, then return the way you came.

High this summit is not. However, at about 228 feet below sea level, the Salton Sea is one of the lowest places in the United States, so the vistas are pretty darn good.

■ ALGODONES DUNES
Algodones Dunes Trail
3 to 6 miles round trip

In the mid-eastern Colorado Desert is a slice of the Middle East—miles of sand dunes that rise out of the desert floor like a mirage.

California's largest mass of dunes, known variously as the Imperial Dunes, Sand Hills, Algodones National Natural Landmark, and Glamis Dunes extend 45 miles northeast from the Mexican border along the eastern edge of the Imperial Valley.

Passage of the landmark California Desert Protection Act in October of 1994 gave wilderness designation to some 22,000 acres of dunes, formerly known as the Algodones Outstanding Natural Area. Off-highway vehicles continue to be allowed to swarm over the southern two-thirds of the dune system, while nature-lovers may walk in peace through the wilderness.

Dune-walking over the breathtakingly beautiful sandscape is a joy, particularly in spring when the foredunes are festooned with desert wildflowers.

The dunes emerged long ago when a series of lakes existed in the Salton Sea basin; when these Colorado River-fed lakes dried up during drought years, winds carried their shoreline and bottom sands southeastward and deposited them as dunes.

While constant movement of sand, summer temperatures reaching above 110°F, and annual rainfall of less than 2 inches are not environmental conditions that would seem to encourage life, a splendid diversity of plants and animals have adapted, indeed thrive, in the harsh dune ecosystem.

The ubiquitous creosote bushes on the edge of the dunes are accompanied by smaller, more unusual flora extending into the heart of the dunes: desert buckwheat, witchgrass, sandpaper plant, and the silver-leafed dune sunflower.

What little water reaches the dunes—the scant rainfall and some flash-flood runoff from the nearby Chocolate Mountains—gives rise to often stunning spring wildflower displays. Evening primrose, purple sand verbena, and orange mallow splash color on the sand.

Spring is when the desert lilies bloom. Clusters of the large, white funnel-shaped flowers adorn tall (nearly 6 feet high) plants. Desert lilies can usually be

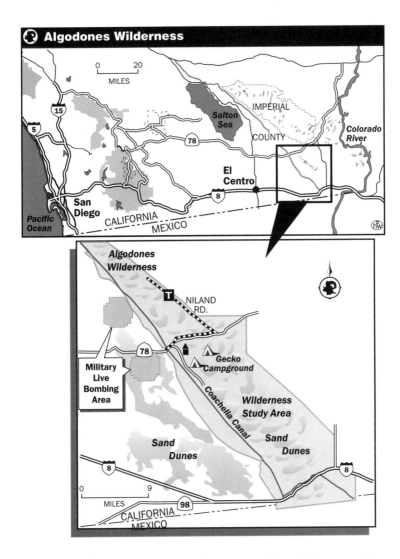

found growing in large numbers on the north side of Highway 78, across the road from the BLM ranger station.

Some unusual creatures call the dunes home. The banded gecko, a small lizard, has notched, interlocking eyelids that keep sand out of its eyes; if sand does manage to land on its eyeballs, its extremely long tongue can lick them clean. Geckos are mostly nocturnal and are thus rarely seen; however they're sometimes heard. One of the few lizards with a voice, they can be heard calling on spring evenings—presumably for a mate.

The Couch's spadefoot toad, which uses its shovel-like hind feet to burrow in the sand, dwells on the east side of the dunes. These toads may hibernate ten months, then emerge by the thousands after a rain to lay their eggs in shallow pools of water.

No trails cross the dunes. The best hiking is in the wilderness area north of Highway 78. Begin at the ranger station and hike north into the dunes or better yet, hike west into the dunes from Niland Road.

Two campgrounds are found near Highway 78, but they're "weekend cities" oriented to the needs of the thousands of motorized dune riders who arrive here in winter and spring. More mellow camping alternatives for environmentally minded dune visitors are the BLM's Long Term Visitor Areas located off Interstate 8 east of El Centro.

DIRECTIONS TO TRAILHEAD From Interstate 10 in Indio, exit on Highway 111. Head southeast past the Salton Sea to Brawley. Drive east on Highway 78 some twenty miles to the western edge of the dunes and the BLM's Cahuilla Ranger Station and visitor information center. You can park at the visitor center, cross Highway 78 and walk north into the dunes.

To really get away from it all, continue east on Highway 78 for 6 miles past the visitor center to the hamlet of Glamis. Turn left on unsigned Niland Road, the well-graded dirt road just west of the railroad tracks, and drive 5 or 6 miles. No developed parking exists; leave your vehicle in the sandy area between the road and the railroad tracks.

THE HIKE From Niland Road, you'll walk 1.5 miles west to reach the main part of the dunes. Because few prominent landmarks (natural or built) exist in the area, pay attention to the route you take. It's easy navigating toward the prominent dunes, but much more difficult finding your way back to where you left your vehicle.

■ MESQUITE MINE
Mesquite Mine Overlook Trail
1 mile round trip

Nineteenth-century prospectors probed the Chocolate Mountains and found "gold in them thar hills," but their discoveries were but a fraction of the precious mineral that was hidden in the rock hereabouts. Today the Mesquite Mine, California's second-largest, produces more than 200,000 ounces of gold a year.

Faint-hearted environmentalists should skip this trail, which presents the mining industry's view of the controversial practice of "heap leaching;" that is to say heaping ore in large mounds and washing it with a cyanide solution which leaches, or dissolves the gold out.

If heap-leaching and the fact that the mine moves millions of tons of "waste rock" around a year doesn't make a conservationist cringe, there's more: the mine operator supported a proposal to bring freight-trains full of Southland garbage here to dump in the holes it's dug.

Mesquite Mine Overlook Trail, open 8 AM to 4 PM daily, climbs an iron-wood- and palo verde-dotted slope for a view of the Chocolate Mountains to the north, the Algodones Dunes to the west, the vast surrounding desert and of course the huge Mesquite Mine just below.

DIRECTIONS TO TRAILHEAD From Highway 78, some 10 miles east of the BLM's Cahuilla Ranger Station and visitor information center in the Algodones Dunes, turn north on well-signed, paved G.F.O.C. Mine Road. Proceed 3 miles to the signed trailhead and ample parking, just short of the entrance to the mine.

THE HIKE You can fantasize about owning a gold mine while walking the Mesquite Mine Overlook Trail, a 14-stop interpreted path that explains the operation of a modern gold mine as well as the habits of local flora and wildlife. Let's see . . . 200,000 ounces a year at $360 an ounce equals $72 million. Not bad diggings for Santa Fe Pacific Gold Corporation, the mine's owner.

■ VALLEY OF THE MOON
Valley of the Moon Trail
To Valley of the Moon is 6 miles round trip
with a 700-foot elevation gain

From the jumbled rock formations at the border are views of two countries (Mexico and the United States), two counties (Imperial and San Diego) and two mountain ranges (the Jacumba Mountains and the Sierra Juarez).

The granite outcroppings resemble those of Joshua Tree National Park, though the surrounding Jacumba Mountains are sprinkled with pinyon pine, not Joshuas. On the northern side of the border the mountains are known as the Jacumba range but more internationally minded geographers consider the mountains to be an extension of Baja's 100-mile-long Sierra Juarez.

The Jacumba range trails lead very close to the border; the range's high point, 4,548-foot Blue Angel Peak is crowned with an International Boundary Marker, a 10-foot high steel obelisk. A more unsavory indication of border activity is Smugglers Cove, supposedly where bandits, circa 1875, laid low; local lore also has it that the cave figured in the smuggling of opium and Chinese laborers.

The most intriguing sight to see is a surreal landscape known as Valley of the Moon. Sunset photography around here is superb.

Until the wilderness designation for the Jacumbas, a series of four-wheel drive roads led into the range. Now the cracked stacks of granite, the caves, and the narrow passageways can only be reached by foot.

A second hike in the area that you might consider: from the saddle on the way to Valley of the Moon, you can follow jeep roads and then make a short cross-country climb to the top of Blue Angel Peak. The pinyon pine-spiked summit offers good views of the border country. Hold onto your hat—it's often mighty windy on top. Round trip distance from the trailhead is 5 miles with a 1,300-foot gain.

DIRECTIONS TO TRAILHEAD From Interstate 8, some 90 miles east of San Diego and just west of the Imperial County line, exit on In-Ko-Pah Road. Head southwest along the frontage road for 0.25 mile, then turn left onto an unsigned dirt road. Drive 0.75 mile up the road to a parking area.

THE HIKE Walk up the jeep road to a saddle. A spur road forks left to Smugglers Cave, defaced by graffiti.

From the saddle, veer right at the first junction, left at the second. As the road descends, you'll ignore minor spurs that lead to primitive camps. The road climbs a bit toward minor, but prominent Tahe Peak. Stick to the main road, keeping left and avoiding the spur road that leads to an abandoned amethyst mine.

After winding east, then south around the base of Tahe Peak, you'll turn east once more and descend into the Valley of the Moon.

Explore the lunar-looking landscape via a couple of jeep roads or by navigating among the big boulders. Stay oriented to the road; it's easy to lose your bearings in this strange terrain.

■ PICACHO STATE RECREATION AREA
Stamp Mill Trail
From Park road to Stamp Mill Ruins is 2 miles round trip

Picacho State Recreation Area beckons the visitor with spectacular Colorado River and Colorado Desert scenery. Colorful canyons, rugged volcanic peaks and isolated backwater lakes are among the diverse landforms of this obscure park located in the Colorado River Basin on the California-Arizona border.

In spring and fall, Picacho is the place to view migratory waterfowl, including egrets, blue herons and a multitude of ducks. Perhaps the showiest of the winged congregants along the Colorado River is the Canada goose— a stirring sight and an unmistakable sound.

Hikers often spot large animals roaming the park: mule deer, coyotes and feral burros. Some lucky hikers even get fleeting glimpses of the elusive big horn sheep. Three park inhabitants always seem to be in a hurry, even in the heat: quail, raccoons and roadrunners.

For most visitors, Picacho is a nine-month park. During the mid and late summer months, Picacho is an extremely hot place. Its low elevation and southerly positioning means temperatures routinely reach 105°F to 115°F in high summer.

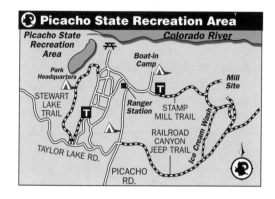

Rangers report that mosquito season extends from April through July. The pesky bugs are particularly thick and annoying on the shores by the area's still backwater lakes.

The park's main dirt road twists through ironwood-filled washes and offers vistas of the mighty Colorado River. Towering above it all is park namesake 1,942-foot Picacho Peak, a plug-dome volcano.

Picacho was a bustling boomtown in the 1890s. Some 700 men worked the mine and Picacho's population soared to 2,500 in the early twentieth century. Steamboats chugged up and down the Colorado, bringing life's necessities to the town, and taking the ore to market. When the Colorado River was dammed, the historic hamlet was flooded.

For the hiker, Picacho offers several signed trails plus numerous opportunities to trek cross-country up beckoning washes. Stamp Mill Trail (2 miles round trip) crosses the park's volcanic slopes and visits Picacho's stamp-mill sites. Ice Cream Canyon Trail tours the tuff and winds among the odd ironwood trees. Above, cacti-dotted canyon walls soar higher and higher and the feeling is that of entering a very special world.

Stewart Lake Trail (2.5 mile loop) crosses an intriguing volcanic landscape as it skirts the shore of (usually dry) Stewart Lake. An interpretive brochure describes the desert flora to be found along this trail, named for early Picacho prospector Clyde Stewart.

DIRECTIONS TO TRAILHEAD From Interstate 8 on the California-Arizona border, exit on Winterhaven Drive/Fourth Avenue and proceed north 0.5 mile to County Road S-24. Turn right and 0.25 mile later, turn left on Picacho Road.

(Yuma is located on the Arizona side of the river. Get provisions here and check out Yuma Territorial Prison State Historical Park.)

Follow Picacho Road (paved for just 4 miles). Near the All-American Canal, Picacho narrows and de-evolves into a sometimes bumpy, washboard dirt road and leads another 18 miles to Picacho State Recreation Area.

To reach the Stamp Mill trailhead, take the road to Lower Dock and soon turn right (east) on the spur leading very shortly to the trailhead and a parking area for a couple cars.

THE HIKE Stamp Mill Trail makes a modest descent over beavertail-cactus-dotted slopes. Enjoy vistas of Picacho Peak and of the Colorado River shore where the town of Piacacho once stood.

About 0.5 mile out, a short side trail leads to the Picacho Jail; actually it's a hillside hollow used by the sheriff to incarcerate the local bad guys and the miners to store explosives.

At 0.75 mile, you'll reach a junction with the right-forking path to Railroad and Ice Cream canyons. Continue another 0.2 mile to the rock walls and rusted ruins of Upper Mill, then a short distance farther to trail's end just above the ruins of Lower Mill.

Ice Cream Canyon Trail explores a colorful canyon tinted with strawberry and spumoni hues. Various cacti—barrel and cholla—dot canyon walls.

"Tuff" is the word for this trail, which crosses beds of the porous volcanic rock. Bighorn sheep sometimes roam the narrow confines of the canyon.

Walk the first 0.75 mile of Stamp Mill Trail then fork right, south, onto Ice Cream Canyon Trail. The path traces the wash bank up-creek, then soon drops to the bottom of the wash. After 0.25 mile, the path meets Railroad Canyon Jeep Trail.

Return via the jeep road for a 4.5 mile round trip hike.

See Map
on Page
251

■ ICE CREAM CANYON

Ice Cream Canyon Trail

Through Ice Cream Canyon is 5 miles round trip

Ice Cream Canyon Trail explores a colorful canyon tinted with strawberry and spumoni hues. Various cacti—barrel and cholla—dot the canyon walls.

"Tuff" is the word for this trail, which crosses beds of the porous volcanic rock. Bighorn sheep sometimes roam the narrow confines of the canyon.

DIRECTIONS TO TRAILHEAD This path shares a trailhead and some trail with the Stamp Mill Trail. Take the road to Lower Dock and soon turn right (east) on the spur leading very shortly to the trailhead and a parking area for a couple of cars.

THE HIKE The path makes a modest descent over beavertail cactus-dotted slopes. Enjoy vistas of Picacho Peak and of the Colorado River shore where the town of Picacho once stood.

About 0.5 mile out, a short side trail leads to the Picacho Jail; actually a hillside hollow used by the sheriff to incarcerate the local bad guys and by the miners to store explosives.

At 0.75 mile, you'll reach a junction with the right-forking path to Railroad and Ice Cream canyons. Fork right, south, onto Ice Cream Canyon Trail. The path traces the wash bank up-creek, then soon drops to the bottom of the wash. After 0.25 mile, you'll pass a junction with Railroad Canyon Trail.

Ice Cream Canyon Trail tours the tuff and winds among the odd ironwood trees. Above, cacti-dotted canyon walls soar higher and higher and the feeling is that of entering a very special world.

One mile from the junction with Stamp Mill Trail, a minor obstacle in the form of a small (4-foot high) rock fall must be climbed. Now the cliffs above the trail are really high—topping 50 feet—back-dropped by cliffs that tower more than 300 feet.

The canyon widens, narrows, then widens again into a peak-surrounded basin, chock-full of palo verde. A short walk across the basin leads to a junction with the Railroad Canyon Jeep Trail.

See Map
on Page
251

■ STEWART LAKE
Stewart Lake Nature Trail
1.5 mile round trip

R ed-rock outcroppings and a little lake, as well as cacti and succulents native to this desert are highlights of a stroll along the Stewart Lake Nature Trail, which comprises the first 0.5 mile of this loop from the park's campground.

What is now the center of the state park was once the land of the native Quechan who lived along this length of river. Nearby Picacho Peak was the focus of much of the tribe's beliefs and storytelling.

This walk offers a good look at vegetation-choked Stewart Lake, and even better vistas of the Colorado River. Perhaps after hiking trails near the river, you'll be inspired to launch a canoe and paddle its many boating trails. The view of the Colorado from the trail is a bit like the one on the river: austere desert mountains lined by green banks.

DIRECTIONS TO TRAILHEAD The signed trail begins by campsites 15 and 16.

THE HIKE Stick with the nature trail, which starts you on a counter-clockwise course amidst mesquite and tamarisk. At the 0.25-mile mark, the trail reaches a bench that overlooks the lake and Colorado River. The feathery-leafed tamarisk, a tree native to Africa, has taken over many of the flats near the river as well as much of Stewart Lake.

Rounding a dramatic rock rising high above the campground, the nature trail offers a chance to see and contemplate Picacho's plant life. Palo verde, ironwood, and cottonwood trees along with sage, mesquite, and many other shrubs thrive in the park.

At the end of its interpreted section, the path begins to climb. Even these volcanic slopes aren't entirely lifeless; hardy plants seem to sprout from the very rock itself.

A mile from the trailhead, the path meets the park road. Turn left and walk alongside the road 0.1 mile until the path resumes on the left. The path returns to the trailhead back at campsites 15 and 16.

CALIFORNIA'S DESERTS FROM A TO Z

A is for Anza-Borrego Desert State Park, California's largest state park by far with more than 600,000 acres of washes, mesas, badlands, slot canyons and palm oases.

B is for Badwater, located at the bottom of Death Valley, 282 feet below sea level, the lowest point in the Western Hemisphere.

C is for Colorado Desert, California's "lower desert," hotter and drier than the Mojave. Occupying the extreme southeastern part of California, the Colorado Desert is a small part of the larger Sonoran Desert.

D is for Death Valley National Park, at 3.3 million acres the largest national park in the continental U.S.

E is for Elephant tree, which features a stout trunk and grows in herds in the Colorado Desert. Its surreal color scheme includes green foliage, red-tan twigs, yellow-green peeling bark, white flowers, and blue berries.

F is for Faults, including the famed San Andreas, which contribute to the creation of the amazing scenery: crazily warped and tilted rock beds, fractured mountains, and more.

G is for Great Basin Desert, northernmost and highest in elevation of North America's deserts; a small part of this vast desert (it covers parts of New Mexico, Colorado, and most of Nevada) extends into California in the north end of the Owens Valley.

H is for Hell, which is what the desert appeared like to early travelers who tagged the land with hellish names: Hellhole Canyon, Hell's Gate, Devil's Chair, Devil's Playground, Dante's View, and more.

I is for Ironwood trees, found in washes and sandy areas. Named for wood so hard it can dull a saw, these hardy survivors can live 300 years and take a millennium to decay in the arid climate.

J is for Joshua tree, a yucca with a twist, whose photogenic contortions are much admired in its namesake national park. Its distribution defines the very boundaries of the Mojave Desert.

K is for Kelso Dunes, among the most extensive dune fields in the West, located in the heart of Mojave National Preserve. They're known as "booming dunes," for the weird rumbling sounds (like a Tibetan gong) they make.

L is for Little Petroglyph Canyon, site of one of the largest concentrations of Native American rock art, some 11,000 images, located in the Coso Mountains and now under the strict security of the China Lake Naval Air Weapons Station.

M is for Mojave Desert, often called "the high desert" for its elevation. Included are the West Mojave with great sandscapes and isolated buttes and the East Mojave, primarily a desert of mountain ranges.

N is for National Parkland. Death Valley National Park, Joshua Tree National Park, and Mojave National Preserve protect nearly six million acres of California desert. A "Three Desert Parks Tour" is becoming popular.

O is for Ocotillo, a 10-foot high shrub with tall spiny stems that produce bright red flowers (after it rains).

P is for Palm, the native California fan palm, which grows only where there is year-round water available. Palm Canyon near Palm Springs is the largest oasis with some 3,000 trees. For every tree in the wild, more than 1,000 have been planted in Southern California.

Q is for Queen Valley, where thousands of Joshua trees thrive in the heart of Joshua Tree National Park.

R is for Red Rock Canyon, aptly named for its towering red rock walls that also come in chocolate brown, black, white, and pink hues. No wonder this canyon located 125 miles north of Los Angeles is a favorite film location.

S is for Salton Sea, California's Great Salt Lake, visited by flocks of Canada geese and multitudes of other migratory waterfowl. Also popular with "snow-birds," humans from colder climes, who winter here.

T is for Tortoise, a slow-moving, prehistoric-looking herbivore that digs burrows to escape the heat. The California Desert Tortoise is the official state reptile.

U is for Ubehebe Crater, one of the more magnificent examples of volcanism in Death Valley. It's know as an "explosion crater." One look and you know why.

V is for Volcanoes, responsible for dramatic, high-speed landscape changes in the California desert. The 32 conical-shaped cinder cones in Mojave National Preserve are particularly fine examples of (recently) extinct volcanoes.

W is for Wilderness, a special status that protects some 3.6 million acres of scenically outstanding and ecologically unique desert (in 69 different areas) from off-road vehicles and commercial exploitation.

X is for Xerothermic, a term applied to desert plants and animals that have adapted to living in a hot, dry climate.

Y is for Yucca, the most common variety being the Mojave yucca (Spanish bayonet) that usually reaches 6 feet or more in height and is often found growing in company with *Yucca brevifolia,* the Joshua tree.

Z is for Zzyzx, formerly a health resort run by eccentric radio minister Curtis Springer from 1944 to 1974, and now the California Desert Studies Center, a field station for research in Mojave National Preserve.

Contacting California's Desert Parks

Antelope Valley California Poppy Reserve
(661) 942-0662

Antelope Valley Indian Museum
(661) 942-0662

Anza-Borrego Desert State Park
200 Palm Canyon Drive
Borrego Springs, CA 92004
(760) 767-5311

Arthur B. Ripley Desert Woodland State Park
(661) 942-0662

Big Morongo Canyon Preserve
(760) 363-7190

Bodie State Historic Park
(760) 647-6445

Death Valley National Park
Death Valley, CA 92328
(760) 786-3200

Devil's Punchbowl County Park
28000 Devil's Punchbowl Road
Pearblossom, CA 93533
(661) 944-2743

El Centro Field Office
1661 S. 4th Street
El Centro CA 92243
(760) 337-4400

Joshua Tree National Park
74485 National Park Drive
Twentynine Palms, CA 92277
(760) 367-5500

(The) Living Desert
47-900 Portola Avenue
Palm Desert, CA 92260
(760) 346-5694

Mitchell Caverns
(760) 928-2586

Mojave National Preserve
222 E. Main Street, Suite 202
Barstow, CA 92311
(760) 255-8801

Mono Lake Tufa State Reserve
(760) 647-6331/3044

Mount San Jacinto State Park
(909) 659-2607/767-4037

Palm Springs South Coast Field Office
690 W. Garnet Ave., P.O. Box 581260
North Palm Springs, CA 92258-1260
(760) 251-4800

Picacho State Recreation Area
(760) 996-2963

Providence Mountains State Recreation Area
(760) 928-2586/(661) 942-0662

Red Rock Canyon State Park
(661) 942-0662

Ridgecrest Field Office
300 S. Richmond Rd.
Ridgecrest, CA 93555
(760) 384-5400

Saddleback Butte State Park
(661) 942-0662

Salton Sea State Recreation Area
(760) 393-3059

Santa Rosa and San Jacinto Mountains National Monument
U.S. Bureau of Land Management
Palm Springs South Coast Field Office
690 W. Garnet Ave., P.O. Box 581260
North Palm Springs, CA 92258-1260
(760) 251-4800

Sonny Bono Salton Sea National Wildlife Refuge
906 West Sinclair Road
Calipatria, California 92233-9744
(760) 348-5278

Tomo-Kahni Village Site
(661) 942-0662

Vasquez Rocks Natural Area Park
10700 W. Escondido Canyon Rd.
Agua Dulce, CA 91350
(661) 268-0840

Web Sites

For **National Parks** information, visit www.nps.gov

For **California State Parks** information, visit, www.parks.ca.gov

For **U.S. Bureau of Land Management** (California public lands) information, visit www.ca.blm.gov

For more about **desert hiking**, visit John McKinney's web site at www.thetrailmaster.com.

INDEX

John McKinney is the author of a dozen books about walking, hiking, and nature, including *The Joy of Hiking: Hiking The Trailmaster Way*. The Trailmaster writes articles and commentaries about walking for national publications, promotes hiking and conservation on radio and television, and serves as a consultant to a hiking vacation company. Contact him at: www.thetrailmaster.com.

California Parks Books from Wilderness Press

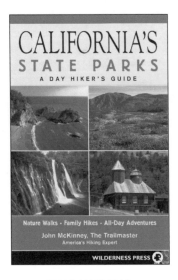

ISBN 0-89997-386-8

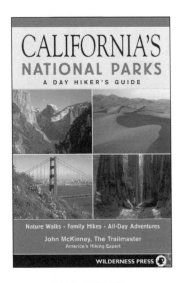

ISBN 0-89997-387-6

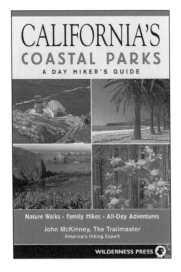

ISBN 0-89997-388-4

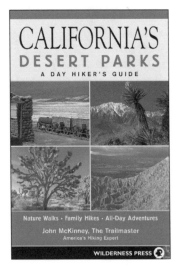

ISBN 0-89997-389-2

For ordering information, contact your local bookseller or Wilderness Press, www.wildernesspress.com.